American Slavery and the Immediate Duty of Southern Slaveholders

American Slavery and the Immediate Duty of Southern Slaveholders

A Transcription of Eli Washington Caruthers's Unpublished Manuscript against Slavery

Jack R. Davidson

◆PICKWICK *Publications* • Eugene, Oregon

AMERICAN SLAVERY AND THE IMMEDIATE DUTY OF SOUTHERN SLAVEHOLDERS
A Transcription of Eli Washington Caruthers's Unpublished Manuscript against Slavery

Copyright © 2018 Jack R. Davidson. All rights reserved. Except for brief quotations in critical publications or reviews, no part of this book may be reproduced in any manner without prior written permission from the publisher. Write: Permissions, Wipf and Stock Publishers, 199 W. 8th Ave., Suite 3, Eugene, OR 97401.

Pickwick Publications
An Imprint of Wipf and Stock Publishers
199 W. 8th Ave., Suite 3
Eugene, OR 97401

www.wipfandstock.com

PAPERBACK ISBN: 978-1-5326-0089-0
HARDCOVER ISBN: 978-1-5326-0091-3
EBOOK ISBN: 978-1-5326-0090-6

Cataloguing-in-Publication data:

Names: Davidson, Jack R., author. | Caruthers, E. W. (Eli Washington), 1793–1865, author.

Title: American slavery and the immediate duty of southern slaveholders : a transcription of Eli Washington Caruthers's unpublished manuscript against slavery / Jack R. Davidson.

Description: Eugene, OR : Pickwick Publications, 2018 | Includes bibliographical references.

Identifiers: ISBN 978-1-5326-0089-0 (paperback) | ISBN 978-1-5326-0091-3 (hardcover) | ISBN 978-1-5326-0090-6 (ebook)

Subjects: LCSH: Caruthers, E. W. (Eli Washington), 1793–1865. | Antislavery movements—United States. | Antislavery movements—United States—History—19th century—Sources. | Abolitionists—United States—History—19th century—Sources.

Classification: E449 .D235 2018 (print) | E449 .D235 (ebook)

Manufactured in the U.S.A. 07/06/18

Contents

Introduction | vii

Preface | xi

Let My People Go That They May Serve Me. | 1

I: The *claim: My people.* **They are** *mine and not yours:* **for you have no right to them.** | 3

1. On creation and preservation | 3

2. The deep and long-continued degradation of the Africans in their own land no reason why they should be enslaved. | 6

3. The alleged ambiguity of slavery furnishes no justification of this practice. | 11

4. Slavery in Egypt. | 12

5. Slavery, if there was such a thing, in Babylon. | 15

6. Slavery in Ancient Greece. | 16

7. Slavery in the Roman Empire. | 19

8. The orderings of Providence furnish no justification of slavery. | 20

9. The Lord's claims on the Africans and all other races and portions of mankind is founded on *redemption*. | 22

10. Differences between servants and slaves. | 23

11. Noah's prediction. | 25

12. Servitude during the patriarchal age. | 28

13. Servitude under the Mosaic dispensation. | 33

14. Servitude under the Christian dispensation. | 43

15. The opinions of learned and good men in its favor is no proof that slavery is right. | 53

16. Slavery originated in avarice, falsehood, and cruelty. | 55

II: The demand: Let my people go. | 59

17. The demand enforced by providences. | 67

18. Human beings cannot be held as property. | 85

III: *The reason* **for the demand or the purpose for which it is made.** | 112

19. Slave Code of the South. | 113

20. According to the present laws and usages of the land, slaves cannot make that entire surrender of themselves to the Lord which the gospel requires and to which the renewed nature prompts them. | 136

21. Under the existing laws and in the present state of society slaves cannot have that equality of rights and privileges which is in the New Testament accorded to all believers. | 142

22. Progress of Emancipation. | 152

23. The influences which the abolition of slavery in these southern states would probably have upon the African Slave trade, upon slavery in other parts of the world and upon the future destiny of the whole African race. | 175

Bibliography | 183

Introduction

Eli Washington Caruthers (1793–1865) was the pastor of Alamance Presbyterian Church in Greensboro, North Carolina, from 1821 until 1861. A disparaging public prayer for the Confederacy is the remembered cause of his retirement after forty years of service. The 1964 bicentennial poster for the Alamance congregation recalls the event that occurred shortly after the bombardment of Fort Sumter in April of the same year and the beginning of the war:

> One Sunday in July 1861, he prayed that the soldiers of the congregation might "be blessed of the Lord and returned in safety, though engaged in a lost cause." A congregational meeting was held, his resignation was requested, and soon the ties were dissolved that had united loving pastor and people for 40 years. Dr. Caruthers was now infirm, and died four years after. He was buried at Alamance where a monument over his grave and a memorial tablet . . . attest the esteem of his people for a pastor faithful, honored and beloved.[1]

During the four years that preceded his death in 1865, Caruthers completed a manuscript, over 400 pages in length, based on the text of Exodus 10:3, "Let my people go that they may serve me." It portrays slavery anywhere as a violation of God's will because "slaves cannot make that entire surrender of themselves to the Lord which the gospel required and to which renewed nature prompts them."[2] Dated 1862 and entitled *American Slavery and the Immediate Duty of Southern Slaveholders*, it was never published and is now in the custody of Special Collections at Duke University.

Shortly after its discovery in 1898 John Spencer Basset wrote that "it is doubtful if a stronger or clearer anti slavery argument was ever made on this continent."[3] The antebellum struggle to theologically resolve the antithetical impressions resulting from the Bible's regulation of slavery alongside its emphasis on the dignity and equality of human beings is a quest usually attributed to northern theologians, especially those of the Presbyterian Church. Mark Noll's account of conservative Presbyterians' failed efforts to "rescue the Reformed hermeneutic from proslavery," as exemplified in the

---

1. Murray, *A History of Alamance Church 1762–1918*, 16.
2. Caruthers, *American Slavery*, 313.
3. Basset, *Antislavery Leaders of North Carolina*, 60.

arguments of Charles Hodge, focuses on the prominent theologians of the North.[4] He has argued that their relationship with their southern counterparts, theological ability, and public influence, best situated northern Old School Presbyterians for developing a theological alternative to the literal, Reformed biblicism underlying proslavery arguments. Despite Hodge's brilliance and influence, however, reviews of his thinking on slavery have called it "poor enough to invite sarcasm" or like "listening to a phonograph record with the needle stuck."[5] Hodge's response to slavery was, in fact, like the rest of his colleagues at Princeton Seminary: "timid, conventional, and unremarkable."[6] Caruthers, a largely unknown Presbyterian minister in a proslavery state, arguably surpasses Hodge and other Old School colleagues, presenting a biblical alternative to the hermeneutics of slavery practiced in American Presbyterianism.

Caruthers's views on slavery were probably known and tolerated by his slave-holding congregation, but when his dissent from the Confederacy became a matter of public knowledge his retirement from the pastorate in 1861 was hastened.[7] He explains his resignation as being "on account of bad health and for other reasons."[8] An early history of the Alamance congregation states that his prayer for the troops "was too much for the people who had risked all for a cause which they hoped to win" and that the congregation met requesting his resignation.[9] No congregational meeting for such a purpose is recorded in the minutes of Alamance church but Caruthers's letter of resignation mentions a proposed meeting for some business." He writes to the elders of the Alamance on July 5th, 1861,

> Partly in conformity with a purpose formed more than six months ago, as you and the congregation are well aware and partly on account of my health which is such at present that I shall probably not be able to preach much for some time, I would through you, request of the Alamance church and Session to unite with me in asking a dissolution of my pastoral relation. I understand that the congregation are to have a meeting on some business tomorrow, but I am too unwell to attend. Please bring my request before the church that the application

---

4. Noll, *America's God*, 413–17.

5. Guelzo, "Charles Hodge's Antislavery Movement," 299–326, 324; Barker, "The Social Views of Charles Hodge," 5.

6. Calhoun, *Princeton Seminary*, 328.

7. Troxler, "Eli Caruthers," 95.

8. Caruthers, *Richard Hugg King and the Great Revival in North Carolina*, x.

9. Scott, "A History of Alamance Church," 92–93.

may be made to Presbytery as soon as possible and oblige your friend and servant. [10]

Caruthers's signature ends the letter. While not conclusive, the timing and content of the note implies some connection between his public prayer for the troops and the proposed meeting. He may have sensed trouble when he learned of the meeting and ended the conflict with a resignation. If a meeting had been planned it could have then been cancelled. Described as one who had "no sympathy with the Southern Confederacy or anything connected with it," the lifelong bachelor now became reclusive, according to his contemporaries " a sort of wanderer" and "little understood." During the last years of his life even longtime "friends were estranged from him in consequence of his unwavering devotion to the American Union."[11]

A minister with ecclesiastical and historical interests, Caruthers authored several books focusing on the American Revolution period in North Carolina. His biography of David Caldwell, *A Sketch of the Life and Character of the Reverend David Caldwell, D.D.*, was the first of several installments on Revolutionary history. Caldwell was Caruthers's predecessor in ministry, a self-taught doctor, and perhaps the most famous educator of his era in the South. An essential figure in any history of North Carolina, Caldwell was the courageous proponent of independence whose reputation was only heightened by the burning of his library by British troops in 1781. In this work Caruthers created the singular resource for the study of this remarkable minister, "among the most illustrious of American citizens." [12]

Another two volumes, *Revolutionary Incidents and Sketches of Character Chiefly in The "Old North State,"* and *Interesting Revolutionary Incidents and Sketches of Character Chiefly in The "Old North State," Second Series* are Caruthers's presentation of the strife between the Tories and the Whigs in what can be described as North Carolina's first civil war in the context of America's bid for independence. These volumes record history that would be lost apart from Caruthers's research involving interviews of veterans and those who remembered them, numerous accounts of cowardice and courage, and a detailed vindication of the actions of the North Carolina militia in the Battle of Guilford Courthouse.

When Caruthers died in November of 1865 at the age of 71, he left behind two manuscripts. *Richard Hugg King and His Times*, subsequently published in 1999, recounts the story of King, a farmer turned evangelist,

10. Minutes, Session of Alamance Presbyterian Church, 30 July 1861, Greensboro, North Carolina.

11. Wilson, *The Presbyterian Historical Almanac*, 6:350.

12. Caruthers, *A Sketch of the Life and Character of the Reverend David Caldwell*, iii.

and his role in the revivals of Western North Carolina. The other manuscript, *American Slavery and the Immediate Duty of Southern Slaveholders*, kept with Caruthers's other papers in Special Collections at Duke University, remained unpublished until now, and is presented here with minimal editing.

Preface

THE FOLLOWING WORK WAS written at the request of a particular friend who expressed a desire that I would write of my views on the slavery question and that, if the state of public sentiment should not admit of their publication, by the voice or by the press, while I lived, I would leave them to speak for me when I was gone and for the gratification of such friends and acquaintances as might feel an interest in knowing what I had thought upon this subject. If it had been designed for the press it would been more methodically and correctly written; but bad health and other circumstances do not admit of transcriptions or anything more than a few verbal corrections. It was written with haste and carelessness which the object in view seems to justify; but the unpolished style and the unmethodical manner in which it is written will not trouble a candid and earnest enquirer after truth, provided the reasoning is fair and the arguments sound.

As all the publications on this controversy, North and South, had long appeared to me radically deficient and unsatisfactory, I threw them every one aside and undertook to investigate the subject anew for myself. In the prosecution of my task, I had to employ many other arguments which have been commonly used wherever slavery has existed, at least in Christian countries, because they are suggested by natural reason, conscience and those feelings of justice and humanity which may be said to be universal but I have made the Bible as my main source of proof. The fundamental principle, that we can have no right to hold any thing as property without an *express* grant from the Creator, which I have made the basis of all my arguments, is one which, so far as my recollection serves me, I have not heard from any speaker nor seen in any publication, but of its truth and fundamental importance and intelligence the reflecting reader must judge. It was necessary however, to contrast the unjust, unchristian, and inhumane laws of the south, relating to slavery with the teachings of the Bible and the original instincts of our nature. In writing the work I had the Revised Code of North Carolina, the first Constitutions of the "Old Thirteen States" with one or two less important publications before me; but am indebted to Stroud's *Sketch of the Laws Relating to Slavery* for the enactments in the Slave Codes of other states. As already stated my thoughts were written down, *currente calamo* and are of course somewhat desultory but for that no further apology is necessary, as they were designed for the private perusal of friends, at some future time.

There are some "hard things" in it and if there were not it could do no good; for an evil of such extent, enormity and long standing cannot be demolished or removed by a little smoother talk. The whole truth must be told and told with an earnest spirit. If people are allowed the right of freely discussing this and every other subject which concerns the common welfare, truth will soon be triumphant and the result will be glorious; but however strongly the facts and arguments and Bible authorities may be felt by those who think their interest will suffer by abolition, the language is not abusive or was certainly not intended to be so; for neither my disposition nor my principles allow me to employ harsh or vituperative language.

Let My People Go That They May Serve Me.
Exodus 10:3

1862 (Original pagination in margins)

THE STATE OF PUBLIC feeling, North and South, in regard to slavery and the terrible calamity which it has brought upon the country, seem to be a loud call in Providence for every fair-minded and patriotic man to consider the subject with more calmness, impartiality, and thoroughness, than he has hitherto done. Much has been said and written on both sides; but it has been so much under the influence of interest and passion that it could produce only mutual animosity and bitter strife. From first to last something must have been radically wrong: for honest, dispassionate, and soberminded controversy never produces such results. The Scriptures have been, with apparent confidence, appealed to, for and against, and nearly all the passages that were thought to have any bearing on the question have been cited and expounded; but with so much ignorance or willful perversion of their meaning that the controversy served only to increase the exacerbation of feeling until it has involved the two sections of the union in a civil war of the most bloody and destructive kind.

If in the able and protracted discussions which have taken place on this question, in the pulpit, on the stump or the rostrum, from the press and in every way in which men usually communicate their views to others the passage quoted above has been used on either side, it has escaped either my notice, or my recollection; but it has long appeared to me, especially when viewed in connection with the Covenant of redemption, as on of the most decisive and important in favor of a prompt and universal emancipation that is to be found in the oracles of revealed truth.

It has been taken, however, not as a text for a sermon, in the technical sense of that term; for, in a sermon of the usual length, or even of double the ordinary length, little more than a synopsis of the arguments could be given; but we design to use it as the basis of a brief discussion on American slavery and the immediate duty of southern slave holders. As we have in it the *claim*, the *demand* and the *reason* for it, or the purpose for which the demand is made, it includes the whole subject, in whatever aspect it may be viewed and whatever may be its consequences, proximate or remote but with the urgency of the case before us and with a multiplicity of other cares and duties bearing upon us all the time, we cannot promise to be very connected nor to go much into a detail of facts.

I. The *claim: My people.* They are *mine and not yours:* for you have no right to them.

THE PREFERMENT OR ASSERTION of a claim implies a right, real or supposed, and the usurpation of that right by others. Pharaoh's claim to the service of the Israelites was utterly unfounded because their God had sent them there for a very different and much better purpose; and so is the claim of all slaveholders to the services of their slaves entirely false and consequently sinful. It is founded in neither reason nor authority. They have no right that can made good in the court of heaven, nor at the bar of reason or before their own consciences, if properly enlightened and suffered to speak to minds free from the blinding indifference of interest, prejudice, or passion; but God's claim is valid and cannot be disputed. This right is absolute and will be maintained against all opposition from men or devils; for it is founded—

1. On creation and preservation.

Every man feels that, so far as other men are concerned, he has a perfect right to the fruits which he has grown by his industry, to the animals which he has raised, to the implements or machinery which he has formed by his ingenuity from materials furnished by the Creator and to the land which he has inherited from his ancestors or for which, according to the municipal laws of the country he has paid a fair price; but God's right is absolute: ours is derived and therefore imperfect. If he has made every thing out of nothing and has given to all men their existence and everything which makes existence either comfortable or desirable, he certainly had a perfect right to employ or dispose of everything as he pleases. This he always has done and always will do; for he is continually asserting his claim to everything and no man can hold any of his earthly possessions any longer than God permits nor can he retain his hold on life an hour longer than God upholds him in being. Mankind, the most important part of the creation, were made in the image of God and were designed especially to manifest his glory and to enjoy his favor. Made of one blood, as they all were, and constituting as they were designed to do and ought to do, one harmonious family living together in mutual sympathy and acts of kindness, for one to compel others, who have not his strength and have not enjoyed his advantages, to serve him all their life without compensation and to entail that compulsory service upon his unborn posterity, is unjust, inhumane and criminal before high heaven. It is robbing them of their birth right and invading the prerogative of God. According to reason, therefore, or the light of nature, no man and no set of men have a right to make slaves of others without an *express* grant from the Creator, which, on the ground we now occupy, no man will be hardy enough to claim.

7   All this is so evident that, we presume it will be questioned by no candid and fair minded man; and hence our revolutionary ancestors, in their noble Declaration of Independence said, "We hold these truths to be self evident, that all men are created equal, that they are endowed by their Creator with certain inalienable rights; that among these are life, liberty, and the pursuit of happiness." By saying that "all men are created equal" they obviously, meant that they are created equal merely in regard to civil and religious rights; for they are the main subject of this ever memorable *Declaration,* which has hitherto excited the admiration of the old world and will stand the test of philosophy, revelation, and experience. More than a quarter of a century ago some Southern politicians of a high mark, in and out of Congress had the

8   effrontery to contradict this assertion of our revolutionary patriots by saying that all men, instead of being created equal, come into the world with very unequal powers of mind and quite as unequal advantages for mental, moral, and social improvement. This we regard as indicating a disingenuousness and a subserviency to personal and local interests altogether unworthy of American statesmen. The inequalities in physical strength, in mental capacities and external advantages are inequalities which the Creator has made to subserve his own wise and beneficent purposes; but the inequalities which exist in their civil and religious rights,—the right of conscience and the right being heard, personally or by the representatives, in all the enactments and discussions which affect their welfare; and the right of employing whatever power the Almighty has given them for their well being—these are inequalities which man has made and which immensely increased the degradation and wretchedness of our race.

9   *Natural differences among men furnish no justification of slavery.* These differences tho' greatly diversified and of almost endless gradations were designed to subserve the most wise and benignant purposes, which we may not always perceive or comprehend but which we cannot doubt. Besides, if left to the unrestricted operation of those laws which the Creator has established the *inequalities* would not be of long duration in any one line of descent; for the strong and the feeble, the gifted and the weak minded would soon change and vicissitude, variety of phenomena and uniformity of design characterize all the works and operations of the divine Being. The hills are as important in their place and the lofty mountains, the rivulets

as the majestic rivers and the lakes as the mighty oceans, but must not be removed nor arrested in their course. The smallest asteroids have an important purpose to answer in in the solar system as well as the mightiest orbs but must be left free to revolve in their appropriate spheres. The fruit on the same tree in your orchard is all of the same size and no two flowers in your garden are precisely of the same hue. No two men or women are, in every respect exactly alike, but are marked by perceptible differences in strength and stature, in features and complexion, in capacity and temperament, in circumstances, tastes, and dispositions. All nations have their peculiarities of intellectual, moral and social character and if these were all properly under a Christian influence they would form a grand and harmonious whole; but to enslave and degrade a part from generation to generation is more absurd and far more wicked and pernicious than the Chinese practice of cramping the feet of their female children and confining them for life to the juvenile size.

Whatever God has ordained in the way of general laws, whether recorded in his written revelation, or impressed originally on their minds, or established in the material universe, was designed for the good of the whole and for all alike; for these general laws, however they may be for a time, obstructed in their operation by the depravity of men or by temporary circumstances, will under his gov't, eventually work out their appropriate results. In the present condition of humanity unceasing alternations of depression and elevation are indispensable to the progress of society and to the present manifestation of God's justice, goodness and mercy to this apostate world. Families and individuals which in the last generation and perhaps thro' several preceding generations, lived in the vale of poverty and were treated with contempt, are now wealthy, talented and prominent if not for most in the community to which they belong, while those who were wealthy, trusted and honored are now poor, ignorant, and worthless. All this is according to the unvarying laws of the human race, for those who have acquired or inherited wealth and favor and high position gradually lose their intellectual enterprise and are left behind in the race of improvement and of social advantage, in the second or third generation, if not in the first; but those who find themselves neglected on account of their poverty and ignorance, having the strongest inducement and the only *sufficient* inducements to a full and vigorous exercise of their powers, and overtake their places in the foremost ranks and give the most effective impulse to the great work of civilization. What is true of individuals is true of nations; for nations are composed of individuals. They have their rise, decay and dissolution and from the same causes which produce these changes in families and individuals but when one nation or tribe makes slaves of another and compels them to do work which they ought to do themselves, they so far counteract the divine goodness and hasten their own disgrace and union.

13   **2. The deep and long-continued degradation of the Africans in their own land no reason why they should be enslaved.**

This plea is commonly made by the advocates of slavery with boldness and with apparent confidence; but it is utterly futile and there is often, at the very time, an obvious consciousness on the part of those who make it, that it is insufficient. Of this the reasons or explanations given are sufficient proof, for it is asserted that they are the most degraded portion of mankind; that they are incapable of civilization; and that a state of slavery is the best state for them. All this we deny and call for something more than bare assertion.

According to the ablest and best writers on the Ethnology, the south sea islanders are a more degraded people than were the Caffres and Hottentots and therefore, by parity of reasoning, they are the people that ought to be enslaved, but this has not been noticed by slave holders.

14   If the most degraded are not be enslaved why should those in the next stage above them be thus treated? Where is there any authority for such a proceeding? If we have to give an account hereafter for all we do in this life we ought to be very certain that we are right, especially in a matter which so materially affects the comforts and welfare of untold millions in their present and unborn generations. *If it is more blessed to give than to receive,* would it not be more nobler more generous, more magnanimous to elevate their condition and consequently to increase their enjoyment, as it would do immeasureably, than to confine them down, as by an adamantine chain, in the neighborhood of the brutes! Is there any consistency in sending the blessing of liberty and civilization, often with much toil and at great expense to other

15   benighted nations, while they are kept in bondage and darkness in the lowest depression and the very furnace of affliction here in our midst?

What length of time sanctions wrong and oppression? Were the men who first enslaved the African race, or even those who first brought them to a perpetual bondage, men of integrity, of humane feelings, of generous impulses and of pure and unselfish patriotism? Were they men whose example we could regard as worthy of imitation and as giving some color of sanction to their conduct? Was not the gov't which established the institution here by force ruling our forefathers at the time with a rod of iron? And did they not soon after denounce it as iniquitous, tyrannical, and cruel? What moral right have we then on this ground, to hold them in bondage? What authority can

16   we plead in justification of tyranny so wanton, cruel, and unreasonable that,

if practiced on any other portion of mankind we should be horror struck at the recital? Why is the black race thus despised rather than the olive, the copper colored, or any other other? Why should those with nappy hair or any other distinguishing peculiarity be confined to a cruel and hopeless bondage rather than those who differ from them? Their extreme degradation on the coast of Africa is owing to the abominable and accursed slave trade; for modern travelers tell us that in the interior of the country, tho' shut out from intercourse with the civilized world, they look like a superior race. Shall we then make one of the most flagrant and enormous crimes in the world, that of the slave trade, justifying another which is only an outgrowth from it, and committed on the same principle? We want an answer which will satisfy enlightened reason and unbiased conscience.

If we have a right now to enslave the Africans on account of their degraded condition, when did we get that right? Or when did they reach the point in their course of deterioration at which we were allowed to seize them and hold them in such an absolute, oppressive, and perpetual bondage? They were not always thus degraded and inferior to the rest of mankind, nor did they become so at an early age of the world. For long generations they appear to have been the superior race and, to the admiration of the literary and scientific community, the mutilated and long buried monuments of their greatness have been brought to light on the Nile, the Tigress, and the Euphrates. The empire of Assyria was founded by Nimrod, a grandson of Ham and the empire of Egypt, for centuries, no less famous than that of Assyria, was founded by Mizriam the second son of Ham. Tyre and

Sidon, those flourishing cities on the Mediterranean coast, which, for many hundred years, were so famous for their wisdom, ingenuity, and enterprise, their manufacturers, commerce and wealth, were soon founded by caravan or some of his descendants. According to history, the posterity of Ham was much more talented enterprising and progressive than those of either Shem or Japhet. Dispersing more widely and with less delay, they seized upon the most important places and took the most prompt and judicious measure to their possessions secure. Some settled around Persian Gulf and in the Southern parts of Asia. Cush, the oldest son, occupied an Arabic land on the Red Sea, in or bordering on what is called lower Egypt and including Ethiopia whence they spread over the torrid zone of Africa and became the black race. Canaan seized upon Syria and the country which has ever since borne his name but was frequently afterwards called the promised land. Mizraim, as we have seen, occupied Egypt and Abysinnia. Thus we find them, in a little time, holding firm and secure possession of all the most important points that were then known or could be readily ascertained: The head of the Persian Gulf, the mouth of the Tigris and Euphrates, the river

Nile, with its widely extended and fertile plains, and the fine harbors of Tyre and Sidon which they founded large, flourishing and permanent empires, cultivated the arts and sciences, became famous in arms and carried on a world wide and most profitable commerce, while all the rest of mankind were engaged in hunting, or tending their flocks, or whiling away the hours in idle amusements.

When the Roman empire was in the zenith of its power, many of the Africans were still a warlike people and did not hesitate sometimes to contend in arms with the mistress of the world. Every school boy can talk about the fame of Carthage, an African city which was founded by a colony from Tyre, 848 years before Christ and was, for a long time, the rival of Rome. During a period of less than two hundred years between 400 and 200 B.C. they had quite a galaxy of men who were celebrated for their enterprise and generalship. There were six African generals, during that period by the name of *Hamilear*, all of whom were more or less distinguished and some of whom were more than a match for the ablest of the Roman commanders. There were two or three by the name of *Hasdrubal* who gave their sworn enemies, the Romans, a great deal of trouble, and were overcome at last only by superior numbers and discipline. There was more than one, we believe, by the name of *Hannibal*, ; but there was one of that name, a son of Hamilear the V, in the order of the time, who was certainly one of the ablest generals of this age to which he belonged: and there were other names of note in history to which we cannot now refer.

In the early ages of Christianity the gospel had quite an extensive and thorough influence along the Nile and over all the northern part of Africa. Flourishing churches were established in every town and neighborhood where there was a population sufficient to maintain them and for a series of generations they had many learned able and popular preachers who contributed greatly to the suppression of error and the establishment of truth. A number of the most learned, pious and useful ministers which the church has for centuries, where African bishops and their names will occupy a prominent place on the pages of history to the end of time. Although they were descendents of Ham they were not thus regarded as an inferior race, but their ministers and churches had as much influence on the general faith and order of Christendom as those of any other country until Rome got the ascendancy.

From history it appears then that all nations are greatly indebted to the race of Ham; for they were the intrepid, earnest, and successful pioneers in the march of improvement. For centuries after the Deluge and after the dispersion from Babel, while the other races were spending their time in comparative idleness and indifference about the future, engaged in the chase or tending their flocks or whiling away the hours in idle amusements, the bold and enterprising sons of Ham were engaged with an industry, perseverance and success equal to those of modern times in founding empires, building cities and establishing governments; in the more important occupations of life—agricultural, ship building and commerce; in all the mechanical and fine arts—music, painting, and statuary. Had it not been for them we know not how long the posterity of Shem and Japhet would have been dwelling in tents, aspiring after no higher attainments and dreaming of no higher enjoyments than belonged to a shepherd's life. Now we would like to know when or how they became so degraded as to justify us in regarding them as an inferior race and in buying and selling them, without respect to age or sex, or to the conjugal and perpetual relations, like cattle in the market? Have we no veneration for them on account of the distinguished leadership which they took us as a race, in the improvement of society? Is the treatment which they have received from us worthy of a great and magnanimous, a free and professedly a Christian people? True, they have lost the Christian privileges which they once enjoyed and that may be considered as the main cause of their deterioration. So have other portions of mankind, such as Babylon, Syria, Palestine and Asia Minor, at least in a great measure, and have in the same proportion, become insignificant and worthless. Ham's descendants, if we may judge from Abraham's intercourse with the monarch of Egypt and from his and Isaac's intercourse with Abimelec, king of Gerar, retained a knowledge of the true God much longer than any other portion of mankind except that one branch of Shem's family to which the promise was made: and the Christian churches and ministers in Africa retained a commendable soundness in the faith longer than those in Asia and Europe. Should we not then honor them as a race for what they have done, or for what God has done for them and by them? And it surely does not become us to treat them thus with contempt and rigor, without a cause for ancestors were once every little if any better than the Caffres or Hottentots of the present day. In the time of Caesar, not long before the Christian era, their priests, the Druids, offered human sacrifices and the people could have been such very little lower in superstition and wretchedness. Other Roman writers of that age tell us that the Anglos and Britons and the Germans, from both of whom, we, the Anglosaxons, the traducers and oppressors of the Africans have descended, were exceedingly ignorant, superstitious and degraded. The Romans, though greatly addicted to superstition and grossly immoral, held them in contempt and regarded them in as an inferior race; but without any solicitation or reward from them, the gospel, with all its hallowing, ameliorating and civilizing influences was sent to them by Christians in the south of Europe and that, in a long series of ages, has gradually raised them to the front rank among the civilized portions of mankind. It was a slow process, however, and those who have not read and reflected on the subject, may be surprised, if not incredulous, when told that it has required near fifteen hundred years since they first received the Bible as a revelation from heaven and a free gift from the church, to attain their present elevation of character and of social enjoyment. It is only about two hundred years since the most favored communities began to understand their civil and religious rights and little more than three quarters of a century since these rights were embodied in a declaration of independence on all monarchical power. Nor is it two generations since two thirds or four fifths of the people in this free and enlightened country were the slaves of many absurd and ridiculous superstitions. Your grandfathers and grandmothers can tell you how the people generally believed in signs and portents, in fairies, witches, ghosts and hobgoblins, how observant they were of lucky and unlucky days and how they were frightened out of their wits by the an eclipse of the sun, the appearance of a comet, or a play of meteors in the heavens. Then if this boasted and boasting Anglosaxon race with an open Bible in their hands and with the ameliorating and humanizing influences of Christianity steadily bearing upon them all the time have been fifteen hundred years in arriving at this present low stage of progress, how dare we say that the Africans, who have been, for long centuries shut out from this light of heaven and from these benign influences and have been moreover debased and stupefied by that abominable traffic, the slave trade, are an inferior race? How can we in justice, or reason, or common honesty, say they are incapable of civilization and are so inferior as to justify us in making slaves of them from generation to generation and buying and selling them, like other domestic animals in the market? Even if they were as inferior as the advocates of slavery assert, they certainly have as good a right to the free use of whatever power the Creator has given them as the weak minded among the white or as those who have been more liberally endowed. *He who is unjust in that which is least is unjust also in much.*

He who will rob another who has not strength to resist him, or who, in a trade will take advantage of another's ignorance is unjust, not only to him, but to God and to the community in which he lives, for this wrong use he makes of the powers which have been given him for a very different purpose. If their inferiority, as a race, supposing it were true, would justify us in making slaves of them, a similar reason would justify us in making slaves of the South Sea Islands and many other portions of mankind. I find nothing in the Bible, in reason, or in common sense and the nature of the case that gives any kind of sanction to slavery on this ground. And the fact is if this principle were carried out it would result in universal misrule and wrong and oppression and violence would once more fill the earth.

3. The alleged antiquity of slavery furnishes no justification of the practice.

It has been asserted every where and by men of high standing in every department of public life that slavery always has existed in the world and that it always will exist at least until the millennium and probably to the end of time. If this were true it would be no proof that slavery is right and that we or any other people can perpetuate it without woeful criminality, for on this ground every enormity that has ever been perpetuated might be justified. Sin has been in the world very nearly as long as the race of man and the outgrowths of his depraved nature, rank and deadly, have been developing themselves in every conceivable abomination and in every possible form of injustice and oppression. The first born of Adam was a murderer and a fratricide; and except so far as the restraints of grace and Providence prevent, man has been, in all ages and all lands, tyrannizing over his fellow men and the world has been often *filled with violence*. It is strange that men of talents, extensive learning and hopeful piety, would, in this nineteenth century and in this land of boasted freedom, science and general intelligence, resort to such an argument; for it would be equally valid, in favor of every atrocity and every wrong that has ever been committed; but it shows either a conscious want of more substantial arguments or a careless indifference in regard to truth. If the question can not be settled by a fairer process of reasoning or by authority which cannot be controverted it had better be given up, for bare assertions, such as are under consideration, which may be met by counter assertions, or may be made just as available in favor of every species of vice, only betray the weakness of the cause or of the advocate.

But we deny the assertion and ask for proof. We contend, on the contrary that, among barbarous tribes and in the early ages of the world such slavery as we have here in these Southern states, could not possibly exist because they had no civil govts of sufficient strength and maturity to establish and maintain such an institution. We are told that before the Deluge, the earth was filled with violence but there is no intimation of slavery.

That form of violence was rather not known, or the sacred writer has passed it over in silence and there is no proof. Civil govts arbitrary despotisms as they appear to have been—began to be formed at an early age after the "destruction of all flesh," but not for two or three generations after Noah left the ark; and, in that time, considering the longevity of men, in the first

32 centuries of the post diluvian perio, that part of Asia where they lived must have been densely populated. According to the earliest accounts we have, the tribes and nations of a remote antiquity which were generally engaged in war, considered that they had a right to do what they pleased with their captives taken in battle or in their maurading expeditions and they disposed of them in different ways. The manner in which our western Indians have treated their prisoners may be taken, perhaps, as a sample of the manner in which captives taken in war have always been treated by rude and barbarous tribes. Some they put to death on the spot, some they reserved for a time, leaving their fate to be determined by circumstances; Some, after being kept for a time were permitted to leave in peace and return home and a few were adopted by an aged king or queen, a king's daughter or a chief warrior, and incorporated into the tribe. Avarice had not then got such entire possession of mankind; but humanity, caprice, and admiration of a captive's heroism had more influence.

33 In a rude state of society the passions are predominant and hence among all barbarous or uncivilized tribes such strange and otherwise unaccountable alternations of sternness and relenting, cruelty and kindness. They are all the time passing from one extreme to the other and their proceedings in the treatment of captives, as in everything else, were not not governed by any deliberate and permanent system and, of course, they had nothing like slavery as it is understood and practiced in this country. It is to the nations which had formed a regular and permanent system of government, such as Eygpt, Babylon, Greece, and Rome that we much look for that species of despotism called slavery, if it is to be found at all in the ages of human life and progressiveness; and, it is believed that whatever of the kind can be found among them from first to last, will compare favorably with that which we have in the Southern states.

34 4. Slavery in Egypt.

As the early history of that country is still involved in much obscurity and as a minute inquiry into this subject is not necessary to my purpose, I shall content myself with the account given in the Bible of their condition and treatment of the Israelites while there. About six hundred years or a little more perhaps after Noah left the ark, Jacob went with his family into the land of Pharaoh, where they became servants and were detained in the house of bondage two hundred and fifteen years while Joseph lived and probably for a short time after they were not oppressed, but were treated with much lenity and kindness. From the first some of the most active among them were employed to tend Pharaoh's cattle; but this was neither oppressive nor humiliating; for it had been their occupation from their youth up to that time. Sometimes after the death of Joseph, other men got in power and a change was gradually made for the race.

It is said that a king arose who knew not Joseph and that he began to treat them with rigor. Two acts of cruelty are related, at which the feelings of a Christian community now revolt, but they appeared to have been confined to the monarch who was on the throne when they were brought out with the high hand and the outstretched arm of Omnipotence. Previous to that time they had been employed, at least the most athletic and vigorous part of them, in building the pyramids and other public works; but the Pharaoh who so pertinaciously, refused to let them go when the demand was made upon him and whose obstinacy proved his ruin, ordered that the male children should all be put to death as soon as they were born and that the men should still furnish their full total of brick, but without having straw furnished them as had formerly been done. Both of these seem to have been precautionary measures for his own safety and were not acts of wanton cruelty. He apprehensive that if they became too numerous they would attempt to usurp or subvert the government and he thought it prudent to take such steps in time as would effectually preclude the possibility of such an attempt. He wish to retain them in his service and at the same time prevent the danger he had or fancied he had reason to dread. By destroying all the male children in infancy he aimed to prevent their increase by requiring of the men such an oppressive service to subdue their spirits so that they would not have the heart to engage in such an enterprise. There is no intimation of an edict that their bondage should be upon them forever and probably he thought of nothing more than holding them under authority while he lived. The acts specified were acts of great barbarity; but Pharaoh was a heathen monarch, who knew not Jehovah the only true God and that was an age of war when life was little regarded, when no means were thought to be unlawful for retaining power.

With this view of the matter we can understand how it was that not withstanding these atrocious acts, there was still so much in their lot that was favorable. Their domestic relations were not interfered with, husbands and wives, and parents and children were not separated and bought and sold to the highest bidder like cattle in the market so far as any intimation to the contrary is now recollected they were exclusively the property of the government and that no "bills of sale" were ever given of them to private individuals, they owned no land, because from the time of Joseph, the lands belonged to Pharaoh and the people were his tenants, but they were not, like our slaves, so far outlawed that they could 'hold no property of any kind; for they had cattle in abundance, and they had money, jewelry, and other property; they were artisans well skilled in all the mechanical arts- in tanning, dressing, and dying skins, in architecture and in fabricating implements of husbandry, in working gold, silver, and brass, in spinning weaving and making up fabrics of a fine and elegant texture. The Egyptians were not forbidden to teach them the use of letters, or were they forbidden, as the slaves are here, to teach one another; their genealogies of tribes and families appear to have been kept with a great deal of accuracy; many of them were quite intelligent and they had, from the first, a government of their own, for Moses, on a brief notice, assembled their elders or princes and heads of tribes and families, when he went to inform them of the Commission which the God of their fathers had given him for their deliverance. When Moses in his little ark of bulrushes was exposed to death on the Nile, Pharaoh's daughter adopted him for her son and employed a Hebrew woman, who happened to be the child's mother, to nurse him until he could do without a mother's care and paid her for her trouble, then had him carefully educated in all the learning of Egypt and intended to make him, it is said, her successor to the throne.

From these facts it appears, that, excepting the two acts of cruelty above specified, which were evidently designed as precautionary measures, for the safety and perpetuity of the government and, in that age of war and rudeness, when life as not valued any where, was not regarded by the world as very conservable, the bondage of the Israelites in Egypt was greatly preferable to that of our slaves in these southern states, where not sort of respect is paid by the law, and the executive officers to the conjugal and parental relations any more than if they were beasts; where they are sold under the hammer, like horses and mules to the highest bidder where no negro, however industrious, honest, and meritorious; can legally own a cent's worth of property. Where they are not allowed even to teach one another how to read. Where they are forbidden under heavy penalties to intermarry with whites, to the fourth generation inclusive though one of the parents in each generation may have been a white person; and where they can not be freed even for the most meritorious services, except on such conditions as make it a farce or a mockery, but the whole race are doomed to the most abject servitude and while sun and moon endure. In Egypt the Israelites had a number of rights which were certainly respected by the monarch and by all in authority among which was that of being adopted by the heir apparent to the throne and made his successor. At least, this was not forbidden or it would not have been done and this with fact with others which have been mentioned shows that their condition was nothing like so wretched and hopeless, though they were subject to a heathen government, as that of the

African race in this country. Occassionally there may be found a humane and Christian master who shows his servants all the lenity he can and generally they are not overworked; but we speak of the laws and of the positions in which they placed by the legislative enactments of the country.

5. Slavery, if there was such a thing, in Babylon.

Here again we shall confine ourselves to the account given us in the Bible respecting the captivity of the Jews and their condition in the land to which they were carried. They are not represented, we believe, as being in the "the house of bondage" or "in the furnace of affliction" as when they were in Egypt, the land of the Pharaohs; but are generally spoken of as captives, "the captives at Babylon" because they had been taken prisoners in war and carried to the land of their captors and kept there for a time at least, against their will. The hardship, in their case, consisted not so much in any oppressive service that was required of them nor in their absolute subjection to the will of another, as in the loss of certain religious and social privileges of inestimable value, which they had long enjoyed and of which they were no deprived as a punishment for their abuse of them. The mass of the people were no doubt, made servicable to the king in some way or other, whether by cultivating his lands or working on his public buildings, we are not informed, but we hear no complaints of bondage or oppression. They remembered their former days and contrasted them with the present. They thought of the light hearted amusements and associations of childhood and youth. The school houses where they learned to read God's own account of the wonderful works which he had wrought for their forefathers; of Jerusalem, the sacred city, the joy of the whole earth; of the glorious temple and of its priesthood, its sacrifices and its services; of their holy Sabbaths, their new moons and their solemn assemblies when the tribes all repaired to the dwelling place of the Most High with their oblations of every kind and after a season of thanksgiving, of penitent confession and social gatherings, returned home joyful in the God of their salvation. They thought upon these things and were sad. They set by the streams and hung their harps upon the willows and wept when they remembered Zion, but this was of short duration and the greater part of them soon engaged in the usual occupations of life. They bought and sold, they married and were given in marriage; they sowed their fields and gathered in their harvests. From aught that appears to the contrary, they became in a little time, contented with their lot and were busily employed in the industrial and profitable avocations of life. Daniel and his three friends, Hannaniah, Mishael, and Azariah, were soon promoted to offices of trust and responsibility. Daniel was virtually made prime minister; for he was next to the king; and the other three were made governors of provinces. Esther was made queen of the empire and Mordecai was promoted to great riches and honor. When their enemies sought their destruction they were allowed "to stand for themselves" or to use the right of self defence and to destroy all that came against them.

These facts without going further into detail, show the manner in which the captive Jews were from first to last, treated in Babylon and as the same treatment substantially was continued thro' a change of dynasties and under several different kings from different nations. We have referred to their history while in the land of their conquerors to show our readers how, we believe, prisoners of war were "usually" treated by the civilized but heathen nations of antiquity. They were certainly not deprived of all their rights as human beings and used and disposed of as the other domestic animals, but they were stimulated to exertion by the hope of reward, their powers were developed without restriction and like other citizens, they were employed in the service of their country in whatever way they could contribute most to its prosperity and welfare. All this might be confirmed by a reference to other conquered nations in those ancient times, but it is unnecessary.

6. Slavery in Ancient Greece.

The accounts given us on this subject by Thucydides, Plutarch, and other Greek writers are contradictory exaggerated and unsatisfactory, which can be accounted for only by supposing that for a time, the treatment of slaves, who were, in the first instance, prisoners of war, was not regulated by established laws, or that the cruelties which were said to be practised were only partial and were attributed to the pride and passions of individuals in spite of the laws. Even this enlightened and Christian country numberless acts of cruelty have committed on the slaves, but which, owing to the negligence of executive officers on the difficulty of getting sufficient proof, this in direct violation of legislative enactments, were suffered to go unpunished, and much more must this have been the case in that age of semibarbarism. In the heroic age when masters in Athens claimed to have the power of life and death over their slaves, they were often treated, under the influence of individual passion or caprice with great barbarity; but humanity triumphed and a law was passed that they should not be punished until by a legal and fair trial they had been proved to be guilty. In that rude age when war was a trade and men were accustomed to deeds of atrocity, when life was not valued except for purposes of war, when pride and ambition of military prowess were the ruling passions and when no other restraints than those of necessity or of public sentiment and expediency were put upon a vindictive spirit, acts of great inhumanity, as might be expected, were frequent and monstrous, but with the progress of intelligence and refinement the claims of humanity came to be more and more regarded and the condition, especially of the servile class, was greatly ameliorated.

The slaves of Sparta were called *Helots* and from their number, their treatment and their ultimate influence on the country they have occupied a conspicuous place in history. The Spartans were, for a long time, the most warlike people of Greece and their civil polity was modeled through out with a view to cherish that spirit and to maintain that character. The young men from childhood to full maturity had a training which was calculated to inspire them with courage and make them as efficient as possible in war. For this purpose it was necessary that they should be exempt from the common occupations of life; but this could be done without a servile class who should cultivate the lands and perform the menial duties that are indispensable in every civilized community. Such was the part assigned to the Helots; and we need not enquire whether the Dorians, when they conquered the country, found them in a servile country or reduced them to such a condition and kept them in it as long as they could. That these were occasionally treated with barbarity by the governmental authorities and that they were not sufficiently protected by law from the cruelty of individuals, or what we term mob law, is more than probable; for the facts are stated by some of their best historians; but these irregularities were such a might be expected to occur, once in a while, among a people characterized by all the ungovernable passions and all the recklessness incidental to a state of continual warfare and under a government which was not only defective, exceedingly so, when compared with the governments of Christian nations at the present day, but essentially military in its constitution and in all its enactments when an act of inhumanity was perpetuated by the government, which was very scarcely done, it seems to have been prompted by a mistaken notion that it was necessary to the safety of the commonwealth and when done by individuals or small parties it appears to have been owing to the lawlessness of excited passions.

The condition of the Helots or slaves in Sparta when compared that of the master portion of the community, was greatly superior to the condition of the black in this country when compared to that of the whites; for they had many important rights and privileges of which our slaves are wholly deprived.

In the first place, in the cultivation of the soil which was the general employment, their *interest* was made to bear upon them as an encouragement to industry and economy; for after paying the owners a moderate rent, which was all that was required of them, they might have a considerable surplus for their own use. They could live plentifully and then add, more or less, according to circumstances, as many of them did, to their stock in hand.

In the next place, no restrictions were laid upon their acquisition of knowledge; but they were encouraged and aided in their efforts to learn what the citizens generally had learned and many of them became as well educated as any other class of society.

In the third place, many of them accompanied their masters when they went to war, chiefly as attendants, but were furnished with light armor and were expected to give assistance in cases of emergency.

In the fourth place, on occasion of peculiar danger and difficulty they were taken into battle as "heavy armed soldiers" but then if they did their duty, they were ever after free men.

In the fifth place, those that were raised with their masters sons always had their freedom given them as a kind of honorary distinction; but were not allowed the privileges of citizens unless they attained it in the regular way, which could be easily done and was generally done by all the better part of them.

In the sixth place, the natural relationships of life were not nullified by legislative enactments but they were undisturbed in their domestic relations and their children might grow up like olive plants around their table. The husband and wife had no apprehension of being torn asunder and separated to a returnless distance, nor of having their children forced from their fond embrace and sold off under the hammer and with as little remorse or feeling of any kind, on the part of sellers and buyers, as if they had no souls and no attachments.

In the last place, there was a way open, a prescribed, simple and well known process, by which any of them who were so disposed, could obtain all the rights and privileges of citizenship, as many of them did, and then they were, to all intents and purposes legally and practically, on an equality with the native born citizens.

The above facts, which have been gathered from Thirlwall's history of Greece and from Anthon's Classical Dictionary, are exceedingly important, because they shew that their slaves in heathen Greece, two or three hundred years before the coming of Christ had many valuable rights and privileges which are wholly denied to the slaves in this professedly Christian and Protestant country. A reference in often made to the Helots of Sparta for the purpose of shewing how much better off the blacks are in this country than their slaves were in Greece, as if the people in this boasted land of Bible Christianity and of boasted intelligence and protestant freedom, in the nineteenth century, ought to take their lessons of justice and humanity from a heathen community more than two thousand years ago; but if we make a fair allowance for the crude notion of liberty and self government then entertained, and for the powerful causes which more often producing ungovernable outbursts of human passion and the absence of sufficient motives to keep them in proper bounds, the comparison will be greatly in favor of the heathen probity.

7. Slavery in the Roman Empire.

In Rome, as in most other nations of antiquity, when war, rapine, and plunder were universal, it was a maxim that the conquerors had an absolute right to the conquered and all who their clemency spared were reduced to a state of servitude. During the period of its rising greatness, the conquests of that singular republic or kingdom, whichever it may be called, so "diverse" from all others, were so rapid and so intensive that their slaves became very numerous. All nations and tribes that did not peaceably submit to their authority were regarded as enemies and an enemy might be killed or spared at their pleasure. During their career of conquest, their prisoners who were sold as slaves, were treated, sometimes by the constituted authorities and oftener by their masters with wanton cruelty partly to keep down anything like an insurrectionary spirit which they had much reason to apprehend and partly to gratify their inordinate love of power.

At first, we presume, they had formed no settled plan of treatment for their slaves and had no express reference to the perpetuity of the bondage in the same line. It was only the barbarous tribes however who were thus treated, for the more civilized nations even allowed their liberty and gradually incorporated into the empire and permitted to enjoy all the rights of citizenship. But when they had conquered all the nations of Asia and the young empire, in its vigorous growth and iron strength had become mistress of the world they had no other supply of slaves than their natural increase they were taken under the protection of government and a more humane treatment was secured to them. Masters had long possessed the power of life and death over their slaves; but "this power was now taken out of private hands and given to the magistrate alone. The subterranean prisons were abolished; and, upon a just complaint of intolerable treatment, the injured slave obtained either his deliverance or a less cruel master."

55   Regular marriages were generally encouraged amongst them and, in ordinary times, at least, the could have their families about them without the fear of premature separation. They were often employed in war and fought in their ranks like other soldiers; for in the war with Hannibal, the state purchased, on credit, of their masters, eight thousand, were divided into two regiments and there was no charge against them of cowardice or inefficiency in any respect. They were employed on other occasions and, for ought that appears to the contrary, always made good soldiers.

Instead of any prohibition by law or public sentiment they were encouraged to learn and were, in fact, carefully taught in all the arts and sciences of the country; for they were the teachers of their masters children and must have well instructed themselves. Many of them were much better educated and more intelligent than their masters; and it remained for Protestant Christianity in this land of freedom and in the nineteenth century to forbid their intellectual development and to chain down their immortal mind in darkness.

56   But a much higher privilege was still within their reach; for masters could emancipate their slaves when they chose; and any slave might by rendering himself agreeable or useful, obtain the inestimable boon of freedom. The humanity, avarice, or ambition of masters for a time set so many of their slaves free that the higher orders became alarmed for their safety or distinction of their rank, perhaps too, for the purity of the Roman blood and a law was passed that the honorable distinction should be confined to such slaves only as, for just causes and with the approbation of the magisterial should receive such a solemn and legal manumission. Although this entitled them only to freedom, but excluded civil and military honors, a way was prescribed by which they could obtain all the rights and privileges of native born citizenry. Such, according to Gibbon and other writers was slavery in ancient Rome, warlike and always warring, stern, fierce and reckless of life, that frightful monster of cruelty, as represented in the vision of the prophet; and we think it manifest that their condition when compared with the master portion of the community was much better than that of our slaves when compared with the corresponding class of the whites.

57   **8. The orderings of Providence furnish no justification of slavery.**

There are few words in our language that are in more frequent use and few that are more oftener perverted or misapplied. By the term Providence we generally mean that constant and absolute good which God exercises over this world and all that it contains. This includes, of course, his control over humans and all other agencies and his employment of these agencies to accomplish his own purposes. Man has a *will* or the power of choice; but all his affections or desires which determine his volitions are depraved and, so far as permitted, he is continually going wrong. The Lord permits every man to go so far in his own blind and perverse way as to manifest his character and teach him, if he will learn his dependence; but he says, *The wrath or wickedness of man shall praise him and the remainder* or what would not be for his praise, *he will restrain.* He permitted the inhabitants of the old world to [proceed] with their violence and other crimes until they could be borne no longer and then destroyed them all by a flood.

He permitted the inhabitants of Sodom and Gomorrha to indulge in their abominations until they were ripe for ruin and then swept them with the broom of destruction. He suffered the Canannites to go on in their idolatry and sensuality until the *measure of their iniquity was full* and then commissioned his own people to exterminate them from the earth. He permitted Judas to betray his master and then sent the traitor to his own place and overruled the act so as to accomplish the redemption of mankind. In like manner he has permitted that curse and disgrace of modern Christendom, the African slave trade and the slavery which has supported it; but nothing except the perversity of man would ever construe that into a sanction of the nefarious deed. *for he is not tempted of evil neither tempteth he any man.* Moses said to the people of Israel, *Secret things belong unto the Lord your God; but the things which are revealed to you and your children.* By secret things he meant the orderings of God's providence, which are not revealed but of which we are for most important reasons left in ignorance until they occur.

Providence has permitted all the fraud and injustice, all the lust and ambition, all the tyranny and oppression, all the crimes and abominations that have been committed in the world or they would not have been committed, but will any Christian say that these crimes are therefore justifiable? If he only withdraws the restraints which he usually exercises over men, their passions will soon burst out and rage with destructive fury; and he sometimes leaves nations communities and individuals to take their own way *until their iniquity is found to be hateful*, or until they find utter ruin starring them in the face. So he suffered the French nation, in their infidelity and pride of intellect, to banish the Bible, the ordinances, and every form of religion until they were compelled, as the only refuge from extermination, to recall them again. So he has done and so he will do, with the nations or communities which attempt to hold their fellow men in bondage and counteract his merciful designs towards the race of man. This question of duty must always be decided by a reference to great great moral principles, or, which is the same thing, to the inspired oracles of revealed truth, and not by the permissions of Providence. It is strange how inconsiderately and unmeaningly the term is generally used; for Providence is made to favor every successful undertaking whether right or wrong. If a man has prospered in his efforts to accumulate property, tho' it has been been by taking advantage of those who are ignorant of business or less crafty than himself, Providence has certainly favored him; If an army has been victorious in battle Providence has certainly been on their side and he is complimented with an anthem of praise and thanksgiving. Alexander, Ceasar, and Napolean; those scourges of humanity, all thanked the gods for successes and so did the Roman Catholics in all their horrid butcheries of the Protestants. Slave holders talk very fluently about the wise and kind Providence which brought the negroes into this country to be civilized; but as an army when unsuccessful in battle has nothing to say about Providence, they have no notion of giving them up or of thanking Providence for taking them away.

9. The Lord's claim on the Africans and all other races and portions of mankind is founded on *redemption.*

Every man thinks he has such a right to what he has purchased with his money as well as to what he has fashioned by his skill or acquired by his toils and sacrifices, that it cannot be taken from him by fraud or violence, without gross and manifest injustice; but when the whole world was under condemnation and led captive by the devil at his will, Jesus Christ *gave himself a ransom for all to be justified in due time.* The covenant of redemption runs thus; Ps 2:7. *I will declare the decree; the Lord hath said unto me, Thou art my Son this day have I begotten thee. Ask of me and I shall give thee the heathen for thine inheritance and the uttermost parts of the earth for they possession.* Psalm 72 is throughout a prediction of the universal homage which should be said of the righteousness and peace which should everywhere prevail. It was promised to Abraham, Gen 22:18, that in his seed all the nations of the earth should be blessed—and Jacob on his death bed, said to his sons, by the spirit of prophecy, *the scepter shall not depart from Judah nor a lawgiver from between his feet until Shiloh come; and unto him shall the gathering of the people be* Gen 49:10. Jesus Christ himself said that if he were lifted up he would draw all men unto him; and the Apostle says that, *every knee shall bow to him and every tongue shall confess that he is Lord to the glory of God the Father.* To the Christian reader it is unnecessary to multiply quotations from the Bible, for the great object of his faith and prayers and efforts is the universal reign of Jesus Christ in all the glory of his mediatorial kingdom when *all kings shall fall down before him and all nations shall serve him;* but if all nations were included in the cov't of redemption and destined to shew forth his praise here as well as hereafter, no man and no act of men have a right to claim the services of any portion of his purchased inheritance.

Every nation since the day of Pentecost, that has acknowledged Jesus Christ to be the only Savior of the lost and the rightful sovereign of the world, every nation that has received the Bible as a revelation from heaven and has, in its most solemn transactions of a governmental kind required an oath to be taken on it in all cases of witness bearing and of induction into office, has come into the same relation to him into which the Jewish commonwealth was brought at Sinai. Other heathen nations all stand pretty much in the same relation to Him in which the descendants of Abraham, so far as they were then included in the promise, stood to Him before their deliverance from Egypt, with this single and obvious difference that the church, in its ministry and in its membership, received a commission before the risen Redeemer left the earth, to go and carry the light of the gospel to them that were sitting in darkness and proclaim an immediate and eternal deliverance to all who were in bondage to sin and Satan.

The commission was to elevate their character and increase their rational enjoyment by giving them the light of revelation and of science and by bringing them to the knowledge of salvation through the mercy of our God and thus inspiring them with the hopes of immortality; but not to enslave them and keep them in ignorance, degradation and wretchedness, from generation to generation, without any crime alleged and without any authority whatsoever from the Lord whom they profess to serve. As redemption, however, is purely a matter of revelation, or becomes known to us only by revelation, we are now on Bible ground and must appeal to the law and to the testimony. Hitherto we have been arguing from reason or the light of nature; but now we must go to the oracles of truth and abide by their decision. The advocates of slavery appeal to the Bible and, as truth ought to be our only object, some enquiry into the teachings of inspiration on this important subject, if conducted with a right spirit can do no harm, prove all things and hold fast that which is right.

10. Difference between servants and slaves.

All the interminable and fruitless controversy in the world is owing to the of precision in the use of language. Words which are very different in their meaning are used as synonimous or interchangeably and the same word is often used in very different senses. Some who may be sincere in what they profess to believe and zealous for truth never take pains to ascertain and define language which they use, especially those terms on which the controversy turns, and others use such words in a vague or indefinite sense with the design of producing confusion of ideas and giving plausibility to the wrong side. Every lover of truth and fairness, when engaged in argument, has found the advantage of defining terms and whether right or wrong, it should always be done. In this case, we regard the distinction between *servant* and *slave* as on of vital importance and we hope that the reader will bear it in mind as he goes along. According to our best Dictionaries and our best writers and speakers, a *servant* is one who serves another freely and usually for a stipulated reward or compensation. A *slave* is one who renders a compulsory service and without any compensation. Most languages ancient and modern use different terms to designate those two classes of dependents, because they had both servants and slaves and therefore needed appropriate or distinct terms for them. Webster says, *a servant,* from *servans* is one who attends another for the purpose of performing menial offices for him, or who is *employed* by another for such offices, or to labor for the other. A *slave* from the German *sclave,* or the Danish *slaves* is one who is *wholly subject to the will of another.* Every slave is a servant; but every servant is not a slave. Strictly speaking we are *all servants;* for we must serve one another or we could not live; but this service, whether it be menial or otherwise, ought to be voluntary in capacity for higher occupations and external circumstances will always place some in the position of servants; but they should have the full benefit of whatever power they possess.

Conditioned as we are in this world there are all sorts of work to be done and there must be all sorts of people to do it; but it is neither just nor wise to confine the drudgery, or the menial business of life to one race or give one portion of mankind. the rich feeling no necessity of exertion and perhaps enneverated by luxury, become remiss and lose their mental enterprise while the lower classes have every possible inducement to exert themselves and left free from restraint, will exert themselves to the uttermost. From the most important discoveries in science, philosophy and astronomy; the most useful inventions in the mechanical arts, such as the Steam engine, the Telegraph, the reaper, the sewing machine, the cotton gin and others and the most admired specimens of the fine arts—music, painting and sculpture, the world is indebted to men who were absolutely poor or in very moderate circumstances. They became renowned, acquired fortunes, and advanced to a high position in society. In this way all the progress of mankind has been made; but their posterity, in the next or following generation, deteriorate and, sinking to the bottom, give place to others.

In ancient Rome, Gibbon says, they had both servants and slaves, and nearly as many of the one as of the other. This is an important fact, which may be of use to us hereafter, and the reader will do well to keep it in mind. *Servants* are recognized and their duties, while remaining such, are distinctly pointed out in both parts of the Bible; but *slavery* in our sense of the term, I have not been able to find there, from the first of Genesis to the end of Revelation. To all the gradations of society which he designed should exist among men he has given full and plain instructions in regard to their duty; but to those who have been reduced to permanent bondage and oppression by the avarice, ambition, and cruelty of their fellow men, he has simply enjoined submission until he has provided a way for their deliverance. This is not in accordance with the avowed belief of a majority in the southern states, but it is the sentiment of the Protestant world generally and we think time will prove its correctness altho' the subject may have been discussed by a thousand writers and speakers, men of learning and eloquence, it is not exhausted and the discussion ought to be continued without let or hindrance until the question is finally settled.

11. Noah's prediction.

Those who undertake to a advocate the cause of slavery say, in substance, that Noah, by the spirit of prophecy, uttered a malediction on the posterity of Ham and that we are, therefore justifiable in reducing the Africans, who are his descendants, to a condition of slavery and in availing ourselves of their muscular strength for purposes of gain. It seems that after the Deluge had subsided and the earth had become reproductive, the old patriarch became a husbandman, planted a vineyard and made wine, of which he drank too freely and became intoxicated. We presume that he was not acquainted with the intoxicating properties of the wine and was thus *overtaken in a fault*. This is probable from his well known character for imminent piety, and from the fact that he is not charged with a repetition of the same act; but be this as it may, when he awoke from his state of insensibility and knew that his younger son, Ham, had treated him in his exposed condition with unbecoming levity, he gave utterance to the following language: *Cursed by Canaan, the servant of servants shall he be to his brethren. And he said Blessed be the Lord God of Shem, and Canaan shall be his servant. God shall enlarge Japheth and he shall dwell in the tents of Shem and Canaan shall be his servant.* If these words were interpreted literally, the curse would seem to be exhausted when the Canaanites were all destroyed by the people of Israel, except one clan, the Gibeonites, who for a flagrant crime, were reduced to a state of servitude; but if we understand the language as including all the descendants of Ham, which we would hardly be warranted in doing by the ordinary rules of exegesis and are justified, if at all, in giving it such a latitude of meaning only by the event, the following enquiries would will arise: Was it a command or a simple prediction? If a command, did it become binding immediately, or at what time afterwards? No respect was paid to it and no attempt was made to obey it for more than eight hundred years and then in relation to a very small branch of his posterity.

71   That the descendants of Shem and Japheth did not understand it as a command appears from the fact that none of them made any attempt to subjugate any part of Ham's posterity until the Israelites more than eight hundred years afterwards, receive a special injunction to subdue and exterminate the people of Canaan. Is the command binding on all the descendants of Shem and Japheth—our western Indians, the Esquineans and the south sea islanders? Or only on such portions of them as are civilized? How is that ascertained for it does not appear on the face of the record and we are not allowed to travel beyond that in search of evidence. I make this remark because I have met with men, professional men, representatives in our legislation and members of the church, who, when I asked them if they understood that language of Noah as a *command* replied in good earnest, "Why certainly, what else was it?" So little have the people of this country and even legislators and prominent members of the church inquired into the teachings of the Bible on this subject.

72   If it is a simple prophecy, on what principle are we to aim at its accomplishment? A prediction of good is a promise and a prediction of evil is a threatening or a warning. It is our duty to do all the good we can and of course, to desire and seek and rejoice in the fulfillment of every promise; but it is equally our duty to take the warning given and do all we can to avert from ourselves and others the calamity which it imports. If Noah's prediction justifies us in the enslavement of the Africans all who acted as agents in executing the great judgments of heaven on a guilty world might make the same plea; for it *was foretold* and in the same prophetic style that the woman *should* be subject to the man and that he should *rule* over her: that the king whom the Israelites desired should oppress, impoverish and make them wretched; that Judas should betray his master; that Nebuchadnezzar should destroy Jerusalem and the carry the Jews captive to Babylon; and that Antichrist the Pope of Rome should sit in the temple of God as God and do every cruel and abominable thing.

73   We certainly occupy a very strange position in the history of the church and even of a Christian and Protestant nation. Did any Christian people before, who had a revelation from heaven in their hands and a

knowledge of the living and true God in their hearts undertake either to destroy or subjugate a large portion of their fellow beings without an express commission from the Almighty? But we do not pretend to have any such commission; yet we have taken upon ourselves the cruel and perilous task of enslaving four millions of the African race and of entailing that bondage upon their unborn and unoffending posterity without any limit as to time. You say they were forced upon us us at first and therefore we are not to blame. True, they were in the first instance, forced upon our forefathers by the British government but have since, in the full exercise of liberty and independence, made their sin our own. A son while subject to the authority of his father may be compelled to do many things which are unjust or even cruel but if he persists in them after he attains his majority, he alone is responsible and is chargeable with perpetuating the iniquities of his father. The Jews in the time of Christ said if they had been in the days of their fathers they would not have been partakers with them in the blood of the prophets and, in proof of this, as they seem to have alleged, they *build the tombs of the prophets and garnished the sepulchers of the righteous . . .* but because they persisted in the same hypocrisy and in the same or similar acts of injustice and cruelty, they proved themselves to be the children of of their fathers and were filling up their measure of iniquity: See Matt 23:30–32. For almost three generations the people of this country have had it in their power to disown those acts of the British government and to free themselves from the odious sin of slavery; but in theory and in practice, in their legislative enactments and in every practicable way they have gone far beyond the intentions of the British government and tho' professing great veneration for the memory of our forefathers who protested against it they have made the sin their own and in a more aggravated form.

74

As already shown in part and will be more fully shown hereafter, we are far in advance of any other civilized nation in the absolute and perpetual despotism to which we have subjected four millions of the human race and this we have done entirely from motives of avarice. Contrary to all the claims and sacred impulses of justice, humanity, and religion, we have undertaken without warrant or authority to be the executioners of a prophetic malediction and Providence permitted us to go about as far as we can go. The people of Israel never thought of either destroying or enslaving that branch of Ham's posterity called the Canaanites until they were expressly commanded by the God of their fathers to do so; and then they seemed reluctant, from feelings of humanity, to comply with the injunction in its full and literal import; but we have gone without warrant and without reluctance or remorse. In this matter we occupy a position similar to that of Pharaoh, the haughty monarch of Egypt in fulfilling the prophecy to Abraham that his seed should

75

be in bondage four hundred and thirty years, and to that of Nebuchadnezzar in Judea fulfilling the prophecies of Isaiah and Jeremiah respecting the destruction of Jerusalem and the captivity of the Jews, and to that of Judas in fulfilling the prediction of the Psalmist that he should betray his master and to that of the man introduced into the church, that overgrown power foretold as Antichrist or the man of sin, that of the Pope in fulfilling the predictions of the Bible that he would murder the Hugenots, the Waldenses, and other witnesses of the truth. We do not mean to compare the religious portion of our community who are slave holders to all or any of these men in moral and religious character; for, being under the blinding influence of self interest, they have not taken an intelligent and impartial view of this subject and are not fully aware of the position which they occupy under the moral government of God in relation to it, but if we were slave owners and advocates of the institution as it exists in these southern states, we should be very shy of founding a plea for it on Noah's prophetic malediction on Ham's distant posterity or on any other prophecy in the Bible.

12. Servitude during the patriarchal age.

Ever since there has been any discussion in this country on the humanity and justice, or the inhumanity and injustice of slavery which has been from the time of its introduction to the present hour, its advocates have alleged in their defence that Abraham had a great many servants, some bought with his money and some born in his house; and they seem to have taken it for granted or to have thought that an unreflecting and credulous public would take it for public that these servants were slaves ; but this was a grievous mistake. They were not *slaves* but *servants* and the term slave is not found, we believe in our translation of the Bible, probably because the translators did not find any word, of corresponding import in the original. If however Abraham was a *slaveholder* according to the southern import of that term, it would not prove slavery to be right for he did some other things which would not be justifiable at the present day. E.g., He got a child by his servant maid and surely Christian people will not assert that his example can justify them in the same practice.

But in this age of rail roads and telegraphs many have found out that all men are not "born equal" not even in a civil and political sense and that all men do not posess an "inalienable right to life, liberty, and the pursuit of happiness." Those revolutionary men belonged to a more rude and unimproved age; and the present generation, in the more literary and philosophical regions of the south, have taken much higher ground. It has been asserted of late, in what ought to be, and is considered by a large portion of the community, as high authority, that Abraham was in very deed, a slave holder; that "the first organization of the church as a visible society, separate and distinct from the unbelieving world, was inaugurated in the family of a slave holder, that the very first persons to whom the seal of circumcision was affixed were the slaves of the father of the faithful"; and that it was sanctified by Moses and the prophets, and by Jesus Christ and his Apostles. If these assertions were all true we should have to give up the point in dispute; but before we do that we beg leave to make a few simple, common sense remarks.

In the first place, they are bare assertions, unsupported by facts or testimony of any kind and we can take no man's assertions without proof. In the next place, they are rendered highly improbable by a number of circumstances mentioned in the history and entirely obvious to the plainest reader. For example, those in the employ of Abraham are not called slaves but servants and, has been shown above, there is between these two classes a radical and essential difference. They were servants, rendering a voluntary service and for a compensation such as ever have been and ever will be in every civilized community.

One of them, Eleazar, of Damascus, was to be his *heir*, in case he should have no children of his own, but has such a thing ever occurred or could it occur in the south? If a master here, in any of these states were to *will* his property to one of his slaves, we imagine it would not be noticed in a court of record or in the Registry office and would become the scoff of the land. When the Patriarch went to drive back the invaders of Sodom and the other cities of the plain he armed his *trained servants* and took them to the battle. This was putting a confidence in them which cannot be put in our slaves or any others and such a thing would not be thought of in this land of bondage and degradation.

The supposition that Abraham's servants were slaves, as we understand the term, is rendered improbable by his general deportment so far as known to us, and from his magnanimous conduct on some occasions, recorded in his history. Would he who , when he went with an armed force to repel the invaders of his country, lifted up his hand to Jehovah, the Most High God, the possessor of heaven and earth, that he would not take for himself, from a thread to a shoe latchet, and that he would take anything from those whom he delivered, lest it should be said they had made Abraham rich—would *he* take the unwilling services of scores and hundreds of his fellow beings for nothing? The assertion, if it didn't amount to a libel on the character of the good old patriarch is so improbable as to create some doubt as to the candor and strict impartiality of its authors.

[Beginning here and until page 109, the pagination of Caruthers's manuscript repeats or is omitted.]

As I was finishing the last paragraph a minister of the gospel called upon me in my study and in the freedom of ministerial intercourse, some conversation ensued about the subject on which I was writing. After stating to him the substance of what I had just written—the impossibility in his circumstances of Abraham's making slaves, in our sense of the term, of three hundred and eighteen armed men and entailing that bondage upon their unborn offspring, he said he thought it was very possible for a man of great moral power, like Abraham, to make slaves of even a greater number of ignorant and superstitious heathen but my reply was and is that, without waiting to controvert his position, which is not at all necessary to my purpose, the cases are not parallel; for assuredly Abraham's servants or employees, were not heathen sunk in ignorance, vice and superstition.

The supposition of many learned men which is not improbable, is that they were converts to his faith in Mesopotamia, having been brought to the knowledge of the truth by his instructions and had followed him to the land of promise, as Ruth followed Naomi, for the sake of his religion and of his Christian fellowship; but however this may have been, they were certainly not poor ignorant heathen. They knew all he knew; they were acquainted with the revelations which he had received and with the covenants and promises which had been repeated and confirmed to him in the most solemn manner by sacrifices. They knew that his posterity was to inherit the land of Canaan and that the Messiah, the great deliverer of mankind from the consequences of their apostasy, in whom all the nations of the earth should be blessed, was to descend from him. His God was their God and his faith was their faith.

The idea seems to have been common among Christians that Abraham had all his servants old and young, circumcised on his faith but this we regard as a considerable mistake. He had his own children circumcised, on his faith, at least Isaac, and so did his adult servants. When a household is now baptized, the adult members who have children of their own, are first baptized on profession of their own faith and then present their children for baptism. So did Abraham's household; but all must be circumcised and brought within the Covenant or not continue with him.

In my early boyhood I heard of some Christian slaveholders who while laboring under the above mistake, were so conscientious that they had all their households including their slaves old and young, baptized on their faith, which had the good effect of causing them to send their negro children to school, to catechize them with their own children on Sabbath evenings and to treat all their slaves with more respect and kindness, but if a man were now to bring up all his slaves old and young for baptism, as he believed in imitation of Abraham's example, it would only excite a smile of pity or of contempt.

The Canaanites spread over an extent of country not half as large as that of North Carolina, were separated into some seven or eight petty divisions like the tribes of our western Indians or the Highland clans of Scotland each with its king, laird or chieftain; but they had no combination, no federal union, no mutual cooperation or settled principles and no efficient arrangements for the general safety hence the Israelites cut them off in detail and there was no confederation among them, except on one or two occasions, when a few of the small tribes united temporarily in self defence.

Abraham was stranger or a sojourner among them living in the land by sufferance and keeping in favor with them by his peaceable demeanor and by rendering them assistance when occasion offered or when duty required as when he armed his trained bands of servants and volunteered to assist two or three of the neighboring chieftains in repelling an invasion of their territory by the northern and eastern hordes under Chederloramen; but he had no other claim on their protection, for it does not appear that he had formed any permanent league with them, offensive or defensive. He did not even own a foot of land in the country until, in his old age, he purchased of Hamor a small lot in which to bury the aged companion of his long and toilsome pilgrimage. He was a lone shepherd removing from place to place and pitching his tent for the time being wherever he found the most eligible situation or the best pasturage for his flocks.

Under such circumstances, how, on earth, could Abraham make slaves of 310 armed men and entail that bondage upon their unborn generations? He had servants or persons employed to tend his flocks and just because he had no body else to do it they are sometimes called servants or sometimes *herdsmen*. When certain angels and the Lord himself visited his tent in disguise there was no parade of slaves in attendance, running to and fro and waiting on the table; but he simply told a *young man*, one of his employees to butcher a calf and he assisted in the preparation, while Sarah herself made and baked the cakes.

When he died, so far as anything to the contrary appears, these servants were at liberty to go where they pleased and seek employment elsewhere; for there is nothing said about any bequest or testamentary disposition of them. When he sent away Hagar with the child which she had by him, a child who appears to have been dear to his heart, he did not give him a female slave to wait upon him. When he put away his sons by Keturah, his second wife, he gave them portions; but there is no mention of slaves. Isaac, who had been divinely appointed as sole heir to the promises, inherited the whole of his father's property, except the portions which had been given away; but there is nothing said about slaves as a prominent part of the inventory.

True, Isaac had servants for a time, to tend his flocks and for the same reason that his father had them, viz. because he had no body else to do it, but there is no intimation that he had inherited them from his father. He might have employed some who had been in the service of his father and whom he had known in his youth, but after his sons became old enough to take their place, we hear little or nothing more of them. When a southern slaveholder makes his last will and testament, his slaves form an important and often the most important part of his bequests; but when Isaac made the final disposition of his property, there is no mention of his slaves. It cannot be supposed that he gave them to Esau and it is pretty certain that Jacob got none of them; for he left the home of his birth and the scenes of his youth, a lone fugitive and on foot with his staff in his hand and a budget of clothes and provisions on his back, and did not return to the land of promise for twenty years when he had servants enough of his own.

When he returned to Canaan with his wives and children after such a long absence, Jacob was rich in flocks and herds; and, like his father and grandfather, he had had servants employed to take care of them only because his children were yet too young but when his sons became large enough to take charge of them, there is no further mention of his servants; what became of them? Nobody can tell; but when when he went down with all he had, into the house of bondage not to return until he was carried back, there is no intimation that he sold his slaves for a round sum of money or that he sold them at all, it is very certain that he did not take them with him. The truth seems to be that they were only hired servants, as soon as his sons were sufficiently grown to take charge of his flocks, there hirelings were dismissed and sought employment elsewhere. All this we think so obvious that no further comment is necessary and that if anyone should assert that he sold them in the land of promise or that he bequeathed them to his sons on his death bed, in the name of truth and humanity we ask for the proof.

We regard it as an act of gross injustice to the memory of those venerable patriarchs, who had received the promises and who looked for a better country with a heavenly city to charge them with being slaveholders or to say of them that they compelled any portion of their fellow beings, sons and daughters of Ham, or any of them to serve them for life without compensation and that they enacted this degrading and oppressive bondage upon their unoffending offspring. It would have belied the whole tenor of their lives in other respects, their justice and humanity, their pure and large minded and unselfish patriotism. They would have scorned such a thing to slander their character by such an imputation. We know that a man may become so biased by interest or by passion or the prejudices of education that the clearest and most forcible arguments will have no effect upon him; but with this fact before us we have been for years amazed at the perverseness of the sophistry employed and the unfounded assertions made on this subject, from the stump and the forum, the pulpit and the press by the southern advocates of slavery.

13. Servitude under the Mosaic dispensation.

The first thing observable in regard to this dispensation is that it was *peculiar* and it is represented in the Bible. The Israelites were a peculiar people, separated from all the world by peculiar institutions and were destined to answer a peculiar purpose. Nothing like it had before been given to mankind, nothing like it them existed anywhere else in the world and nothing like it would ever be known again. Of course, there was much in it that could not be transmitted to other nations and to future ages.

We may remark again that it was designed to be *temporary* and to continue in force, no longer than the purpose for which it was given should be accomplished. The moral law and the import of its temple and priesthood, it rites and ceremonies, which represented Christ and his salvation, were the substance, or that which concerned all mankind; but every thing else was local and temporary, confined to that people and to that age of the world.

It may be further remarked that a number of things were *permitted* under that dispensation which had not been allowed from the beginning and which are forbidden under the more full and spiritual dispensation of the gospel. A man was permitted to have more than one wife, or a wife and some concubines; any man might, at anytime, put away his lawful wife by simply giving her a bill or writing of divorce intent, and if a man died without children, his brother was required to marry his widow and raise up children to the deceased husband. These and a number of other things were peculiar to that dispensation, having never been allowed before nor since. If it could be shown therefore that such slavery as we have here was permitted or sanctioned in the law of Moses that would be no proof of its lawfulness in this age of far greater light and freedom; but for the satisfaction of plain common readers, who have neither the time nor the means nor the ability to investigate subjects of this kind we may bring to their notice very briefly, what we find respecting it in that wonderful book.

91   That a servitude, in some respects a little hard and irksome, existed under the law of Moses there is no doubt and it was of nothing more than might have been expected, if it was not unavoidable in that age of man and rudeness, when their knowledge of the divine character and government was so imperfect, but not withstanding the disadvantages of that people when compared with ours, in regard to the intellectual and moral culture, their servitude had none of the most odious and oppressive features which characterize our slavery.

    There were among the Hebrews three distinct classes of servants and they were obtained in different ways; by war, by purchase from the heathen, by debt, by the commission of theft, by birth and by voluntary consent; but they all had certain inalienable rights and privileges secured to them which are denied to our slaves. None of them were in an hopeless condition; for there was a way by which they or their children might in due time, regain their freedom and a restoration to all the immunities, rights, and privileges of citizenship. Those obtained in any or all of the above ways must have been comparative by few, nothing like equal to the demands and much the larger number of their servants were obtained as servants have long been obtained in the northern states and in other countries by voluntary contract.

92   The Gibeonites and perhaps one or two small towns allied with them were doomed to a peculiar kind of servitude and do not properly come under the denomination of Hebrew servants. As the penalty for a willful and flagrant crime it was ordered that for the future, they should be employed in cutting wood and drawing water for the temple services; but no other drudgery was required of them and they belonged under exclusively to the commonwealth. They never became the property of individuals and no mention is made of them, we believe, after the time of Solomon. Of course their case can afford no argument in justification of slavery and we need take no further notice of them. Respecting the Hebrew servants in general to whatever class they belonged, whether that of foreigners or that of native born Jews, and in whatever way obtained, whether by war or purchase by poverty, crime or voluntary contract, it may be remarked:

> That their masters were required to treat them with great humanity and kindness. See Lev 25:39–55, and many other places.
>
> That the master who slew his servant, whatever might have been his orgin, should be surely punished, if he died within a day or two. See Exod 21:20, 21

That if the master injured his servant in his eye or his tooth, by which it is generally understood to be meant, in any of his limbs or members; he must give him his freedom. See Exod 27:26, 27

That on all their sabbaths and festival occassions their servants of every description, their servants should be allowed an entire cessation from all their labors. See Exod 20:10.

That they should be allowed to attend and share in all those feasts which were made from the secondary tithes. See Deut 12:27, 28; 16:13, 14.

That the owners were bound to instruct them in the knowledge of the true God and to have them circumcised if it had not been done before (see Gen 17:10–13) in consequence of who they were allowed to remain in the land and so far incorporated with the nation as to have the seal of the covenant affixed.

That a man might marry his servant maid, whether she had been obtained by war or by purchase, and make her his wife but if he became dissatisfied and sent her away, she must be free and he could have no further control over her; so he might betroth such a servant maid to his son, but if the son repudiated her she must have her freedom. See Exod 27:7–11.

That a servant of foreign birth, in whatever way obtained, could at any time become a proselyte to the Jewish faith and worship and consequently be entitled to all the freedom and other privileges of native born Israelites. At such has long the opinion of the Christian church and we recollect no intimation in the Bible to the contrary.

That a Hebrew who had become a servant for debt or for theft could not be made to serve more than six years; for in the seventh year he must be restored to his liberty with some compensation for his labor, or with presents of considerable amount, with the wife whom he had married before his servitude; but if his master had furnished him a wife he could not take her with him. See Exod 21:2–21; Lev 25:1–17.

That servants of Hebrew birth might acquire and possess or dispose of property to a considerable amount. See Lev 25:49; 2 Sam 9:9.

That in the year of jubilee all servants whether of Jewish or foreign birth as it seems to be now understood by our own best Hebrew scholars, were set at liberty, when their forfeited estates, if they ever had any, were restored to them and they returned to the full and secure enjoyment of all the rights and privileges that ever belonged to them: Lev 25:29–42.

That altho' they might buy servants of the heathen they were not vindable and therefore were not property and we recollect no intimation that they might sell their servants of any kind or traffic in them and make them chattels like horses or mules or any thing else and therefore they were certainly not *slaves*. There was no such thing as entailed bondage among them and they could not hold their fellow beings whether Jewish or heathen as property. The servitude of the patriarchs was adopted by Moses with some modifications and hence as Israel's sons by his servant maids were legitimate and became patriarchs, heads of tribes and heirs of the promises as a Jew might marry his servant maid and consequently his children by her would be native born citizens and heirs of the promises.

95 After what has been said hardly any verbal criticisms are necessary and more than a very few would be out of place.

The Hebrew word, *obed,* always translated *servant,* is said by our most learned men to e derived from a verb which means to cultivate the ground or to labor, for example, Gen 2:4–5; 3:23; 4:2, 12. *Cain was a tiller or worker, of the ground.* Exod 20:9: *Six days shalt thou labor.*

> In process of time, it frequently meant to labor for another, but voluntarily and for wages. Mal 3:14; Gen 29:15, 27; 20:2, 10.
>
> Sometimes, to labor for another by *force*. Gen 14:4; Deut 20:17; Gen 25:23; 27:40; Lev 25:11.
>
> Both politically and personally. Gen 15:13, 14; Exod 1:13—14:12; Jer 5:19; 17:4.
>
> Person at servitude in general. Exod 21:2, 6; Lev 25:39, 40.
>
> Often it meant to serve God: Deut 6:13; Josh 22:5; 1 Sam 7:3, 4; Ps 72:11; and to serve *idols:* Ps 97:7; Ezek 20:39; Deut 12:2, 17:3; Judg 10:13; 2 Kgs 21:3; Jer 22:9.
>
> In some instances is meant labor imposed on others. Exod 1:15; Lev 25:4; 22:13; 25:14.

The noun usually means one who labors for another, either for him or by compulsion. It is familiarly used, like our word servant as an expression of deference, politeness or humility. Gen 33:5, 12; 44:27; Isa 36:11; Ps 97:34; 20:7, 8; 25:24–31; 28:2; Dan 1:12; 2:7. But it was not then used in important cases when duty was concerned. Dan 3:16–18.

It is often used in addresses to the supreme Being, as in Gen 18:3; 1 Kgs 8:28–32; 1 Chron 17:17–19; Ps 27:9; 31:26; Dan 9:17, and the verbal noun is used to signify a *servant of God*. Ps 34:22; Neh 1:10; Ps 105:26, 42; Num 4:42; Isa 32:17; 1 Chron 9:13.

The noun *servant*, it is said, is never used to designate the Antediluvians. When God entered into covenant with Noah, he and his sons were freemen. The curse predicted by Noah *obed obed*, a servant of servants, grew directly out of sin; but there was no word in Hebrew for *slave* or Noah would have used it in this prediction.

This predictive curse is no proof that *slavery* was intended; that it was either in Noah's mind or in the divine purpose; nor even that he was then inspired any more than when he planted his vineyard; but all this is inferred from what afterwards took place. We believe there is no allusion to the prediction of Noah in any other part of the Bible; and therefore the advocates of slavery, even on philological grounds, assume too much. Traffic in human beings, it is supposed, can in truth be, or was, a speedy outgrowth from idolatry.

This prediction, it is believed, was not intended in a personal sense, but infers to the subjugation of nations. See Gen 27: 29, 37; 25:23. After Gen 9:25 the word *obed* is not used, in the Bible for 500 years and when used in reference to Hagar and others of that age it could not mean slaves. There are two words in Hebrew which are used to designate female servants and which correspond to *obed*. They are used interchangeably or sometimes the one and sometimes the other, and are both applied to Hagar. Gen 16:1-8. They are often translated and should be in almost every case translated *handmaid* or *maidservant*. See Gen 12:16; 21:10; 30:43; 31:33; Exod 11:5; 20:10; 23:12; Deut 5:14; 12:16; 15:17; 16:11-14; Exod 21:7, 27, 32; Judg 9:18; Ruth 2:13; 3:9; 1 Sam 25:14, 25, 27, 31, 41. 2 Sam 14:15; 6:20, 22. Job 31:13; Gen 34:9, 10, 11, 16. The words are both applied indifferently to maid servants whether Jewish or heathen—and for both the Septuagint translation has *paidiske* which is the Greek word for maid servant.

In the New Test. *paidiske* is once contrasted with *elutherias, free* (Gal 4:22) but everywhere else, we believe it is translated *servant, maid,* or *damsel*. See Matt 26:29; Mark 14:66, 69; Luke 12:45; 22:56. John 18:17; Acts 12:13, 16. The word *douli* is used only three times—Luke 1:38, 48; Acts 2:18—in all of which it means *servant* of the Lord or *handmaid* of the Lord. The word *paidiske* doesn't appear to mean in any case, a *slave* or *bondservant* but a *hired* servant; or perhaps, in some age, as white children in this country are often bound out during their minority. Abraham has servants *bought* or obtained with his money and some *born* in his house, or in Hebrew phraseology, *sons of the house*. Is Israel a *servant*? Is he a home born slave—a child of the house? Or, is not Israel a son? Why then is he spoiled? All bought with money and all born in the house were circumcised and all who were born there had peculiar privileges.

These few criticisms, which might be extended to any length may serve to amuse the common reader in his leisure hours, provided he will be at the trouble of hunting the references and of studying them in this connexion; but to pursue them much further would only confuse ordinary readers and render the work unprofitable. They go to prove, however, that the statements made above are correct; and if more should be desired they may, if Providence permit, be forth coming hereafter. In times like the present, when there is an entire break up of former organizations and when change is making in all the business habits of life, people have neither time nor patience for literary investigations. What they need and desire is brief and common sense presentations of truth, addressed to the understanding and conscience. They may have been heretofore prejudiced my education and blinded by interest and rendered insensible to reason by excited passions but when emerging from the ruins of such a convulsion as has lately taken place and when about to reconstruct the old fabric or rather to construct a new one they will be free from such biases and will listen with more calmness to the voice of truth and mercy from the throne on high.

We cannot go further into this part of the subject at present and it is not necessary. But there was one kind of servitude, a life long servitude, allowed by Moses which deserves a passing notice. It must have been of rare occurrence and is of no great importance in itself; but it becomes interesting from the fact that it shows the aim of the inspired lawgiver to grant the people as much liberty as their advancement and the condition of the surrounding nations would admit. In fact it proves that, so far at least as they were concerned, no such thing as compulsory service even for life was tolerated; and it also furnished a test either of principle or of personal attachment, according to circumstances.

The law was in the following words: *And if the servant shall plainly say, I love my master, my wife and my children; I will not go out free. Then his master shall bring him unto the Judges. They shall also bring him to the door, or unto the doorpost; and his master shall bore his ear thro' with an awl; and he shall serve him forever.* Exod 21:5–6; Deut 15:16, 17. After this profession and ceremony he was bound to serve his master forever or while he lived; but it was a matter of choices: There was no compulsion; for he made his determination freely and in full view of all the consequences.

We need not discuss the mooted question whether any free man has a right to give up his liberty, or, if in servitude, to refuse it when offered to him, for in matters which involved no fundamental principle of religion, the Mosaic institutions were adapted to the age in which he lived. People of little information and feeble minds are incapable of comprehending general principles or of appreciating the most important privileges but their passions are strong and their attachments are warm. In the case above stated a man who understood the value of freedom and prized it above every thing else, would, however sincere and ardent might by his affection for his family, either forsake his family, or trust to Providence and his own exertions for obtaining their liberty, also in due time; but one whose enjoyments were chiefly of a social and animal kind; whose powers were incapable of much development and to whom liberty would be of little value if he had it would rather remain with his wife and children under a good master, especially as the law did not allow him to be sold than to have them in servitude and be free himself. The few cases of this kind that occurred must have been only exceptions to the general rule and could not prove that the lower classes, except in some chance cases of mental imbecility or hopeless poverty, were converted in a state of perpetual subjection to the will of another nor that they did not accept of their freedom when it was within their reach.

The assertion has been commonly made in the south not only in their social circles, but by authors and public speakers, that the slaves are contented with their condition and do not want to be free. This assertion is contrary to the strongest instincts of human nature and we know it to be untrue unless it be with such as have been kept in gross and barbarous ignorance. These slave owners themselves have now had some opportunity of knowing if they did not know before, that it was false; and they stand convicted before the world of misstating the facts for the sake of their own interest. Some of the more intelligent blacks have said to me, years ago, that they were not anxious to be free and kept here without any advantages; for they knew with what hardships they would have to contend if placed here in poverty and ignorance where they would have to contend with the wealthy and educated whites. They knew that if they would have no land of their own to cultivate, no houses to live in and nothing to go upon their condition would not be very desirable. They would have to depend on renting houses and would often find difficulty in getting them; for not many whites would want them on their premises. There they would be obliged to depend upon hiring themselves out by the day or the month in order to procure the means of paying their rent and supporting their families, but the whites, in that case, would employ them only in crop time or when necessity required; dishonest whites too would cheat them out of all they made and their condition would still be one of poverty, ignorance and degradation. In these circumstances they could not have all the civil rights and social advantages more than a name; and in all this they shewed their good sense; but they always added that if the white folks would give them their freedom and send them off to themselves where they could have a territory and a government of their own they would be mighty glad of it. To say then that they are contented with their bondage is false and to make that a plea for keeping them in subjection is a slur on humanity. It is not strange that a few, on perhaps in a thousand, who had been set free and sent off to the North or to Liberia, have returned to their former owners and requested to be taken back into bondage. We have known of families, from the eastern part of this state, who, after removing to the rich lands of the west and remaining there for a year or two, returned on foot and assigned as a reason for it that they could get no way there to eat. The Israelites at Sinai, after all the stupendous miracles which had been wrought for their deliverance, in the house of their bondage and at the Red Sea, made a god, called for a leader and resolved that they would return, *in mass* into Egypt. Yet they learned better in due time and became the greatest, freest, and most prosperous nation in the world.

On a review of the above facts, we need not ask the intelligent and reflecting and candid reader to say whether there was any such cruel and despotic slavery under the Mosaic constitution as we have in these southern states. When we have a *law* that secures to a negro man the enjoyment of his wife and children. Where is there a *law* which requires every slave, male and female, to be carefully instructed in the Christian religion or which even *permits* any of them to be so far instructed in the language of the country that they can read the Bible. Where is there a *law* which exempts them from labor on all the sabbaths and great festivals of the country and that gives them liberty to share freely in the provision made for even our national anniversaries? Where is there a *law* giving them freedom and a right to all the privileges of citizenship on their becoming proselytes to the Christian faith, or their becoming true believers in Jesus Christ and children of God? Where is there a *law* with one exception and a poor one it is, as will be shown in another place—which gives them the least hope of freedom on any terms? Can one ray of hope and gladness dawn upon the dark and dejected mind of a southern negro? Is there a jubilee for the degraded drudging and cheerless slave, on this side of heaven?

Considering the rude and warlike character of of the age in which the Mosaic institutions were given and their peculiar, local and temporary nature, it is strange indeed that a Christian and protestant people, who are always boasting of their freedom and intelligence, should attempt to find a reliable or satisfactory justification of southern slavery in the patriarchal and Mosaic institutions. If what we have stated above be true, that all protestant nations who receive the Bible, without vote or comment, as a revelation from heaven stand in the same relation to God into which the Jewish people were brought at Sinai; that the heathen nations, having been redeemed by

Jesus Christ and their conversion, in due time, secured by covenant promise, sustained to him before their deliverance from bondage; and that all true Christians, whatever may be their race or their complexion or their disadvantages are brethren in Christ and belong to the household of faith, the whole weight of the Mosaic system, in its true spirit and import, is against "the peculiar institution" of the south.

There were some other facts and regulations connected with this subject, as we learn partly from the Pentateuch and partly from other portions of the Bible, which were of a favorable kind and which ought not to be passed by unnoticed. It appears,

> That a servant who was found competent, trusty, and discreet had charge of his master's domestic affairs and was called the *steward*. It was his province to direct the other servants in their work and to lay in food and raiment for the household. See Gen 24:2; 47:6; 1 Sam 21:7; 1 Chron 27:29, 30; Ruth 2:5; 1 Cor 4:1, 2; 1 Pet 4:10. Sometimes a female servant who was capable and trustworthy had of all the *indoor* business. 1 Tim 5:9.

> That it was the duty of the servants, or some of them, ordinarily, to teach their masters children; and such seem to have occupied the place of private teachers in the families of our rich planters before the establishment of free schools.

> That a slave who had fled from another nation and sought a refuge among the Jews was to received with kindness and not given up or returned to his former owner by force. See Deut 23:15, 16.

> That kidnapping or manstealing was punished, as it is here and should be every where, with great severity. See Exod 21:16; Deut 24:7.

> That when a man had been sold to another for debt or any other cause, he might redeem himself if he could, or nay of his near kindred might redeem him by paying for the unexpired time of his servitude until the year of release. See Lev 25:47–55.

> That there was no law prohibiting emancipation and that a master might at any time, without committing any offence against "the peace and dignity of the *state*" or hurting the consciences and patriotic feelings of his fellow citizens, give full scope to the human and generous impulses of his own nature, by relinquishing his claim and "letting the oppressed go free."

> That there was in short, no enactments designed to render the bondage of any class as perpetual, degrading and absolute as possible; but that

so far as predictable or expedient under the existing state of things, provision was made for the improvement of their condition for the elevation of their character and for their speedy and full restoration to all the rights and immunities which belonged to the chosen race.

The very few slaves, who, after having been set free and sent to the north or to Liberia, have returned to their masters, are, like the marriages over the country, so much talked about that the number appears much greater than it really is; but these scattering cases, so far from proving that they do not desire liberty or that the great mass of them are satisfied with their bondage, only proves the hardship of their condition; for having no land of their own and no resources of any kind and not receiving sufficient assistance or encouragement from the more favored population around them, their return was a matter of expediency or of dire necessity. We advocate their speedy and complete emancipation, but in a human and judicious way. We insist that, as they have by their labor paid for the raising or purchase, two or three times over, when masters, from the impulse of kind feelings, set them free and send them off to enjoy the priceless boon of freedom. They also furnish them with the money of subsistence and of improvement until they learn to manage for themselves and each acquire something of their own.

But in regard to the case of voluntary servitude under the Mosaic law, we may remark that the was no other hardship in it than the necessity of leaving his wife and children or remaining in bondage. He had his choice and that was a matter of vital importance. We need not discuss the necessity or propriety of such a law at that period of the world's history, in the moral condition of the surrounding nations, but it was far more human than any enactment in the slave code of the southern states. Whatever a chosen individual master, one in a thousand may do with a favorite slave there is no legal provision for giving him his choice, either to go out and free or remain in bondage with his wife and children, nor even to remain with them upon any terms. Rare exceptions made by individuals cannot be here taken into the account while the laws and the general practice pay no regard whatever to the attachments of the slave; but he may, at any time, as the caprice or the interest or the necessities of his owner require, be born from the objects of this fondest affections, sold under the hammer and like any other animal and then borne off to a returnless distance from all that is dearest to him on earth.

14. Servitude under the Christian dispensation.

The servitude allowed by the law of Moses as we have seen, was essentially milder and far more favorable to that class of the community than the slavery known among the civilized nations of more modern times and especially in this land of boasted light and liberty; but that being a dispensation of great darkness and bondage when compared with the spirituality of freedom of the latter day glory, surely no Christian can suppose that Christ and his Apostles would sanction a more rigorous bondage than that of the old economy. So far as I now recollect, it has not been alleged by any Christian writer or speaker, who could be regarded as a man of ability and fair minded ness, that the *spirit* of the gospel tends to bondage in any respect, or that there is found in the New Testament, an express *command* making it the duty of church or of the Christian nations to enslave the unevangelized portions of the mankind. It has indeed been said of late by men of high standing in the church that slavery always has existed and always will exist; that it arises out of the necessity of circumstances and will probably exist in the millennium. These assertions require proof and they may pass for what they are worth. Their authors have, so far, drawn off from the Bible and taken the ground occupied by mere worldly, ambitious and self-seeking politicians. The question now is, not what reason alone, biased as it is by passion and worldly interest may dictate, nor what temporary and even varying circumstances might seem to justify; but what Christ and his Apostles have taught.

We need hardly remind the reader here that the Roman government, under the Emperors, was a very despotic one and that it then extended over the civilized world, nor that, as stated in Gibbon's *Decline and Fall of the Roman Empire*, the Roman people during this period, had both *servants, and slaves,* and in nearly equal numbers. The import of these terms as they are used in the New Testament and the aspect in which the whole subject is there presented would require and volume; but this we shall leave for others of more leisure or of more ample means, and make a few such plain and obvious remarks as are necessary to our purpose.

From the preceding remarks it appears that no such thing as entailed bondage was allowed among the Jews; that native born Israelites could not be made to serve longer than the seventh year which was the year of release; that all servants, whether of native or foreign birth, went out free on the morning of the Jubilee; that a Jew might marry his servant maid, whether bought or captured from the heathen, and true, as the Sons of Jacob by his servant maids became incorporated with the chosen race; and that no Israelite was allowed to sell his servant, however obtained nor even to deliver up a run-away servant, Jewish or heathen, to his former master.

Of course, they were not property; they cannot be bought nor sold like cattle in market; their masters were required to instruct them carefully in the true religion and might give them their freedom at any time. In every case "a door of hope" was open for the servant and there was full scope for the generosity of the master.

This servitude, tho' it belonged to a much lower degree of civilization and religious knowledge was as superior to our slavery as day is to might or as virtue is to vice; and most assuredly the condition of that class of men and women has not been made worse by Christ and his Apostles. Would He whose advent was announced from heaven in the rapturous strains of *glory to God in the highest and peace on earth, good will to men,* enjoin more rigorous bondage than Moses who, in that age of darkness, war and oppression, delivered the law amidst the lightenings and terrors of Sinai, would He who came to preach the gospel to [the] poor and the broken hearted, then proclaim liberty to the captive and the opening of the prison to them, that are bound, who enjoined it upon all that hear the gospel *to break every yoke* and *to let the oppressed go free*—would he, by his own teachings or by those of his inspired Apostles, sanction such absolute and degrading and hopeless bondage as we have in these southern states?

If He who was the personification of mercy, come to free his people from the burdensome rites and ceremonies of the law, which had been given by divine appointment, words surely not approve a ten fold more irksome and oppressive bondage enforced by men and for the mere purposes of gain. No intelligent and sober thinking Christian can for a moment suppose that the Lord of Glory who "came not to be ministered unto, but minister and to give himself a ransom" for us that he might make all men free in the highest and fullest sense, would thus rivet the chains of despotism on any portion of the human race and entail that bondage upon them from generation to generation.

105 In the early stage of this controversy between the North and the South on the slavery question and while it was confined mainly to theologians and literary men, much stress was laid on the word (*doulos*) which is of very frequent use in the New Testament and is uniformly translated *servant*, or some other English turn of the same import. It was contended on one side that it properly meant a *slave* (from deo, to bind) and should have been so rendered; but the other side maintained that among the Greeks and Romans too, it had a great latitude of meaning to designate all of what ever grade, who were dependent on others and obliged to be wholly or in a great measure subservient to their will. The best Greek lexicons suggest that it primarily meant a *house born* slave but define it as designating both *servants* and *slaves* or those whole of this servile class whatever may have been its

original import, it had in the time of the New Testament writers a variety of application and must have been used by the Greek community to designate all who were *subservient, submissive* or *obedient* to others, for it is so used in the New Testament wherever written in the common language of the country; and that such was its extended import at that day will be manifest from a few references and collation.

The noun, in the feminine gender is applied by Mary to herself at the annunciation (Luke 1:38) and is properly translated handmaid, that is, one obedient and devoted to the service of the Lord. Also in Acts 2:18 in the masculine gender it is applied to men who are bound, employed or engaged in anyway to attend upon or serve another Matt 8:99; 13:2 *and to my servant, do this and he doeth it.* Matt 10:24. *The disciple is not above his master, or teacher nor the servant above his lord,* where the comparison between the condition of a servant and that of a disciple or scholar shows the kind of subjection in which the former was held. See also 1 Cor 7:21–23. John 13:16; 15:20; Phil 2:7. Sometimes it means one who is devoted or addicted to anything. John 8:34; Rom 6:16, 17. 2 Pet 2:19. Sometimes it designates one who yields a servile assent to the opinions of another 1 Cor 7:23. Often it means one who is merely an agent, attendant, or assistant to another Matt 18:23; 29:29; Eph 6:6; 1 Pet 2:16; 2 Cor 4:5; John 15:15. Sometimes it means the Apostles and all other preachers of the gospel Rom 1:1; Gal 1:10; Phil 1:1. These references might be multiplied to any extent but the common reader can generally get the precise meaning of the word from the connection in which it stands and we need not dwell longer on this part of the argument.

This plan of managing the controversy determined nothing and was soon abandoned. Owing partly to the poverty of the language and partly to the different significations which words acquire but a careless or ignorant use of them, few questions of importance ever have been or ever be determined by etymologies and verbal criticisms. Those ought not and cannot be overlooked, but they are not the main reliance because it is difficult if not utterly impossible to determine merely by this process whether a writer uses a given word in its primary, secondary, or tertiary meaning and there a man who has paid any attention to this matter will always endeavor to obtain the precise meaning of a word from connection. This is the main dependence of our best lexicographers and dictionary makers; and hence we find in an unabridged dictionary of any language a great many quotations from approved authors to confirm the definitions given. A word may have half a dozen or more shades of meaning and all of them different from that which it had in its original or which we would give to it from its derivation. So it was, in the time of Christ and his Apostles with the word in question (*doulos*) which was applied to all who voluntary or involuntary attended upon another or rendered him a service which depended upon his dictation and to all who became so devoted to any person or practice as to have no independent will of their own. When politicians engaged in this controversy and made it the occasion of bitter and acrimonious debate in the halls of Congress the status of their question was changed and the arguments were drawn by northern presses chiefly from the great principles of justice and humanity, from the moral character and government of God, from the doctrines, spirit, and precepts of the gospel, from the original instincts of our nature and from the inalienable rights of man found to be indispensable. It was contended by the advocates of emancipation that as God is infinitely good and no respecter of persons, he endowed all men with the same inalienable rights and designed by the gospel to deliver them from all kinds of oppression to elevate their character and condition and to increase as much as possible their rational and social enjoyment; but inquiry now is what did Christ and his Apostles teach in regard to slavery?

That we may ascertain, if we can, in what, aspect slavery was regarded by the Lord and Savior himself, whether as a "human institution" or as one of injustice and oppression, we must observe the despotism, which consists in the exercise of absolute power over others, is just the same in its nature, whether, it is exercised by one man over a nation or by one man over another man; for the number cannot change the nature of the control to which they are subject nor alter its bearing upon their comfort and welfare. This, we think, is too obvious to be disputed or to need further comment but the New Testament treats all forms of despotism alike; for they are all in direct opposition to its spirit and design. Despotism, tyranny or the subjecting of others to the will of one man is unjust and cruel to them; for it is depriving them of rights which the Creator has given them. It is impious; for it is usurping or attempting to usurp the prerogative of God and frustrating, so far it can be done by man, his beneficence designed in the arrangement of his providence and in the provisions of the gospel. There is a perfect harmony between the constitution of the universe in all its parts and the providential and moral government of God. All tyranny, injustice, and oppression of the weak by the strong are the outgrowth of depravity and are of course contrary to the gospel of the grace of God, the great design of which is to deliver us from this inherent depravity and from all its physical, social, and moral results.

The direct aim of all the doctrines and requirements, the promises and threatenings contained in the revelation given us is to make every man feel that to his own master he stands or falls; that he is accountable to God alone for the use he makes of his powers; and that if any other mortal or any other created being interposes his authority and claims the control of these powers, he is at war with the Almighty and is rushing upon *the thick bosses of Jehovah's buckler.* The full conviction waked up in every man by the truth and the spirit of God has led millions to the stake as witnesses for the truth and has produced all the firm, rational, and effective resistance that has ever been made to oppressive and tyrannical governments. The heartfelt conviction that *it is better to obey God than man* is the originating and sustaining cause of all the sacrifices and efforts that have been made for freedom at the stake and on the rack, in legislative halls of protestant Christendom and in the modern battlefields of Europe and American.

There are many explicit and most important commands which the whole slave population of the south are virtually forbidden by our laws to obey or an obedience to which, on their part, is rendered utterly impracticable by the laws and by the claim which theirowners make on their whole time and strength. What the Savior said to the Jews in John 5:39 he says now to us all: *search the Scriptures for in them ye think ye have eternal life and they are they which testify of me*; but if we say, by our municipal laws and by our practice that the slaves shall not search them or, which amounts to the same thing, that they shall not be taught to read, we interpose between them and God and assume the whole responsibility of disobeying the command and of preventing the immense advantages which would result to them and others from an intelligent and honest obedience. The master or some other, whom he directs or permits to do it may read a small portion of the Scriptures to them occasionally on the Sabbath, the only rest day they have; but for that there is no command whatever. The command is addressed to them as much as to us; but we put it out of their power to obey. You say, They are unable to read: very true; but why are they unable we have made them so or kept them so; for every thing that could be done has been done by legislative enactments to prevent them from learning.

111

The New Testament requires of every man an entire consecration of himself, soul and body to the service of God; and hence the Apostle says, *I beseech you therefore brethren, by the mercies of God that ye present your bodies a living sacrifice, holy, acceptable unto God, which is your reasonable service* (Rom 12:11). As God made and redeemed the whole man, soul and body, he has a right to both and requires of every man a whole sacrifice but we say by our laws, and by our practice that we will have their bodies while they live and the Lord may have their souls if he chooses. The devil it seems, contended with Michael the Archangel for the *body* of Moses; and, if we may judge from the tenacity with which they hold on to them, slave owners, or many of them, would contend, not with Michael perhaps, but with Jesus Christ himself, for the bodies of their negroes. The Epistles of Paul abound

112

with passages similar to the one just quoted, as Rom 6:18, 19: *[Y]ield your members servants to righteousness unto holiness.* 1 Cor 10:31: *Whether therefore we eat or drink or whatsoever ye do, do all to the glory of god.* We are required to love the Lord with all the heart and soul and strength; but slaves cannot make this entire consecration of themselves to the former of their bodies and the father of their spirits.

113   The injunction in Jas 3:1: *Be not many masters,* and that in Matt 23:8–10: *Call no man your father upon the earth, neither be ye called masters,* relate to religious or spiritual matters, but the slaves cannot show the Spirit of the gospel; in obeying these commands because if they get any knowledge of the Bible they get it only at second hand and from those who are compelling them to render a life long and toilsome service for their benefit and of whose honesty in this matter they are naturally suspicious. the master portion of the community have assumed the task and the responsibility of telling them what they must believe and how they must live in order to be saved. If this is not having dominion over their faith (2 Cor 1:24), or *lording it over God's heritage* (1 Pet 5:3), it has some appearance of that and is not in accordance with the Spirit of that gospel which brings glory to God in the highest, peace on earth and goodwill to men, which requires us to walk humbly with God, to love others as ourselves, to give all their due, to do good unto all men as we have opportunity to bear one another's burdens and so fulfill the law of love.

114   There have always been *wolves in sheep's clothing* and even good men believe differently and give, publicly and privately, different expositions of the doctrines and duties taught in the Bible. The Apostle says, *Prove all things: hold fast that which is good* (1 Thess 5:21). The command has no stipulations and makes no exceptions; but the slaves are virtually forbidden to comply with this injunction because they are not allowed to make the attainments and acquire the means necessary for the purpose. The responsibility rests somewhere, but not on them. The Bereans were commended as more noble than those of Thessalonica, because they received the gospel with all readiness of mind and search the Scriptures daily to know whether the things which they heard preached were so (Acts 17:11) but here is a nobleness which say the slaves shall not have or shall not be allowed to manifest, and a commendation which they shall not receive and an everlasting advantage which they shall not obtain, for they shall not be taught to read and consequently shall not be permitted to search the Scriptures for themselves.

115   The Christian system are all its teachings and influences is calculated to humble the proud and to raise up the down trodden. Such is the tendency of the announcement that God is no respecter of persons, and that

Jesus Christ gave himself a ransom for all to be justified in due time. Such is the tendency of the doctrine that all who ever be saved are justified fully through the atonement of Christ and regenerated by the Sovereign grace of God. Such too is the design and tendency of the promises and threatenings of the gospel, ministry and of the Christian ordinances which form a common bond of brotherhood and any occasion of universal fellowship for all alike who have been made the children of God and heirs of eternal life. *Let the brother of low degree rejoice in that he is exalted and the rich in that he is made low because as the flower of the grass he shall fade away.*

The benevolence and liberality of the rich, if they attained the maturity of a stronger faith and a richer experience would produce something like what the Apostle terms an equality (2 Cor 8:14). Such an equality that the rich would not look with contempt on the poor and the poor would not feel ashamed in the presence of the rich. From all this kind of Christian liberality and equality the slave are excluded; and in the full import of the injunction, *Let nothing be done through strife or vain glory but in lowliness of mind, let each esteem others better than themselves* (Phil 2:3) they can have or no participation; for although they may thus esteem others, they cannot feel that others esteem them in the same way. Do you ask if I expect you to associate with your slaves on terms of equality? I answer no, not while they are poor and ignored any more than I would expect the rich to associate on terms of equality with the poor, or the learned with the illiterate or the moral with the immoral but I would have you to give them their freedom and all the rights to which they are entitled by nature; to elevate their character and improve their condition, by giving them the same advantages of education which you have enjoyed and by aiding and encouraging their industry Abolish your enactments and regulations for keeping them in ignorance and degradation, which are so hostile to the teachings and the spirit of Christianity. Be consistent in your profession and act up to the requirements of your religion. Do for them what you would wish them to do for you in an exchange of circumstances and you will no longer find any difficulty in admitting them to all the privileges which belong to the household of faith.

As already remarked, Christ and his Apostles treated all despotism alike and with the utmost abhorence, but with consummate prudence and discretion. The Roman Empire was then mistress of the civilized world and had accumulated immense wealth from the conquered nations. Its-government, which was imperial or imperatorial, was a most despotic and cruel one; but they enjoined it upon all Christians to be submissive and obedient *not only for wrath,* or from the fear of punishment, *but also for conscience sake* (Rom 13:7). This great Apostle speaks nearly the same language in his Epistle to Titus, 3:1: *Put them in mind to be subject to principalities and powers, to obey magistrates, to be ready to every good work.* Peter says, in 1 Pet 2:13–14, *Submit yourselves to every ordinance of man for the Lord's sake; whether it be unto them that are sent by him for the punishment of evil doers and for the praise of them that do well.* Others of them used language of the same import; but surely no intelligent and sober thinking Christian can believe that these inspired men intended by this language to sanction the despotic, cruel, and persecuting government of Rome, or to forbid them who thus subjected to change it when could do so without causing some greater calamity.

On the same principle they enjoined it upon *servants* and *slaves*, of whom there appear to have been a number in the church, to be submissive and obedient. *Servants obey in all things your master according to the flesh; not with eye service as men pleasers; but in singleness of heart fearing God* (Col 3:22). *Let as many servants as are under the yoke count their won masters worthy of all honor, that the name of God and his doctrine be not blasphemed. And thou that have believing masters, let them not despise them, because they are brethren, but rather do them service, because they are faithful and beloved partakers of the benefit* (1 Tim 6:1–2). *Exhort servants to be obedient to their own masters, and to please them well in all things; not answering again, not purloining, but showing all good, fidelity; that they may adorn the doctrine of God our Savior in all things* (Tit 2:8, 9). Did they, by the language sanction slavery any more than they sanctioned the despotic government of Rome when they enjoined it upon all Christians to be obedient and to honor those who were in power? The key to the exposition of all these passages is 1 Cor 7:21: *Art thou called being a servant care not for it; but if thou mayest be made free use it rather.* This was as much as he could say with prudence and it was just telling them that liberty was vastly desirable and that if they could obtain their freedom in a Christian way, either by gift or by purchase, by all means accept it as an inestimable boon and they improve it for their own welfare and to the glory of God; but if they could not be made free, they should submit to the allotments of Providence and be obedient to their masters. But their directions to masters are about as explicit as those to servants and they must be overlooked. *And ye masters do the same things unto them forbearing threatening; knowing that your master also is in heaven; neither is there any respect of persons with him* (Eph 6:9).

Master give unto your servants that which is just and equal; knowing that ye also have a master in heaven (Col 4:1). By that which is just and equal, or according to justice and equity must have been meant a fair compensation for their services; but surely no one will say that just what they could eat and wear often barely sufficient and of the coarsest kind, would be any compensation at all. The directions given to servants and slaves, with one or two exceptions perhaps were probably given to such as belonged to heathen or unbelieving masters, and those who had *believing* masters were only servants.

It can't be proved that any of these believing masters were slaveholders; and some learned commentators, who lived and wrote years before the controversy on the slave question here became so rancorous, and think that during the Apostolic age, no slaveholder was ever admitted to membership in the church. It was a matter of so much importance that if an application of the kind had been made it must have engaged the attention of the brethren and reference would have been made to the inspired men who were their guides; but there is no intimation in the wirting of the Apostles that it ever became a mooted question. Members who were able to afford it would, no doubt have servants and men engaged in pubic life, especially in important stations, could not do well without them; but to suppose that the members were slave holders, like the heathen around them and as they are in this country, is inconsistent with that universal brotherhood, the entire absence of anything like invidious distinctions, that mutual sympathy which pervaded the whole mass and that ardent love which made them shrink from no toils and grudge no sacrifice of property or any thing else for the relief of the necessitous.

Many of the remarks which have been made on other portions of the New Testament might be made, with very little modification, on two or three verses in Paul's Epistle to Philemon and as much stress has been laid on the sanction of slavery supposed to be found in this Epistle, we could pass it by without a separate notice. It sees the Philemon was a native Greek and now a man of property, a devoted Christian and a highly esteemed member of the church. Onesimus was a servant, who left his master, "without leave or license," and went to Rome where Paul was a prisoner, but with considerable liberty and living in his own hired house. Probably Paul had shared the hospitality of Philemon at Colosse, where he was then residing, and Onesimus, having seen him there, now sought him out and explained the reason of his coming. Paul instructed him in the doctrines of the gospel and was the means of his conversion. He then advised him to return and made him the bearer of this letter or Epistle to his master.

It has been taken for granted , especially by Southern speaker and writers that Onesimus was a *slave*; it cannot be proved; and this communication of the Apostle certainly furnishes very if not conclusive evidence that he was only a domestic or hired servant. In verse 16, *doulos*, is the word in the original; but, as we have seen, that word was then used to designate either a *servant* or a *slave*; for the wealthy and pleasure-loving Romans, in the heathenish pride and insolence, looked with contempt upon such as were in a servile condition and addressed them all or spoke of them all in the same language. It therefore proves nothing; but in the conclusion, *by Onesimus a servant*, the word translated *servant* is *oiketou*, which mean a domestic, a household servant, an inmate or one living in the house, and even the women and children, which may be regarded as an explanation of what he meant by doulos, servant, in the 16th verse, and this is in accordance with the whole tenor of the communication. In the 18th verse it is said, *If he hath wronged thee or oweth thee outright, put it to my account.* Had Onesimus been a slave this language would have been totally inappropriate; for a slave, being properly himself or regarded as such, could own no property and be under no liabilities except for his labor or his violations of the law. He could contract no debts and could not be said to owe anything. If Onesimus was a slave and had taken anything from his master it must have been by robbery or theft, and would have been so expressed by the Apostle.

It is not said that Onesimus owed his master anything and is merely supposed as a possible case; but if his further service as a slave had been meant there could have been no *if* about that, no supposition and no room for doubt. Is it not obvious, then, that the was not a slave, but a domestic or hired servant, and that he left before he had served out the time for which he was engaged. *If he owes thee aught, anything, put it to my account.* In this view of the matter all is plain and consistent. Philemon might have paid him a part of his wages in advance, as is often done with hirelings, or the absence of Onesimus, just at the time, might have occasioned him much inconvenience and even some loss in his business. If the servant had become indebted to his master in any such way, Paul was willing to assume the payment and made himself responsible by writing the obligation with his own hand. [See v. 11] and intimates that if Philemon chose to retain Onesimus s a servant he would find him more profitable since his conversion than he had previously been, becaue more honest, faithful and trustworthy. In v. 13 he insinuates that he might have retained Onesimus to attend upon him in the bands of the gospel and only declined it on the ground of courtesy and good fellowship, which he might have done, perhaps, without any violation of law or usage, if Onesimus was a domestic, or a hired servant who could not be compelled ot stay with any man longer than he pleased, but not if he was a slave; and what is said in the following verses has long appeared to me incompatible with the supposition that he sustained such a relation.

The suggestions and commands in these three verses (15–17) that the running away of the servant had providentially become the occasion of his conversion in order that Philemon might receive him forever; that he ought now to receive him, not *as a servant* but *as a brother beloved*; and that he should receive him on his return as he would receive the Apostle himself, seems to contain a courteous and extremely delicate intimation that Philemon should no longer regard Onesimus as a servant to be ordered about and treated as an inferior, but as a *freeman* entitled to share in that equality which was the spiritual birthright of the whole brotherhood and in all the rights and privileges belonging to the household of faith, but however that may have been, there is certainly nothing in this Epistle, so full of the spirit and kindness of the gospel that gives any sanction to slavery in the proper sense of the term.

15. The opinions of learned and good men in its favor is no proof that slavery is right.

That "a few do all the thinking" is a trite remark which is verified by facts and needs no comment. There are comparatively few who are capable of thinking for themselves and forming an opinion of their own making a thorough investigation of any important subject, or of solving great and difficult problems in any department. Comparatively few have the capacity or the mental discipline, the means or the leisure requisite for such investigations and fewer still have the resolution and the perseverance- The multitude take their opinions upon trust from the educated few and feel very little concern to know whether they are right or wrong.

On the slavery question ninety nine out of a hundred know nothing except what a few politicians and preachers have told them and of what they have read and heard they recollect only what is favorable to their interest. Whoever tells them and makes it appear plausible that they have a valid right to slave property, they will believe him and will fight it our to the last, without any earnest and prayerful enquiry into the real merits of the question. If any thing is said in doubt of the justice and humanity of the institution the reply is that good and reliable men, preachers and others, who have read a great deal and ought to know have shown that slavery is sanctioned in the Bible and is therefore perfectly right. It has convulsed the nation like an earthquake and deluged the country with blood, yet millions are making no inquiry into the moral character of the institution and are determined to risk their lives and everything they have in defense of their slave property, just because a few men whom they consider learned and good men, have been slave holders and have said the found authority for it in the Bible. Learned and good men are only men of like passions with other men and are just a liable to be blinded by prejudice or swayed by interest. Learned and good men have hone more good in the world and more harm too than all other classes put together. From David king of Israel down to

George III, by the grace of God, king of Great Britain, France, and Ireland, learned and good men believed and taught the multitudes to believe in the divine right of kings but the patriots of '76 asserted and proved it too that there was no such right, but that for three thousand years the world had been under a delusion.

127   The preachers, the most learned and best men they had and not the common people, made popery. For a thousand years, the preachers, the most learned and best men they had, believed and taught the Christian church universally to believe that the Pope was the vicar of Christ upon earth and that the y whole world ought to obey him but Martin Luther and his co-adjutors proved that he was Antichrist and delivered the half of Christendom from his tyrannical power. For generations, the preachers, learned and good men believed and made the protestant churches believe that balls and dancing parties were only an innocent recreation and a fine accomplishment for young people but now all the evangelical denominations in the land have denounced them as the offspring of vanity and fraught with interminable mischief. So it has been with distilling, the habitual use of spirits, and many other things.

The gospel ministry is the great means ordained of heaven for the conversion of the world, and when they are properly endowed with the gifts of the Holy Spirit and confine themselves with earnestness and self devotion, to the appropriate work they do more good than all other classes of mankind put together; but when they go wrong, as they very liable to do they produce more evil than men and devils combined.

128   All that I have read or heard from Southern men on this subject is one-sided. Probably nineteen twentieths of the preachers in the southern states, including all denominations, own more or less slaves and some them own large umbers and they are just as liable to be swayed by interest, custom and the influence of politicians and of "the uppertendom" as other men.

It is not strange, then, they should come in defense of slavery, nor should pretend or really imagine that they find the institution sanctioned in the Bible; but always and in every situation where a man's interests or his educational prejudices are concerned, his impartiality and his willingness to know the truth and acknowledge his wrong, are to suspected. Under these circumstance and in view of the desperate depravity which still belongs to the best of men, the fact that learned and good men generally in the south, or those who are respected to be such, have advocated slavery and been blind to the evils of the institution—its injustice, oppression and inhumanity is no proof that it is right; nor can it release others from their personal responsibility in this matter, or from their moral obligations to make an honest and thorough investigation for themselves and those who rely on the opinions of such men do an immense injury to the present and coming generations, they shame reason, trample on humanity, undervalue truth and bring a reproach upon religion

16. Slavery originated in avarice, falsehood, and cruelty.

A man invested with power, whether limited or unlimited, may from mere selfish motives, adopt measures or engage in enterprises, of a public nature which are based on sound principles and which may result in extensive and permanent good. In such dases the end does not justify the means and he will not be acquitted before a higher tribunal; but if he acted on no moral principles and if his motives were of the basest kind, calamity and wretchedness, if not utter ruin must be the consequence. The institution of slavery commenced without any right motives or any correct moral principle and it has remained unchanged, in its essential character and in its bearing upon the social welfare to the present day.

History informs us that neither the African slave trade nor the colonial slavery of England would ever have been permitted had it not been for the gross falsehoods and misrepresentations of those who first engaged in the enterprise. Gain was their only object and fraud and lying were the means which they employed to accomplish their purpose. The governments of England and France were made to believe that the natives of Africa *embarked voluntarily* and that the object of these traders in taking them to the colonies was to civilize them and convert them to the Christian faith. They pretended that their only object was to benefit the Africans themselves and promote the cause of Christianity in the world. In this way "Queen Bess" of England, in whose reign the excrable slave trade began, was deceived, or she never would have given her consent; for she had in the commencement serious scruples of conscience in regard to the lawfulness of the trade. With her comprehensive and penetrating mind she seems to have anticipated the evils to which its continuance might lead and the unjustifiable means which probably be adopted to obtain the consent of the Africans of force them to leave their native land; for she revolted at the thought of either fraud or coercion. Accordingly when Captain, afterwards, Sir John Hawkins returned from his first voyage to Africa and Hispaniola, to which latter place he had carried a number of Africans, she sent for him and, as we are told, expressed much concern lest any of the Africans should be carried off without their free consent, declaring at the same time that "it would be detestable and call down the vengeance of heaven upon the undertakers." Hawkins promised to comply with the injunctions of Elizabeth but he neither kept nor meant to keep his word; for when he went to Africa again he *seized* as many of the inhabitants as he could and carried them off as *slaves*. "Here," says an English writer, "began the horrid practice of forcing the Africans into slavery, and injustice nad barbarity, which as sure as there is vengeance in heaven for the worst of crimes, will sometime be the destruction of all who encourage it." The people, Christian people of England and America had not become hardened by familiarity with the crime and although they had only a glimpse of the extent to which the trade would carried in order to supply the slave market and the shocking barbarities with which it would be attended, spoke what they thought.

So it was in France and so it was, we believe in every other Christian nation. Labut a Roman Catholic missionary, says in his account of the American island that Louis XIII was very uneasy when he was about to issue the edict, by which all Africans coming into his colonies, should be made slaves, until he was assured that the introduction of them in this capacity, into his foreign dominions, was the readiest way of converting them to the principles of the Christian religion. Then, the African slave trade, of which slavery is the instigating cause, commenced in avarice, falsehood, and deception; for if the Christian governments of that time had only known what was the real object, they never would have given it their sanction and this country would not have been cursed with the "peculiar institution" of the south.

But slavery and the slave trade are only parts of the same system and they are supported on the same principle. If one is unjust, cruel, and inhumane, so is the other. Abolish slavery and the slave trade ceases. They are something like distilling and the use of spirits, except that in slavery under our laws, it propagates itself and needs only occasional supplies from a broad; but we are now officially concerned with the undeniable fact that slavery has the same moral character and must come under the same condemnation with that terrible scourge of humanity, the African slave trade; for it is an act of injustice and wanton cruelty to kidnap and bring the Africans into bondage it must be equally unjust and cruel to hold their unoffending offspring in the same bondage. If there is any immutable distinction between right and wrong, surely wrong can never become right nor can injustice lose it character by continuance in wrong doing.

Slave owners in the west Indies had no constitutional or legal right to hold them as property; for it was not recognized by either the constitution or the laws of Great Britain. To transport the Africans with their free consent and for the humane purpose of Christianizing them violated no moral or fundamental principle; but to force them into slavery and compel them to labor without a reward was an open violation of the constitution and of all constitutional laws then in force. Slavery never existed in England and never can exist there while their constitution and laws remain unaltered. If Elizabeth had given Hawkins or any other man permission to force them away and make slaves of them, it would have been made null and void because unconstitutional and illegal. The royal consent was given and the first acts of Parliament were passed for human and Christian purpose; but *the beginning of which is like the letting out of water*—where it has once got a start it is not easily stopped; And as the *charters* given the colonies no more recognized slavery than the Constitution and laws of England all the enactments of the colonial legislations on this subject were unconstitutional; for those enactments were required to be made agreeable to the laws and statutes of Great Britain. According to those laws and statutes no man could be compelled to labor without a reward; and every man must be tried by his peers or equals but the slaves were compelled, they and their unborn posterity, to labor without reward and were not allowed to be tried by their peers. Moreover by the constitution and laws of England every man had a right to bear testimony against anyone who had wronged or injured him; but by the colonial laws a slave was not allowed to bear witness against his master or any white man. The master might overtask him or beat him and cripple him for life; but the poor slave had not redress; so that almost any fundamental principle of the British constitution, law, and statutes was violated by the colonial legislation and all their enactments in regard to slavery ought to have been declared null and void. This was, in substance, the view taken of this subject by Clarkson, Wilberforce, and their compeers who advocated and effected the abolition of slavery in the west Indies. To a British community it was irresistible and ought to be so to all American freemen.

134

Every intelligent reader knows well that the slave code of colonial legislation has been continued and greatly increased in severity. All the fundamental principles of our constitution and laws are not violated by our legislative enactments and so far as civil rights are concerned, the slaves are not treated as human beings. If a white man is injured by another he can bear testimony and have redress; but a slave is forbidden to bear testimony against any white man. He may be overtasked, beaten unmercifully and even crippled for life, but he must bear it all in silence. If a white man is charged with any violation of the laws, he just be tried by his peers, but a slave must be tried by his *superiors*. If a white man commits treason against the state the constitution and law allow him a fair trial; but if a slave shows any disposition or makes any attempt to resist the laws, he is sure to be hung and oftener than otherwise, without judge or jury. If he makes any attempt to resist his master, no matter what may be the provocation, the master may kill him and have no penalty to fear. In most cases he is allowable a trial

135

by jury the only semblance of a right that he can claim, but the jury, the lawyers, and all concerned in the trial belong to a different race and are either slave owners or belong to the master portion of the community. True, if a master treats his slave unmercifully or treats him with wanton cruelty he may be subject to a slight penalty; but as the slave is not allowed to bear testimony against a white man; it can seldom be proved. So there is or was a law in this state to punish a man for wanton cruelty to his horse; but as the horse could not bear testimony, it could seldom be proved and the poor brute has had to suffer in silence.

As slavery originated in falsehood, fraud, and violence, it must be abandoned or be perpetuated by injustice and oppression. They must have their freedom and be allowed to enjoy all the rights, immunities and privileges of other men or be treated more like beasts than human beings. They must be emancipated and before very long, and of this all who pay any attention to the signs of the times, are beginning to be satisfied. They will be emancipated and will in the life time of many who are now beginning to act their part in society; for if such will not listen to the voice of reason and humanity, conscience and the Bible. The will interpose by his providence as he has often done in past times.

II. The demand: Let my people go.

As in Egypt and everywhere else, the demand is made by express communication and enforced by his Providence; but, here, and there, both are done by such ways and means as existing circumstances require. Egypt was an idolatrous country sunk in superstition and without the means of obtaining the needful information Pharaoh was a heathen monarch and knew nothing of Jehovah, the only living and true God. The Israelites, the children of the Covenant made with Abraham and the people who were now to be delivered from their bondage, had no written revelation, no true prophet and no *teaching* priest, until the Lord raised them up such for the purpose of instructing them and of acting as their guides to the land of promise. It was necessary, therefore, that Jehovah should adapt his communications and the operations of his Providence to the condition of both, the oppressed and their oppressors. It was [also] proper if not absolutely necessary, that he should make his will known to all concerned by the very men who were destined to act such a conspicuous part in the great movements about to be made and that he would enable them to give such proof of their divine mission as ought to satisfy even the proud monarch of the land.

Now we have full and complete revelation of all we need to know and we have been amply furnished with all the means and facilities we ask to aid us in coming to a full understanding of its import. We have had liberty of conscience and sitting under our own vine and fig tree, while there were none to molest or make us afraid, we could study it morning, noon, and evening. We have had an educated and spiritual ministry, whose sole business it has been to study the Bible and expound it to the people; and he has vouchsafed the influences of his Spirit to the Amercian Churches in larger measure than he has done, since the days of the Apostles, to any other land. We are not to look fro any special or direct communication respecting our duty. In Egypt it was necessary that he should make such manifest displays of his power as were necessary to convince an ignorant people and the proud monarch of a great hearth nation, of his existence, of his government over the world and of his justice, truth, and faithfulness to his promises; but now while he sends us to the oracles of inspired truth, the recorded revelation which he has given, for knowledge of our duty in every thing, he shapes the course of his providence in every act of judgment or of mercy according to the circumstances in which he has placed us as accountable beings.

139   The passage which we have placed at the head of this discussion is explicit and positive. It has no condition or limitation and makes no allowance for the interest or convenience of those on whom the demand is made. No time is allowed to sell them off or to make the best arrangements that can be made to prevent an entire loss or sacrifice of their value but a prompt and unreserved surrender of them is required. The traffic is an unlawful traffic and the gain which you have made by their labor is the gain of oppression. Recollect that all nations, the Africans included were given to Jesus Christ in the covenant of redemption and they belong to him. His right is supreme and will be maintained. You have no valid claim to them and you must *let them go*. The determination must be made forthwith and the actual delivery of them must be made as speedily as practicable, or the consequences will be sad and calamitous. We have no commission to make the demand; but it is made in the Bible and we only state what we find therein written.

140   You may say and no doubt many will say that you never received the passage in this light and you don't see how a demand made upon Pharaoh, King of Egypt more than four thousand years ago can have any bearing upon slaveholders at the present day. Why then was it recorded by the pen of inspiration? Merely as a historical fact to gratify an idle curiosity? Then you have read your Bible to very little purpose and have very disparaging notions of the infinite Being. He never does anything in vain and the whole transaction in Egypt is fraught with the most important instruction God has recorded nothing in his word that is not important to us and he has never done anything in his providence that was not designed to teach us a lesson of warning or of encouragement. *All Scripture is given by inspiration of God and is profitable for doctrine, for reproof, for correction, for instruction in righteousness* (2 Tim 3:16). *For whatsoever things were written afore time, were written for our learning that we through patience and comfort of the Scriptures might have hope* (Rom 15:4). *Now all these things, judgments sent upon them for their rebellions, murmurings and sins of every kind as a people, happened to them for ensamples and they are written for admonition upon whom the ends of the world are come* (1 Cor 10:11).

141   If the passage in question has been overlooked, in its true import, for more than two hundred years, it is not the only important one that has shared the same fate. The Apostle says, Rom 3:28, *There we conclude that a man is justified by faith, without the deeds of the law. Knowing that a man is not justified by the works of the law, but by the faith of Jesus Christ, that we might be justified by the faith of Christ, and not by the works of the law, for by the work of the law shall no flesh be justified* (Gal 2:16). For a thousand years these passages with scores of others teaching the same doctrine, were overlooked or misunderstood and misapplied by the whole Christian world, except in a

little handful, who were concealed in the valies of Piedmont and now known as *witnesses* for the truth; and men and women everywhere else sought to be justified by penances, deeds of charity, counting their beads, crusades, persecution of heretics and the merit of departed saints. The Savior told the Jews (Matt 23:9; see also 8–12; 20:25–28) to call no man father or master, upon the earth; but for a thousand years the whole Christian community, few exceptions, as millions still do, called the pretended and lying occupant of Saint Peter's chair, *Pape*, father, their sovereign lord, the vice gerant of Christ upon earth and the dictator of the terms on which they were to be saved. For long centuries the whole of Christendom interpreted Paul's directions about submission to the *the powers that be* as requiring submission to any form of government however despotic; and to the this day not half the world have learned to think rightly upon the subject. Similar remarks might be made on many other passages; but they will occur to every intelligent and reflecting reader without further reference or comment. The mass of the Christian communities feel so little anxiety to know the *whole* will of God and to have respect unto all his commandments especially where their interest is concerned, that they slumber on in a state of security or indifference until they are roused up and compelled to think *search and try their ways,* to enquire for the right way and to put away their iniquities, either by a mighty outpouring of the divine Spirit or by some wide spread and distressing calamities which bring their sins to remembrance. 142

The whole tenor of the Bible is a demand on all who are holding others in bondage and oppression to give them up and leave all free to serve God with whatever powers he has given them; but there are some passages which may be cited as corroborative of the one which we have placed at the head of our remarks. 143

In Ezek 18:4 the Lord says, *All souls* that is all persons, all men and all women, *are mine: the soul* the man or the woman, *that sinneth shall die.* Masters often compel their slaves to do wrong by violating the Sabbath, by aiding them or others in the commission of many crimes which we need not name and by assisting them in accomplishing plans of fraud and deception. E.g., a shrewd active young negro man is sometimes thoroughly drilled in all the arts of gambling and by playing the violin round the gambling table, altogether unsuspected, and by giving his master intimations which he understands, of the the cards in his opponents hands, enable him to win every game. This is only one a a thousand ways in which they are often the willing or unwilling abettors in the commission of the most flagrant crimes. In all such cases the master is accountable at the bar of God for the acts of his slave; but the text quoted above implies that according to the principles of the divine government every one must be left free to act on his 144 own responsibility and be made to feel that *To his own master he stands or falls.* Even Christian masters or masters who are members of some church, often make their slaves do things on the Sabbath, and on other days too, which are palpably wrong and injurious to the interests of vital piety; but to whatever extent this may be true of them, slaves are compelled, in ten thousand instances every day, by their ungodly masters to commit every species of iniquity, from what many would consider as little desecrations of the Sabbath to the most flagrant immoralities. In fact, I have often known people to make their slaves do things, on the Sabbath as as on the other days of the week which they would be ashamed to do themselves and which their consciences would not let them do. Such things, so far at least as impenitent masters and mistresses are concerned are inseparable from the institution as it now exists and God is demanding the surrender of them to his service. All men and all women, all human beings are his, and woe to those who infringe upon his rights or dare to interpose, in whole or in part, between any of them and his authority.

145   In Rom 12:1 we read thus: *I beseech you therefore, brethren, by the mercies of God that ye present your bodies a living sacrifice, holy, acceptable to God, which is your reasonable service and be not conformed to this world; but be ye transformed by the renewing of your mind, that ye may prove what is that good and acceptable and perfect will of God. 6:13 Neither yield ye your members as instruments of unrighteousness unto sin; but yield yourselves unto God, as those that are alive from the dead: and your members as instruments of righteousness unto God.* Not withstanding all the disadvantages under which they labor, many of the slaves have become sincere and so far as their condition admitted, consistent Christians; but while they are held in bondage and their masters claim the whole of their time and strength it impossible for them to consecrate their *members* or their physical powers to God in the Spirit and to the full extent of the above requirements. Perhaps you may say as some have said, that servants are enjoined in the New Testament to serve their masters with fidelity and good will and that if they are thus

146   serving you they are serving God. Suppose you are an ungodly man and make them do wrong all the time or whenever you choose, are they serving God in the gospel of his Son? As already shown, those passages in which servants are enjoined to be obedient to their masters were addressed either to *servants* in the proper sense of the term who were rendering a voluntary service and therefore had the disposal of their own time or to slaves who belonged to heathen or unchristian masters. No Christian slave of any intelligence, feels that he can comply with the above requisitions as he wishes to do; for his time and his physical powers are all at the disposal of another and perhaps of a very wicked man who will compel him to work or go errands

on the Sabbath and do a thousand things by which God is dishonored and his conscience is troubled; but the masters authority can't change the extent of the divine requisition so reasonable and so beneficent. Every man and every woman is required to serve *God with his body and with his spirit which are God's;* and those who interpose to prevent such a consecration of himself to God by any human being incurs an amount of responsibility which will some day overwhelm with shame.

Attentive reader of the Bible know that the ancient prophets often reprimanded the Jews severely and denounced the displeasure of heaven on them for treating servants with severity and especially for attempting to enslave them by keeping them or forcing them back into servitude after the year of release. We shall, however, trouble the reader here with only one reference in regard to this matter and leave him to look for others at his leisure. See Jer 34:8–22. It seems that when the king of Babylon was besieging Jerusalem, or approaching it again after he had left it for a time, the king, the nobles, and all who were able to employ servants, had at the instance of the prophet, made a solemn covenant to set all their servants free and give them a final discharge in the last year of the Septenary period, which hwas the year of release; but when that year was past they had forced them back again into service. This was an act of cruelty and a violation of the their solemn engagements. *Therefore thus saith the Lord, ye have not hearkened unto me in proclaiming liberty every one to his brother, and every man to his neighbor; behold, I proclaim a liberty to you, saith the Lord, to the sword, to the pestilence and to the famine; and I will make you to be removed into all the kingdoms of the earth.* Such was the doom passed upon them for an audacious and wicked attempt to enslave their brethren. It was not this only crime for which their destruction was threatened; but it was the last enormity with which they are charged; for in a little time the city was taken and burned, the king, the nobility and all the better classes of the people were seized and carried captives to Babylon. This passage furnishes the clearest proof that there could be no such thing as slavery amony the Jews, or that no man would be permitted to enslave his brother, nor to hold him in servitude longer than the dawn of the seventh year, the year of release; for it was God's abhorrence, and that all such attempts would be visited with the same judgments, the sword, the famine and the pestilence, with which *he* punished the worst of crimes; but since Christ has come and paid the ransom which divine justice demanded for all who had been given to him of the Father from every nation and kindred and tongue and people under heaven, all mankind is neither Jew nor Greek, Barbarian Scythian, bond nor free. All that come to him are received with equal freedom and form one common brotherhood.

149   The first company of Jews that returned from Babylon was not very large, but it was several times increased by the accession of considerable numbers. Some seventy years after the first return, ere Jeremiah was appointed by the King of Persia governor of Judea and on his arrival in the city he found every thing in a deplorable condition. The temple was not finished and the worship of God was not fully restored. They were engaged in all the industrial pursuits of life and the shrewd enterprising portion of them were becoming wealthy; but another portion from the want either of energy or good management were in very depressed circumstances. Some had mortgaged their lands, vineyards, and houses that they might buy provisions because of the dearth. Others had borrowed money for the king's tribute by giving a lien upon their lands and vineyards; and many had already sold their son's and their daughters for servants nor could they possibly redeem them for other men had their lands and vineyards. When he heard this he was indignant and took a solemn oath of the nobles that they would no more oppress their brethren and would also restore to those whom they had oppressed and brought into bondage, a certain portion of their land and money.

150   Neh 5:1–12. There seems to have been in the mind of all pious Jews an invincible opposition to *slavery* as we understand the term and the Mosaic system was strongly guarded against anything like an extended and enduring bondage. The idea that, whether rich or poor, they were all brethren fostered and developed as it was by their religious ceremonies, their sabbatical institutions and the teachings of the prophets was in constant and direct hostility to anything like an entailed or perpetual enslavement of each other or even of strangers. This idea is far more prominent and ought to be more practically and fully realized under the Christian than the Jewish system; for we have an infinitely greater and more precious promises; and a more abundant supply of that Spirit whose fruits are love, peace, and joy. The command is to receive one another, without respect of persons and without any such distinctions on account of external circumstances, the want of educational advantages or anything else that does not essentially affect their moral character, as Christ has received from the glory of God the Father.

151   Ever since the apostasy of our first parents the religion of mankind had been the same in its principles and in its practical influence. The modes of worship and the ways and means by which the fundamental doctrines of Christianity, were taught and impressed upon the human mind, have been varied as their condition and circumstances required; but the substance has been the same; *for unto us was the gospel preached as well as unto them;* but in every age and under every form of church polity the *spirit* of the gospel is that of *universal freedom*. The purport of all the communications made,

on this subject, by Moses and the prophets, and by Christ and his Apostles is that no man shall intere with the moral agency and accountability of another; that no man shall undertake to answer in another's stead for the use which he makes of his time and his physical powers; and that no man shall so far bring another under his control, or so far occupy his time and energy as to diminish the amount of intellectual, moral and social enjoyment which religion might afford him. In the most lofty conceptions and in the most enraptured visions of the evangelical prophets the perfect security of every man in his person and in the voluntary occupation of his time, and the universal liberty of thought, of enquiry and of action. The prophet Isaiah often reproving the people for their false pretensions to religion while they were living in the practice of gross immoralities, and especially for their hypocritical fashing and this impious plea for the divine favor on that account. Isa 58:6 says, *Is not this the past that I have chosen to loose the bands of the wickedness, to undo the heavy burdens, and lo let the oppressed go free, that ye break every yoke?* This language is the sufficiently explicit and comprehensive. It is perfectly useless—it is worse than useless for people in this country to say that their slaves are not oppressed or overworked, for slavery itself, especially as it is here legalized and made absolute and perpetual is the worst kind of oppression. Thus the prophet says, *Let the oppressed go and break every yoke.* Some of the English commentators, highly valued and much lauded in this country in the exposition of the above passage, speak of all profession of religion, who "traffic in the souls and bodies of men," or who buy and sell their fellow beings, "as the worst of hypocrites, the most flagitious of knaves and assert that they ought at once to "cast off the mask of religion" and not deepen their perdition by professing the faith of our Lord Jesus Christ while they continue in this practice but we prefer to tell the sinful truth and leave its effect to the divine Spirit.

153
In a most animated and glowing description of the Messiah's universal reign in righteousness and peace throughout the earth the Psalmist says, *He shall judge the poor of the people, he shall save the children of the needy, and shall break in pieces the oppressor. He shall redeem their soul from deceit and violence; and precious shall there blood be in his sight* (Ps 72:4.14). The slaves of this country must certainly be included among the poor, the needy and the oppressed; for if they are protected from the peltings of the pitiless storm and have enough to eat, so have the horses and cattle, but that is a most pitiable condition for human beings to be placed in by their fellow men, often by those who profess to be their brethren in Christ and kept there *per force*, while they can't legally hold a dollar's worth in money or property and are studiously debarred from all means of intellectual learning. The prophecies respecting the latter day glory have all a progressive fulfillment and slavery

must be banished from the earth for *Ethiopia shall stretch forth her hands unto God*—by which we understand to be meant that the African race will believe in Jesus Christ; that they will call upon him in faith; and that he will deliver them as he will delver all his people in every other nation from the hand of the oppressor.

154 As the prophets who spoke of the latter day glory and particularly Isaiah, who is by way of eminence styled the evangelical prophet, were commissioned to make known to the Jews and to all who might read their predictions in this and everything else, we might multiply quotations to a considerable extent but we shall content ourselves, for the present with only one more reference in Is 61:1–2. The prophet represents the Messiah as saying, *The Spirit of the Lord god is upon me; because the Lord hath anointed me to preach good tidings unto the meek; he hath sent to bind up the broken hearted; to proclaim liberty to the captives; and the opening of the prison to them that are bound; To proclaim the acceptable year of the Lord, and the day vengeance of our God; to comfort all that mourn.* Soon after Jesus Christ commenced his public ministry, perhaps on the ensuing sabbath, he went into the synagogue of Nazareth and stood up to read. The book or roll containing the prophecy of Isaiah was handed to him and, opening on this place which was probably the lesson, or part of the lesson for the day, he read it in the hearing of all present; Then handed the roll back to the minister or ruler of the synagogue, took his seat and began his exposition by saying, *This day is this scripture fulfilled in your ears.*

155 From the particulars enumerated in this passage, it had a manifest reference to the year of Jubilee, when there was a general release of all debts and obligations, of all bondmen and bondwomen and of all lands and possessions which had been alienated from the tribes and families to which they belonged; and when Jesus Christ applied the prediction to himself he declared plainly enough that the Jubilee had a typical import but that only gave it a much more important meaning without changing in any respect it literal significance. Most of the prophecies which relate to the Christian age have a progressive import and fulfillment. The return of the Jews from their captivity in Babylon, which is used to signify the return of sinners to God was fulfilled in its literal sense within a few generations after the delivery of the prediction and it is fulfilled in it higher or spiritual sense in the case of every one who is converted from the error of his ways. It is said that the wilderness shall bud and blossom as the rose, which is every fulfilling more and more in both its literal and it spiritual import. It was predicted that the blind should see, that the deaf should hear, that the dumb should speak

156 and that the lame should walk. During the personal ministry of Christ on earth, all these predictions as every one knows, received both a literal and

a spiritual accomplishment. In their higher sense they are fulfilling every day and every where throughout Christendom, in the case of all who are brought out of the darkness of mature into the marvelous light of the gospel. In the lower sense they are receiving a partial accomplishment by the skill of physicians and other friends of humanity for, while, by various contrivances the lame, the halt, the maimed, are enabled to walk, the deaf, the dumb, and the blind are taught to read the Bible and to transact the usual business of life but they are yet to receive a more literal and full accomplishment by higher attainments in medical skill and by the discovery of means which are yet unknown so the prophecy in question has been already been fulfilled to a very gratifying extent and will yet have a universal fulfillment in its fullest extent of meaning; we therefore regard all the texts quoted under this head, historical, preceptive and prophetical as confirmatory of the demand which first made on Pharaoh, king of Egypt by Moses and Aaron and is now made by the lively oracles of God on all, here in America and every where else, who are holding their fellow men in bondage.

17. The demand enforced by providences.   157

The greater prosperity of the free than of the slave states first occurs to us as an important fact in God's providential government of the world enforcing his demand for the unreserved and speedy surrender of our whole slave population. It has thus been stated numberless times on every hand by, statesmen, politicians, and other men of education, who were versed in our national history north and south, that, when our independence was acknowledged by Great Britain and for many years after, the south was, in all the means and reasons requisite for social progress, far in advance of the north. The southern states had a larger population, a greater extent of territory, a better soil, and a more congenial climate and a more extended and profitable commerce; and until within the last two or three years they carried every presidential election and every important measure in congress that they wanted. In a pamphlet entitled, The Five Cotton States and New York, which, as I have seen stated, was written by a Philadelphia Merchant, a man of liberal education and of a very philosophical cast of mind, the author says that for some time after we gained our independence, the merchants of Philadelphia   158
went to Charleston for their silks and finer fabrics of every description, as the merchants of the South, for the last fifty or sixty years, have been going, for such articles, to Philadelphia and New York. What has made such a change? Slavery and that alone; for all the men who had the means and the ability to maintain a growing commerce with other nations to give a strong and

continued and well directed impulse to the progress of society had slaves and cotton or rice plantations which, not only occupied their time and attention, but impaired their intellectual enterprise; but the north have got far in advance of us in everything on a smaller territory they have quadrupled us in population, and on a sterile soil and in a cold, bleak climate, they have made the whole face of the country look like a well watered garden. As the statistical reports have shown, their cereal and other products have annually amounted to far more in value than all the cotton and sugar of the south, which their manufacturers of every kind have exceeded ours probably a hundred fold; because, from one extremity to the other of their barren, naturally barren country, not withstanding their long and dreary winters, theirs is an ever busy and universal industry, a rigid but judicious economy and a bold will directed and untiring spirit of enterprise.

159   In slave countries, the boundaries of science have never been extended and nothing of importance has been added to the stock of human knowledge: No great inventions have made in the useful arts and very rarely has much excellence been attained in music, poetry, painting, or sculpture. All the advances made in mathematics, astronomy, and philosophy, physical or mental, in classical and general literature, and in the mechanical and useful arts have been made in countries where there was no such thing as slavery. We are indebted to the north for every thing we have that is worth having- for all our valuable works on mathematics, science, and on natural, mental, and moral philosophy; on law and medicine, theology, government and jurisprudence; for all our histories, poetry, works of taste and general literature for our books of surveying, navigation, and engineering; for our Bibles, hymnbooks and even our common school books; for our improvements in farming and farming implements; for our improved breeds of horses, cattle, and sheep; for our household furniture and in short, for everything that makes us comfortable at home or that enables us to pursue the business of life with any tolerable degree of success. In the South we may have invented a pretty good straw cutter and a bedstead that affords little or no harbor for bugs, but nothing, I believe, of more importance.

160   Southern men have as good minds naturally as northern men and they always shown it on sudden emergencies or great occasions which gave them a sufficient impulse and called forth the highest and most rigorous exercise of their powers. Hence what are now called or were lately called the "border states" have produced, in proportion to their population, more great orators and able commanders than the north; but it was under the pressure of necessity. Ordinarily they lack the necessary stimulus and spend their time either in idle ness, perhaps hunting, fishing, gambling, and other frivolous or worse than frivolous amusements, or in a light kind of "summer reading" which

gives them no enduring celebrity, no world-wide reputation, and results in no extensive and permanent benefit to the community. The whole north is like a great bee hive, where men, women and children are all going from sunrise to sundown, as busy as bees; but in the South one fourth of the population are little better than drones; and during the warm or pleasant weather, you may find them setting on the benches at every tavern door, some half a dozen, more or less of white men, generally slave holders; or the beardless sons of slave holders, smoking their cigars, cracking the heels of their boots together and talking politics. These are simple and undeniable facts and they speak a volume in regard to the condition of the South.

Throughout the North, pretty generally in town and country, the boy is taught to understand and made to feel that, whether rich or poor he must exert himself and habits of industry, economy, and enterprise are formed as he grows up which go with him through life. Those who have intellectual powers above mediocrity prepare for some one of the learned professions, for scientific and literary pursuits, or perhaps for the application of mechanical philosophy to mechanical inventions and improvements. Early in September of 1861, a gentleman of ability, moral worth, and true-hearted, who had been a member of the Federal congress, asked me in conversation, why it was that the South had so many more men of eloquence and political sagacity in congress than the north? To which I replied that there were two explanations to be given of the fact, if it was a fact. The South generally sent their ablest men to Congress but the North, with few exceptions, sent only their second or third rate men. Talented young men in the south, not feeling themselves under any necessity of intense and long continued application or critical investigations in order to obtain the means of subsistence or to accumulate a fortune, devote their time to the study of constitutions, history, and oratory, diversified with poetry, novels and ballestellure. As free schools are of recent origin in most of these states, comparatively few boys of genius, when only birth right was poverty and ignorance have been so fortunate as to obtain a liberal education and be permitted to evolve their powers under the more propitious influences with which those are surrounded who are born in affluence and many who might have shone with surpassing luster and carved their names high on the temple of fame, have been doomed to pass their life in toil and obscurity, unknown, and unappreciated, like a gem of priceless value buried beneath the tumultuous waves of the ocean or a flower wasting its fragrance on the desert air. Those in the southern states generally who have genius and the means of getting a liberal education in early life are under no necessity of close and protracted application to study, prepare themselves just for public life. Hence we have had so few native southerners who have made very great scientific and literary attainments, or have earned a wide spread and enduring reputation as profound, elegant, and accomplished writers on any subject of general interest and importance.

163   In a land of freedom that state of things is very different; for there a boy of genius is usually discovered and taken out of the rubbish in which his lot was cast and placed where his powers can be developed for his own advantage and that of the community; but there where a young man of a high order of intellect and conscious, on leaving college or at an earlier stage of his progress, make it a matter of serious enquiry and reflection in what pursuit or occupation he can employ his talents to the best advantage. If he is a young man of piety and feels that he ought to preach the gospel he will prepare for the ministry; but if not, the dry technicalities of law, with the little dirty practice that comes into every court, and the uncertainties in the practice of medicine don't suit him. In the sphere of a statesman there is no pecuniary profit to be realized and much petty electioneering to be done, to which a man of refined taste and lofty conceptions will not condescend; but the sphere of science and literature, of art and philosophy, large enough to fill his capacities, varied enough to suit his inclination and grand enough to satisfy his highest aspiration, lies before him and its attractiveness determines his choice. By writing two or three novels, which he can do in

164   as many years, or in less time, he can realize some forty or fifty thousand dollars. The author of Uncle Tom's Cabin made a handsome little fortune by that publication alone; and I saw a statement three or four years ago that Fanny Fern had then realized fifteen thousand dollars from the sale one little volume entitled *Ruth Hall*, and perhaps twice that amount on her other little light and pleasant publications. Washington Irving made a fortune by his writings; so did Cooper by his novels; and Bancroft and Prescot by their histories. Author, of New York has made quite a large fortune by publishing a series of the Latin and Greek classics, with explanatory notes for the use of Academies and colleges. So have others done by publishing as series of mathematical works for the same purpose, or even by publishing a series of English readers for common schools; and others have realized a larger amount by writing for magazines and Quarterly Reviews. Hence such a large amount of the first talent in the country is now employed on the Reviews, magazines, and weekly papers both secular and religious. but in a slave country there is nothing to produce such a full and complete development of all the human powers.

165   For the last thirty five years there has been a gradual but steady recession of the slave population from the north, or from what have been lately called the border states, to the south and a concentration of them round the Gulf of Mexico; which though not noticed by many we regard as a significant fact and one which should claim the attention of all concerned.

Politicians and others who have only a nominal faith in the Bible and many of them not even that, explain this movement by natural causes, or by the shifting zones of trade and business. The say that as slave labor is so much more profitable in the cotton and sugar regions their owners run them off these and employ their capital more profitably in some other way. This may be true, but it is certainly one of the many events which go to make up the course of Providential movements and all of which are necessary to the accomplishment of his purposes. It claims the attention of slave owners and of the governmental authorities to its significance and to the demand made in the sacred oracles for their immediate surrender. Every pin belonging to a building or a system of machinery must be in its place or the whole will go wrong; and in the great system of agencies which are constantly and assiduously engaged under the control of divine Providence in working out the progressive results of redemption, every one must be in his place and every movement must be made at the right time and in the direction, or there will be a failure of the accomplishment.

166

Whether, in this removal of the slaves towards the Gulf, which must be regarded as providential, it is designed to make them ultimately the rightful owners and occupants of the soil, or to make them dominant population and let the remaining whites there disappear by amalgamation; or to have them ready for embarkation for Liberia, when the proper time comes, we cannot tell. This is among the secret things which belong unto God; but it will become known by the progressive unfolding of his purposes. We presume that neither Pharaoh nor his courtiers understood, at the time, the specific design of any one of the miracles wrought for the deliverance of the captive Israelites nor did it enter into their minds that every one of them was as necessary in it place as each and every one of the planets in the Solar System; but it was their duty then, as it is ours now, to take the warning, given and comply with the demand for the total and speedy emancipation of the millions whom they were holding in an unjust and cruel bondage.

The Israelites must have been all collected, by some means or other, into one place so that all could move off together in one compact and well organized body; and whatever disposal is to be finally made, of the blacks, we presume that some place of *rendevous* will be assigned them by Him who claims their services, watches over their destiny and now demands their release. If they are to have a territory and a government of their own on this continent, the cotton and sugar regions of would seem to be the most suitable place for them or if the Lord designs that they shall be returned to their father land, the Gulf of Mexico will be the most convenient place for their embarkation. A large majority of them are there already and in some of the states their relative proportion to the whites is nearly three to one.

167

168 The remainder can soon be taken thither and then they will be ready to occupy those states or the islands in the Gulf of Mexico, or return to Africa, as *the pillar of cloud and of fire* may direct. When the Israelites assembled at their place of *rendezvous*, they had the promised land in view, the land given to them by the oath of Him who cannot lie; but none of them, not even their leaders, knew by what route they should be led nor how long they would be on the way. Although the Holy One of Israel demands the release of the four million now held in a degrading and oppressive bondage among us and will not cease to visit us, at longer or shorter intervals, with the judgments of his hand, he has not told us until they are released where is the land which he has designed for them, nor precisely where nor when nor how he designs to employ them in his service; but our duty is to yield a cordial and prompt compliance with his requisitions and trust him for the results. We are in the midst of great and mysterious movements which we cannot control and the *finale* of which is beyond our ken; but we have the sure word of command and we have the Providence of the God pointing out our course as we advance. Pharaoh and his servants would not take the warnings given them by the divinely commissioned leaders of Israel nor yield to the pressure of the calamities which were coming upon them with increasing severity, until it was too late. Remembering that *what was written afore time was written for our instruction,* let us not be guilty of Pharaoh's sin nor subject ourselves to Pharaoh's ruin.

169 That the free blacks in the North, where there are half a million or not much less could never be persuade, with few exceptions, to immigrate to the colony in Africa, when it was manifestly their interest to do so, ought to be regarded as another significant fact, especially when it is known that they reason which they have always assigned, as stated in the Northern papers a few years ago, was that they did not feel like leaving their native land while their country men were in bondage. Politicians and slaveholders generally who have not reflected seriously on the subject, nor read either history or their Bibles with attention, may sneer at the reason assigned, as a whim or an idle notion; but has it ever been known that such a mass of human beings were governed by a whim or an idle notion for forty years and in the face of every prudential consideration and Moses would not forsake Egypt entirely while his people were in bondage and chose rather to suffer affliction with them than to be called the son of Pharaoh's daughter or sway the scepter over subjugated millions. When Joseph was dying he gave it, in charge to his brethren that they should keep his bones there until their deliverance, as a pledge of his confidence in the fulfillment of the divine promises and they carried them along with them to the land of promise.

That the Lord does influence the minds and hearts of individuals, communities and nations is unquestionable and it must be so; for otherwise he could not govern the world. How he does this we need not inquire—whether by a direct agency or by so ordering circumstances that, while acting only in the view of motives they shall be led to accomplish his purposes either of judgment or of mercy. In all this then is no constraint upon their will and no interference with their moral agency for as they desire none of his ways and are but upon their own course, or do not honestly and fervently ask him for direction, but trust to their own wisdom and aim at the accomplishment of their own plans which are frequently in opposition to him, it is right and fit that he should so influence them by presenting motives adapted to their selfish nature or by placing with their reach such objects of choice as will be most attractive to them, that their fancied wisdom shall be confounded and their selfish designs frustrated, while, without any intention or wish to do so they are doing just what was necessary to the deliverance of this people from their temporal or spiritual oppression and for the advancement of truth, freedom, and humanity in the world.

170

Thus by ordering the circumstances of the Pharaoh so that while acting freely in accordance with his selfish designs and his aversion to the truth, he would be led to persist in his tyrannical purposes, he is said to harden his heart and Pharaoh by voluntarily making the choice he did, without desiring any other direction than that of his own will, is said to harden his own heart but it must be observed these things relate only to the transactions recorded in Exodus. He might not have been thus hardened against all truth and all humanity. If a lone man and his wife when fleeing from famine as Abraham and Sarah did, or a solitary family escaping from a similar calamity had come to his count, he would no doubt have received them with much hospitality and kindness; or if a neighboring nation had been visited in the famine and pestilence he might have contributed liberally for their relief. A man, a church, or nation may in a similar way, harden their hearts as to one thing and not to anything nor anything else. So God may, as he did in the case of Pharaoh, harden their hearts and let them go on to ruin.

171

By ordering circumstances so as to present worldly motives and of sufficient strength, he is said to have brought up the the King of Assyria against the two tribes and made him carry them away captive. In the same way he brought up Nebuchadnezzar against the other two tribes and made him destroy Jerusalem and carry the inhabitants away to his own land. So he has even controlled and led about all the great men and all the little men too, as effectually as if he had *put a bridle in their mouth*, but without impairing in the least their freedom of choice or their responsibility.

172

As everything good in man, however, is from him, he inclines and determines his people in a different way to do his will, whether recorded in his word or indicated by his Providence. His Spirit abides in their hearts; but sometimes more sensibly or in larger measure than at other times. Hence when he has any thing of more than ordinary importance for them to do he is said to *stir them up* or *put it into their hearts* to make the sacrifice or do the work. Of such expressions the whole Bible is full and we need make no references. Whether the sentiment or feeling, or whatever you may choose to call it, on the minds of the free blacks, which has kept them here for forty years against their interest is from the spirit of all truth and grace or not, time must show; but the fact, which is well known, ought to be taken into the account and well considered by all concerned.

173   The opinions and example, the admonitions and warnings of the wisest, purest, and most patriotic statesmen whom this or any other country has ever produced, from Washington down to the present time, lend a strong enforcement to the demand made in the Bible for the speedy surrender of the Lord's people whom he has redeemed and whose services he requires. We naturally turn first to the father of his country whose counsels seem to have and ought to be regarded as having an almost oracular authority; for so far as we have followed them we have had uninterrupted prosperity and so far as we have departed from them we have had cause for bitter regret. In a letter to John H. Mercas, Sept 9th 1786, he says:

"I never mean, unless some particular circumstances should compel me to it, to own another slave by purchase, it being among my *first wishes* to see some plan adopted by which slavery in this country, may be abolished by law."

In a letter to Robert Morris dated April 12th of the same year, he says: "I hope it will not be conceived by these observations that it is my wish to hold the unhappy people who are the subject of this letter in slavery. I can only say that there is not a man living who wishes more sincerely than I do to see a plan adopted for the abolition of it; but there is only one proper and effectual mode by which it can be done and that is by legislative authority and this so far as my suffrage will go, shall never be wanting."

174

In two letters, of different dates, addressed to the Marquis Lafayette he expresses substantially the same views; and in an letter to Sir John Sinclair he said:

"There are in Pennsylvania laws for the gradual abolition of slavery, which neither Virginia nor Maryland have at present; but which nothing is more certain than they must have, and at a period not remote."

On the 17th of March, 1792, he thus wrote to Charles Pickney, Governor of South Carolina "I must say that I lament the decision of your legislature upon the question of importing slaves after March 1793. I was in hopes that motives of policy, as well as other good reasons, supported by the direful effects of slavery, which, at this moment are presented, would have operated to produce a total prohibition of the importation of slaves, whenever the question came to be agitated in any state that might be interested in the measure."

It is well known that he emancipated all his slaves, of whom he had a great many, and for the readers satisfaction we give the following extract from his will and testament:

"Upon the decease of my wife, it is my will and desire that all the slaves which I hold in my own right shall receive their freedom. To emancipate them during her life would, though earnestly wished by me, be attended with such insuperable difficulties, on account of their intermixture by marriage with the lower negroes, as to excite the most painful sensation, if not disagreeable consequences, from the latter, while both descriptions are in the occupancy of the same proprietor it not being in my power, under the tenure by which the lower negroes are held, to manumit them."

When Mrs. Washington learned from the will of her deceased husband that the only obstacle to the immediate emancipation of the slaves was her right of dower, she promptly gave it up, as we are told, and they were at once made free.

In his "Notes on Virginia" Thomas Jefferson who wrote the Declaration of Independence and was afterwards President of the United States, uses the following language: "There must doubtless be an unhappy influence on the manner of our people produced by the existence of slavery among us. The whole commerce between master and slave is a perpetual exercise of the most boisterous passions—the most unremitting despotism on the one part, and degrading submissions on the other. Our children see this and learn to imitate it; for man is an imitative animal. This quality is the germ of all education in him. From his cradle to his grave he is learning to do what he sees others do. If a parent could find no motive, either in his philanthropy or his self love, for restraining the intemperance of passion towards his slave, it should always be a sufficient one that his child is present. But generally it is not sufficient. The parent storms the child looks on, catches the lineaments of wrath, puts on the same airs in the circle of smaller slaves, gives a loose rein to the worst of passions, and thus nursed, educated and daily exercised in tyranny cannot but be stamped by it with odious peculiarities. The man must be a prodigy who can retain his manner and morals undepraved by such circumstances. And with what execration should the statesman be loaded who permitting one half the citizens thus to trample on the rights of the other, transforms those into despots and these into enemies, destroys the moral of the one part and the *amor patriae* of the other; for if a slave can have a country in this world, it must be any other in preference to that in which he is born to live and labor for another, in which he most lock up the faculties of his nature, contribute, so far as depends on his individual endeavors to the evanishment of the human race or entail his own miserable condition on the endless generations proceeding from him with the morals of the people, until industry also is destroyed."

177 During the past generation the whole civilized world has been waking up on the subject of universal freedom and a most gratifying progress has been made on the continent of Europe. The autocrat of Russia has emancipated his serfs and thereby set a noble example for the despotic governments of the nations. Italy, Piedmont, and some smaller states have thrown off the yoke and established a representative government with a limited monarchy. The Sultan of Turkey has been compelled to make important concessions and when Christianity obtains a more general influence over the masses which it will certainly do and in a very few years, they will assert their rights and in spite of everything, establish a free government. The emperor of Austria, though little more than a mere tool in the hands of the Pope, has been forced to grant his subjects some important privileges and immunities sorely against his will, and these are only preparing the way for still larger and higher demands. As the mind of man is expansive and his desires have no assignable limit, if he is permitted to enjoy in any degree the benefits of freedom, he will not rest until he gets the full inheritance.

178 More distant nations are beginning to catch the inspiration and the despots of heathendom have been made to tremble on their thrones. The intellectual, moral, and social powers of men are about the same everywhere their religious and civil rights are the same and the laws of their being, their instinctive tendencies and their desires of acquiring more than they have of everything that affords them security or gratification, are constantly impelling them to advance and to remove whatever obstructions may have been thrown in the way of their progress. Nothing more is necessary for the emancipation of every race and kindred and tongues and people under heaven than to give them that firm and enduring sense of the accountability to God alone, which the Bible teaches, and which will make them understand how much better it is to serve God than man and be ready to go if necessary, as martyrs to the stake or to die anywhere rather than be slaves and renounce the truth. All on whom the light of revelation has only dawned regard liberty as a boon of inestimable price and as the light increases they will rise up and assert their dignity as rational and immortal beings.

179 In early life the development of the human powers is very slow and so it is with the general mind, especially in nations or communities which have

been kept in ignorance and pressed down by the heavy hand of despotic power. Neither great attainments, nor great changes in the habits of a people, are made in a day or a year. There must be time for enquiry, reflection, and experiment. What has been gained must be tested and made secure, or all may be hazarded through ignorance and impudence. Perhaps it would not be best that the down trodden nations of Europe should be all set entirely free at once and left to form a government for the themselves; but, as a child learns to keep the centre of gravity and to walk by the same efforts, they must be allowed to advance as they gain strength and the wisdom of experience. When you see the dawn you know that it will increase to the full radiance of the midday sun and that no power on earth can arrest or hinder its progress; and when the light of life and immortality dawns upon a nation that has been long sitting in darkness and in the region and shadow of death, it is not in the power of men and devils to stay its progress or to spread over them a covering long enough and broad enough to prevent it from reaching their minds. But while the civilized nations of the world are thus bursting their fetters and rising up to the dignity of freemen, shall we applaud them for their courage and rejoice in their success, while we keep four millions here, with their rapidly increasing numbers, in a bondage more absolute and degrading than any other upon earth? Is there any consistency in these greeting while we are lording it over so many of our brethren, the countless numbers, of the same flesh and blood, for whom Christ paid the same ransom that he paid for us, who are heirs of the same promises and destined to the same inheritance and not only lording it over them but doing every thing in our power to prevent them from becoming acquainted with their rights to make their bondage perpetual? Do those providences which are setting the nations of the old world free from their vassalage and placing them in circumstances so favorable to the development of their powers and to their progress in social enjoyment have no significance for us and give no enforcement to heaven's demand for the full and speedy emancipation of the down trodden millions among us? Whether the wicked will understand or not, *the wise shall understand* and the obedient shall be led in the way of safety and uprightness.

The establishment of a colony of blacks from this country on the western coast of Africa and the prosperity which has so far, attended it cannot be viewed in any other light than as providential events of more importance than we can now estimate and as indicating the same wise and beneficent design with those which have been already mentioned. Its founders were men of piety, foresight, and large minded patriotism. Their object was one of pure benevolence and Providence has smiled upon it from the beginning. Like all other enterprises of the kind it had for a time, to contend with difficulties; but these were all overcome and now it appears to be firmly established. Its independence has been acknowledged by the principal nations of Europe and some of them have shown it special favor. England and France have, each of them presented the government with a coasting vessel and have shown a disposition to give the colony such aid and encouragement as will stimulate their energies, enable them to develop their power and to work out a national and political destiny for themselves. The varied products of their fertile soil and sunny climate promise a profitable commerce which is increasing every year. They have men of ability at the head of their government, in the army and in the all the learned professions; they have churches of all the protestant denominations in this country and supplied with a competent ministry; they have schools, academies, and literary institutions of every grade, yet in their infancy it is true, but an infancy that promises a vigorous manhood; they are now on friendly terms with the natives who are manifesting great anxiety to get the civilization of their brethren from America introduced among them; land, according to the statements I have seen, can be obtained in any quantity and upon easy terms. Their increase from births and immigration has been steady and their prospects are as fair as could be expected. Their prosperity has in fact been greater than the first settlements planted in this country attained in the same length of time. They have almost an unlimited extent of territory before them and without any apprehension of such collisions from different races as before the white settlers in the American colonies. I cannot now go into any further detail of facts and it is not necessary. The colony has been established there, in the providence of God; it is composed principally of blacks who were manumitted by their humane masters for the purpose fo sending them with the gospel and civilization to that benighted land, and it has so far prospered.

The African colony has been viewed from the first with intense interest by it friends and with as much antipathy by its foes; for, to the reproach of justice, freedom and humanity, it has had many and virulent enemies in this country; but the wise, the benevolent and the patriotic have given it their support. Nearly all the presidents from Monroe, under whose administration the colonization society was organized, down to the present time have been its cordial friends. The most large minded, far seeing and patriotic statesmen we have ever had, such as Clay and Webster, with many others, contributed to its success their money, the influence of their names and the power of their eloquence. The opposition to it has been by slaveholders in the south and by a few abolitionists in the north. Slaveholders seemed to be afraid that it would prove the capacity of the black for self government and ultimately become an effectual means or agency in working out the abolition of slavery. Hence it received very little support from the south and a few abolitionists at the north opposed it because they thought it would interfere wit htheir scheme of an instantaneous and universal emancipation of the slaves here without any provision for their removal and their further welfare; but by the prudence, energy, and self sacrificing spirit of its friends, with the labor of a kind Providence, it has been enabled to hold its own way and to wax stronger and stronger.

Can we suppose now that the Lord put it into the heart of Dr. Finley and his co-adjutors to form the American Colonization Society, and that he has preserved and prospered it thus far, merely for all the good it has hitherto done to Africa or is likely to do in a century to come without greater accessions of numbers and resources from this country?

All intelligent, fair minded and disinterested men view it very differently and regard it as a suitable preparation made beforehand for the manumitted slaves from this country, the days of whole redemption they now believe to be drawing near. The colonies planted in this country were a refuge for the oppressed brethren in England and all men have regarded that as a providential arrangement. Then why not regard the colony so providentially founded in Africa as a preparation made beforehand for the slave population of this country, when set free and returned to their "father land"? Whatever others do we cannot but view it as a sign of the times and an admonition from heaven of an approaching and general emancipation.

Within a few years after the last war with England, or as soon as the state of things in the country became settled and business revived, politicians began to agitate the slavery question in congress and the discussion grew warmer and warmer every year until it became acrimonious, bitter and abusive. Members condescended to personalities, guarded and fought in the halls of congress. In 1850, if my recollection serves me, matters seemed to have come to a crisis and, in the general apprehension, nothing saved the Union from a sudden and violent disruption but the wisdom, patriotism and compromising spirit of such men as Henry Clay and Daniel Webster. Where only local and temporary interests are concerned compromises answer a good purpose and are, in fact, indispensable; but no compromise can be made at the expense of great moral and fundamental principles that will be of any permanent advantage. The Lord reigns and will maintain his cause in the earth. A compromise of mere human opinions and interests that tramples on or ignores the principle of his moral government must be unavailing and we never had the least confidence in the ability and permanence of any compromises that have been made for the maintenance of slavery.

186   The authors of these compromises acted from the most patriotic and motives but they do not appear to have admitted a full recognition of the fact that the Almighty does always and every where effectually control the agencies of men and will forever maintain his won cause.

Of that insignificant, but violent and reckless party at the north, usually denominated Abolitionists, we have nothing to say; for we never could see that they had very much to do in the great movement which was making towards emancipation. There have been for the last generation, few politicians, north or south, of tried patriotism and unbending integrity, and many of them, without caring a straw for the moral or religious principles involved only made the slavery question a stepping stone to office; but the mass of the people were honest and conscientious. In their view that article in the Federal constitution establishing or rather upholding slavery was directly in opposition to the great principles asserted in the Declaration of Independence, that *all men are born equal* and that all men have an inalienable right to life, liberty, and the pursuit of happiness. This, if viewed merely in a political light, was a gross inconsistency which ought to be rectified and a foul reproach to the nation, which should not be suffered to remain.

187   But they had much stronger reasons for their opposition to slavery and to the "peculiar institution" of the south. They believed, honestly and on good grounds, that it was contrary to the whole spirit and teachings of the Bible; that it originated in avarice and that it was essentially unjust and oppressive. Of course they thought it as much their duty to do all they could in the way of argument and free discussion to accomplish its removal from the land; If the right of petition had not been denied them in congress, contrary to an express provision of the Federal constitution; if the privilege of free discussion had not been prohibited in the south, they would have been satisfied; but these unconstitutional proceedings only increased the irritation.

The politicians of the south, the people too, defended their cause mainly on the ground of interest; for that was the great argument relied on, in and out of Congress. "Cotton was King" and he must be kept on his throne. The world could not do without our cotton; but the whites could endure the labor of cultivating it in that climate, and there fore slavery must be maintained. Their appeals to the Bible, to history, and philosophy were evidently nothing more than the special pleadings of a county court lawyer but they never thought of resorting to force. The argument drawn the sup-

188   posed of pretended necessity of the case was in every body's mouth from the "able divine" and the learned judges and the "eloquent orator," down to the local preacher, the *picayune* politician and the mechanic in his shop. In the north they contended for all the rights specified in the Declaration of Independence and asserted that the word *slaves* is not found in the constitution;

that it was omitted just because it was expected, north and south, by the framers of the constitution and by all others that it would not be long continued as a civil institution and that this was well understood in and out of the convention. In the south they ignored the assertions in the Declaration, that "all men are born equal." and that "all men have an inalienable right to life, liberty and the pursuit of the happiness." The north complained that the fundamental principles of the constitution and of all free government were violated by refusing to receive their petitions in congress and by prohibiting free discussion in the south; but the advocates of slavery asserted that all this was done in self defense and that necessity has no law. Now as the conviction of the northern people increased as it was by investigation, as the grandeur of "king cotton" loomed up before the imaginations of the southerners, any attentive observer, of ordinary sagacity could not fail to perceive that, unless emancipation was speedily commenced, a civil war with all its horrors, must be the inevitable result.

What the Lord did with Pharaoh and his servants he had virtually done before and has been doing ever since with all the nations of the earth and even with his own church and people. He will be glorified by the whole of his creation and especially by the intelligent portion of it. If they will not honor him by having respect to *all* his commandments and by diffusing happiness ot the extent of their abilities, he will, sooner or later, glorify his power and his justice in their punishment. He said he had raised up Pharaoh, put him on the throne and kept him there that he might show forth his power on him; and, as he had determined and said that he would not give up what he regarded as his slave property, the Lord hardened his heart, i.e., ordered circumstances so that he hardened his own heart, or be led to persist in his determination until he was overwhelmed in ruin. Whether his heart was hardened in relation to every thing or anything else and whether he had formed a determination to pursue any other course of such flagrant injustice and enmity is nothing to our present purpose; but here his interest was concerned and avarice and the love of power had possession of his soul. The fact that he was a heathen and thought that he was accountable to no being except himself is no reason why God should thus deal with him alone and let others escape who are guilty of the same or perhaps of much greater enormities. 189

Circumstances were so ordered in other parts of the world that very little was done in the raising of cotton for market until recently and the price of this staple and consequently, of slaves had become so high that people had gone as far as they could go in making what they call their slave property secure and had become fixed in their determination never to give it up. They have been thus led by circumstances to harden their hearts and to 190 resolve, with some show of unanimity, that they "spend the last dollar and the last drop of blood" before they will yield on the part the south. This is confessedly a war for slavery and they have resolved to retain it or perish in the attempt. Every man here is as much a monarch as Pharaoh; for he may, by a word or by the cast of his vote, decide the destinies of the nation; and slave owners are now pursuing a course very similar to that of the Egyptian despot. Whatever may be the proximate results of the present contest, many discerning and sober thinking men among us believe and thought slave owners themselves, do not scruple to say that the final issue will be universal abolition. Pharaoh suffered himself to be deceived by the false miracles of his magicians as many now suffer themselves to be deceived by the sophistry and bare assertions of those who make pretensions to knowledge and religion; yet when he was hard pressed by the plagues sent upon him, he promised to do better and the Lord then gave him sufficient time to fulfill his promises; but he still hardened his heart. When insurrections with some massacre of the whites in one or more of the cotton states, the people and the governmental authorities adopted or talked strongly of adopting measures forgetting clear of them, but, as slaves brought a high price in the market, when the danger seemed to have passed away, their good feelings and resolutions all vanished and they resolved again not to let them go. If they did not expressly retract their promises and renounce the measures which they had initiated, they tacitly left them unaccomplished. Broken promises and resolutions are among the sins for which, as a people, we have to answer but how many have uet believed it. Pharaoh knew not Jehovah, the God of the Israelites and might possibly have thought that Moses and Aaron were impostors. His Magicians could do some wonderful things as well as Moses and by their arts he was deceived and hardened in his wicked purpose. We do not pretend to say that all those preachers and professors of religion who have undertaken to justify were willful deceivers for we have no doubt that many slaveholders were sincere and humble Christians but they were led astray by the interests and other malign influences. Much sophistry has been employed and the teachings of the Bible have been greatly perverted. We admit that the southern people have been in certain sense, acting on the defensive, and those who are acting on the defensive though not necessarily wrong nor always unfair in their statements, are, when wrong, under stronger temptations to do so than the assailants.

Some how or other by the force of custom, avarice, of passion and of circumstances, we have become involved in the terrible calamities of a civil war; and the expenses of this war, including the destruction of property, have already amounted to far more than all the "niggers" in the land are worth. All business has been at a stand still, except that of speculating on property with paper that has been constantly depreciating ever since its first issue and will, before all is over, not be worth more than the rags of which it was made. All the surplus produce in the country is taken to support the army and while the soldiers are living on half rations, hundreds of poor families over the country are starving. At least half a million of southern men have already perished in the war, having been slain in battle or died of disease and how many more are destined yet to perish no one can tell. A great deterioration of morals has already been produced and subjugation, we predict will be the inevitable result. Yet all this might been easily foreseen and prevented by yielding as a Christian people should have done to God's demand and by putting away the evil in time. Avarice seems to be regarded by other nations as the reproach of this country and it is the judgment of the civilized world that the southern people now claiming a species of property to which they have no moral right.

We are in the midst of scenes, the most extraordinary and the most unaccountable that the world has seen in modern times. War, it is true, is not an unusual thing; for the history of the world is little more than a history of the wars that have taken place and the effects which they have produced on society; nor is it difficult to assign the general cause; for, *whence come wars and fightings among you? come they not hence even of your lusts that war in your members?* (Jas 4:1). Human depravity is in general, the cause of all the violence that is done and all the crimes that are committed in the world; but all the wars recorded in history have had their cause in the desire of conquest or in a spirit of revenge for past injustices, real or alleged, in a fanatical purpose of exterminating heretics or in defense of great moral and religious principles. This is not only a civil war and the greatest civil war that the world has known except that which took place in the Roman empire in the time of Julius Caesar and immediately after his death; but this is unique in the proximate causes of its rise and progress. No other war has originated in the same cause; no other war has ever been waged for the same object; and no other war has been productive of the same results; but these are yet among the secret things which belong unto the Lord our God. As soon as the trumpet sounded the whole nation rushed to arms almost with lightening speed and as if under influence of some mighty impulse. In no other war of modern times has either side had as many men in the field or anything like such an amount of preparation. What number of men the Federal government has now or has had I have not learned; but Napoleon I never had as many men in the field at once, by a great deal, as the Confederate government has had for the last eighteen or twenty months nor anything like the amount of artillery and all other military preparation. Ambition, revenge, and fury seemed to have animated both sides, to a greater or less extent and hitherto there seems to have been no abatement of the passion, which first impelled them to the bloody conflict. In ancient times, the heathen nations were in the practice of cursing their enemies, or of very devoutly invoking the vengeance of the gods upon them, which was done with great solemnity and by the observance of certain prescribed ceremonies, and then of cursing them as hard as ever all the time they fighting them.

The conflicts have been bloody and destructive. When three or four hundred thousand men engaged in deadly conflict with the improved artillery and small arms of the present day, the scene was awful beyond description, as if the seven trumpets of revelation had all combined their blasts in one terrific peal of vengeance and destruction. Tens of thousands and hundreds of thousands of southern citizens have fallen and died of disease. As many lives perhaps have been sacrificed on the other side but that is poor consolation and we have nothing to do with it at present. We have heard many say excitingly that we had killed more of the Yankees than they killed of our men; and the two sides, heathen like, have been all the time cursing each other, without form or ceremony, "bell, book, or candle". Now what is all this for? As before stated it is a war for the defense and perpetuity of slavery on the part of the south and for its abolition on the part of the north. Are the slaves all told worth half the lives that has been expended on the sufferings that have been endured? If a gradual emancipation had been commenced only four or five years ago it would have prevented all the horrors of war and all the crimes and sufferings and sorrows to which it has given rise.

The professed object of the northern government and people was to preserve the union—a thing Washington did and which any of our best presidents would have done had there been occasion for it. We have no right to question their motives while the south have been thus fighting a sacrificing their lives and their treasure and everything in defense of slavery and in trying to exalt "king cotton," he has been extending his power into other quarters of the globe and will probably leave us, e'er long, in the outskirts of his vast dominions. British manufacturers and merchants and statesmen have been for the last five years, anticipating this convulsion and have been trying to get up competition in other countries. That they have been successful is proved from the fact that contrary to the assertions of our southern politicians to the contrary, they have got along very well for the last two years without our cotton, and whether that is to be the way in which slavery will be abolished or not—I mean by the unprofitableness of slave labor—England will soon care nothing more for our trade than as an outlet for her manufacturers.

18. Human beings cannot be held as property.

But to all the arguments and admonitions hitherto used, by statesmen and divines, patriots, philosophers and other friends of humanity in favor of emancipation, the general reply of slaveholders has been and is that "our slaves are our property, secured to us by the constitution and laws of the land, and we will fight for them and "die in the last ditch" before will give them up." Very well: What are *constitutions*? In a general sense, a constitution is a system of rules and regulations for the government of a nation, state, or community of any description; or in more definite sense, it is a system of *fundamental* laws in conformity with which all other laws must be made. These articles, however, denominated fundamental laws, are framed or adopted by depraved, short sighted, selfish and erring men, and they are not *all* fundamental in the strict sense of the term; for they have to be frequently amended, expunged, or substituted by others. The Federal Constitution was amended in a short time after it was adopted; and all the state constitutions, north and south at least of "the old thirteen" have been considerably altered and some of them two or three times. An article, in a constitution, containing an unsound principle is like a mass of rotten limestone in a rock wall, or a flaw in a tile deed to property; and may not the in our state constitutions establishing slavery be utterly unsound in its principle? There is no question that they constitution and laws of the land make your slaves your property; for that is the very thing against which we are contending. It is the main object of this discussion and should be the honest and earnest desire of every Christian and every true hearted patriot to ascertain whether that article and the laws founded upon it are in accordance with the great principles of justice and humanity, or whether they are in opposition to the constitution and laws of heaven. Truth can do permanent injury and error can do no permanent good. The crimes and wretchedness of mankind are all owing to their perversity and their obstinate persistence in their own course. The world is in their hearts and they cling to whatever they can get of it with a deadly grasp; and they seem to take it for granted that they have a good and indefeasible right to whatever the constitution and laws framed by our forefathers, tho' wholly inexperienced in the science of self government, allow them to claim as property.

Another question arises here, however, which is of more vital importance than human constitutions and laws and to which every lover of truth and every friend to humanity will feel that the must have a satisfactory answer: What is property? Any thing that men choose to call by that name? Or any thing that they can lay their hands on and hold fast? That would justify all the fraud and villainy, and the robbery, oppression and violence in the world. The strong might enslave or tyrannize over the weak and the intelligent might defraud the ignorant or swindle them out of all they have. Then what is property? Anything that the "constitutions" and laws of the country say shall be regarded as such? These constitutions and laws, as we have seen, were framed by depraved, short sighted and erring mortals, who, in their selfishness and their supreme attachment to the world seemed to think that they had a right to make everything they could, consistently with the peace and good order of society, subservient to the accumulation of property, and they cannot be taken by any man, who feels his accountability, as the rule of duty and the guide of conscience until they are tested by the unerring standard of truth and equity. What is property? What is the abstract or general meaning of the word, apart from all technicalities and without reference to any particular species of property? Or, what is its meaning as ascertained from its etymology and from the multifarious connections in which it is found? We do not ask the question with the design of giving a direct answer or a precise definition of the word; but of exciting the reader, if we can, to enquire and think for himself. Few may have an inclination to do this and with many it may be impracticable; but two other questions are suggested here the answer to which may settle the other without any curious search after etymologies, or a laborious enquiry into the *usus loquendi. How do we get the right to hold any thing as property? And what is the extent of that right?* If these inquiries have been started heretofore and satisfactorily answered by others, we are not aware of it, and would be very glad to find them taken up and disposed of by some one who was more competent to do them justice. Much has been written and well written about property in treatises on Moral Philosophy and Political Economy; but in the few that have come under my notice, the right to hold property seemed to be founded in the posessory instinct of man, or in the necessity of the case.

No Christian who is even tolerably well read in his Bible and who has earnestly desired to know the whole of his duty, need be at much of a loss for an answer to the questions, How do we get the right to hold anything as property? And, what is the extent of that right? Most assuredly we can have no moral and indefeasible right to anything and can justly claim nothing as our own without an *express* right grant from heaven. That grant and the extent of it must be found in the recorded revelation which God has given; and there were only two occasions, one before the Apostasy and one after, on which anything like a general and permanent grant was made. As soon as Adam was created a living soul and felt the wants of nature, the Lord gave him an express right to Paradise, or the Garden of Eden probably an extensive and beautiful country, with all the fruits which grew in it, with the exception of one kind or that which grew on one tree. This was reserved as a test of his obedience; but of all the rest he might freely eat. See Gen 2:16–17. As Adam was constituted the federal head and representative of all his race, this grant was made to the whole of mankind as well as to him but, without an extension of the charter, they dare not claim or use anything else.

After the Deluge, to Noah, who was then the only progenitor of a ruined race and the only inheritor of a sin blighted and desolated world, God extended the grant to all the beasts of the field, pairs of which he had preserved in the ark, to the fowls of the air and to the fish of the sea. See Gen 9:2–3. These were general and express grants made to the whole human race through their representations, Adam and Noah; but it is a matter in all laws, human and divine, for it is necessarily implied in the nature of law, that what is not expressly granted is reserved. This, then, is the only right we have to hold anything as property and the extend to which that right can be maintained. The fruits of the earth, the beasts of the field, the fowls of the air and the fish of the sea, with the earth itself as the source from which the means of subsistence for man and beast are to be obtained include all that has been granted to the children of men by the Creator and all that they can claim as their property. These they may use prudently and in moderation for their comfort; improvement and welfare; but all the rest, the world of intelligent beings, he has reserved to himself. Hence the Psalmist says, *The heavens, even the heavens are the Lord's; but the earth hath he given to the children of men* (Ps 115:16).

When these grants were made there were no nations and civil governments, no systems of church polity and no proscribed forms or modes of worship, no local institution and no divisions of mankind. The rights then granted were for the whole race in all its extent and in its generations. By virtue of these grants every man has a valid right to as much of the soil as he can acquire by an honest industry and to all the fruits, metals and other products that he can bring out of his share. They include an extent and variety ample enough for all the progress and all the enjoyment that are practicable in this life; but every thing above these in the scale of being, the Creator has reserved to himself. As he is the former of our bodies and the father of our spirits and as he has united them together so as to constitute but one person, one moral agent, if we enslave any portion of our fellow beings, our brethren of the same family, and compel them to serve us from generation to generation without reward or compensation, we encroach upon his reserved rights and must take the consequences. The grant of the earth and its products, mineral, vegetable and animal was made to all alike and none can deprive others of their share, or what they might acquire by the free use of their powers, without the most palpable injustice and God will be the avenger of all such. As we have shown the mere local and temporary regulations of the Mosaic economy, of which servitude was one, were only for that people and for a limited time. The whole genius and spirit of the Mosaic institutions was strongly opposed to anything like an entailed or protracted bondage. Even their captives taken in war or servants bought of the heathen could be held in bondage only until the Jubilee or at most for life, but even such servants or bondmen might at any time obtain their freedom by becoming proselytes to the Jewish religion. A man too might marry one of the bond maids or give her to his son for a wife, but if he put her away as he might do any other wife, she was to have her freedom. It would be difficult to conceive how any enactments could be made at that age of the world more decidedly opposed to any thing like an established or protracted bondage; but as those regulations, whatever may have been their import, extended no further, and no longer than that commonwealth, we have nothing more to do with them.

205   Property considered in all it relations and in all its bearing on the progress and welfare of society; is the main subject of human legislation and is therefore nearly allied to the rights of conscience, to the interests of truth and piety, and to the regular harmonious and continued development of the diversified powers which have been given us. Distinct conceptions of its origin, its design and the extent to which it may be held, are indispensable not only to statesmen legislators, the executive and all the functionaries of government, but to all classes of a self governing people; and the ignorance and carelessness which have hitherto prevailed on this great subject, in and out of office, have greatly retarded our progress and brought upon us most distressing calamities. The science of government requires the intense and undivided study of a lifetime; but very few of our office seekers and office holders, in every department, have ever given it one hour's serious attention. In nine cases out of ten or nineteen cases out of twenty, they have thought of nothing but measures—such measures as have been proposed by others or such as they can suggest, and, wise or unwise, all their energies are employed for their success. We would like to know how

206   many of our representatives in the state legislature or in congress could give their constituents a satisfactory explanation of the right by which and of the extent to which they may securely, profitably and with a good conscience hold as property what comes within their reach. Respecting a number of things which are now made property and included in the aggregate rewards of industry. All serious thinking men have their doubts, and misgivings; but as they are made property by the laws of the country, they go in the general traffic and try to persuade themselves that somehow or other, they will be severely punished hereafter. The definition of property given in Blackstone and other standard works in law, though good as they go, are not

satisfactory, at least to an intelligent and reflecting Christian; and we have met with nothing in moral, theological, or political treatises that removes all doubt and apprehension from a well informed conscience. No explanations that have yet been given or that can be devised by human ingenuity, apart from the simply and explicit and authoritative statements of the Bible, will ever be sufficient to quell the fears of the inquiring and to set them forward on a path like that of the *shining light that shines more and more until the perfect day*. Our folly and our misfortune as a people has been that we have never sought a knowledge of our duty from the inspired oracles, but have leaned mainly if entirely to our own understanding

The teachings of the Bible extend to all the interests and relationships of life; and they are the only infallible rule of faith and practice we have. Great principles are distinctly given which are easily comprehended and are applicable at all times and in all circumstances. You may use the fruits of the ground, the beasts of the field, the fouls of air and the fish of the sea; you may have the earth and its products; but on your fellow man you must not lay your hand unless it becomes necessary in self defense or for the prevention of a crime.

The hue and cry which was raised about a generation ago against church and state was as wicked as it was useless. The friends of religion soon proved that the union of church and state, in the sense intended by the authors of the alarm, was impracticable in this country, at least while our gov't retained its republican form and the "hobby" was turned loose and left for some future occasion if it should ever occur; but all all men are naturally opposed to religion and even good people seem afraid that the alarm will be again raised. The Jewish commonwealth, when first formed was a republic and the civil regulations of the Mosaic law were as much a part of the theocracy as the religious department; but every republic, if it is to be secure and permanently prosperous, must be as really a theocracy, a gov't of God, as the Israelite nation. Their can be no dangerous union of church and state in following the instructions which God has given as in his record respecting the foundations, principles and design of civil gov't, or the origin of property, the right by which it is held and the intent of that right. As he is the Creator, all things belong to him and are at his disposal. He has given us express permission to use such things as will be conducive to our well being and no man. *If we would use this world as not abusing it,* we must be contented with what he has granted us and not employ that for the purpose of encroaching upon what he has deserved. If he has given us a grant of the earth and its productions, he has given the Africans and all other nations the same; for it was made to Adam and Noah for the whole race descending from them without distinction or partiality. With whatever local and temporary arrangements he made at different times and for special purposes, we have nothing to do. They have answered their end and have passed away. They concern us no more than the directions given to Joshua, David, Gideon and others in regard to the manner of arranging their armies or of attacking their enemies; but it must be at our peril if we transgress or disregard those commands and ordinances which were designed for the whole race. We dare not encroach upon the rights of others or rob them of their dues nor treat them in any way with cruelty and oppression.

Men cannot hold their fellow beings as property; for they have no right to do it; no express grant has been given to and the Lord will not suffer them thus to encroach upon his prerogative. The institution of slavery, or of absolute and entailed bondage, is the work of civil government and not of individuals; but civil government was instituted expressly and exclusively for the punishment of crimes and the maintenance of justice and good order. It was designed to be *a terror to evil doers and a praise to them that do well;* but nations and communities must be punished here; for they will have no existence, as such hereafter. No truth is taught more fully and forcibly in the Bible; no details in the sacred history are more distressing or more admonitory than those of the desolating judgments of God upon the disobedient nations; *for the nations and kingdom that will serve him shall perish.* Where are all the great nations of antiquity that rose to power and magnificence flourished for a time and then disappeared from the face of the earth as though they had not been? Where is the Israelitish nation once the most honored and the most highly privileged, the most powerful, the most prosperous and the most envied nation on the globe? It has been made a desolation, a hissing and a byword to all the world!

If governments are to administer justice and maintain the cause of the individuals when injured and oppressed, God will administer justice among the nations and maintain the cause of those who are downtrodden, insulted, and despised. *The judge of all the earth will do right;* and, though he may bear long with disobedience and tyrannical abuse of power, he will, in due time, arise to vindicate the cause of truth and righteousness. We must have read history, sacred and profane to very little purpose if we have not seen God reaching among the nations and raising one to be the scourge and often the destroyer of another. It is a maxim of the wise man that the *wicked shall not prosper* and it is no less applicable to nations than to individuals. *The prosperity of fools shall destroy them* and all men are fools who boast of their own wisdom, or trust their own heart or rely upon their own strength. Nations are composed of individuals and the sins of all, respectively, form the aggregate of national guilt. In great prosperity they became *lifted up with pride and fall into the snare and condemnation of the devil.* Pride must be brought down and the arm of the oppressor must be broken. God will not suffer any nation to hold a large portion of their fellow beings in perpetual bondage and to merchandise of the mas they do of their other goods and chattels.

The experiments made in this kind of systematic oppression are highly instructive and should not be overlooked. Egypt tried it and failed to her ruin. Greece tried it and with similar results. The mighty empire of Rome, when in the zenith of her power and in all the glory of her conquests, tried it and eventually sunk under the desperate effort. These were the most civilized nations of Antiquity; they had regular, fine, and established governments; and each of the two last, in its turn, was mistress of the world. Rome had, at one time and for a long time according to Gibbon, a population of about a hundred and twenty million, a much greater number than ever belonged to one empire, except that of China, before or since. That part of the population, denominated slaves, in the proper sense of the term, must have been comparatively a small proportion of the whole; they and the *servants,* Gibbon says, were nearly equal in number, and the two together could hardly amount to much of the whole; and yet the slaves were, at least a prominent cause of her downfall. True, this was effected in a way very different from that in which the old dominion of Egypt was over come by her bondsmen; but it is of no consequence to us in what way or by what means the Lord accomplishes his purposes, either of mercy or of judgment. Everything in creation, winds and tempests, hailstorms and lightening, war, famine and pestilence and the crimes and follies, the overweening pride and the overreaching ambition of those who are to be destroyed or punished, may become, in the hand of omnipotence, the ministers of his wrath. Alexander destroyed himself by the excessive indulgence of his appetites; the unbounded ambition of Caesar fired the indignation of the few remaining patriots in Rome and caused him to be assassinated. Bonaparte's insatiable thirst for conquest and dominion led him into the heart of Russia where he was overwhelmed by the snows of winter and throughout the wide of range of Jehovah's empire he is carrying out his wise designs by such means and agencies as are most suitable and will best subserve the ends of of his Providence and most promote the glory of his grace. Men let their avarice and their love of power and self indulgence carry them too far when they undertake to make a large portion of their fellow beings *property* and entail upon them in their successive generations a degrading and oppressive bondage for the Lord will, at the right time, bring judgments upon their oppression and deliverance to the oppressed.

The lessons of history on this subject are all important and can be neglected by no honest enquirer after truth. All authentic history confirms the teachings of the Bible and shows that the actual administration of the divine government is in strict accordance with the revelation which he has given; for it proves that, as he has given no portion of mankind a right, or an express permission to dominion over another portion permanently, and he suffers them to do it only for a time, as he suffers them to proceed in any other wickedness so far, and only so far as it can be overruled for good and made to work for the praise and glory of his name.

No other nation has hitherto been able to maintain the institution of slavery more than a few generations; but whether in a milder or more oppressive form it has, in some way or other, worked itself out in the course of tow or three hundred years. The Israelites, according to the Bible chronology, were two hundred and fifteen years in Egypt, which, if you reckon thirty six years to generation, will include six generations, and, in the beginning of the seventh, they went out free. During the whole of this time, however, they were *not slaves*, in the proper *sense* of the term; for while Joseph lived they were treated with respect and were kept there by Providential circumstances and merciful kind and not by the laws of the country or the authority of the monarch. After Joseph's death another king arose who had not known him personally nor been well informed in regard to his past services, and cared nothing about him or his religion. He considered the Israelites as his bondsmen and began to treat them with rigor; but he was only preparing the way for their deliverance and hastening the crisis in his own destiny. The Lord would not suffer his people to be long held as property, nor be compelled to serve another at his will and pleasure. Just as soon as Pharaoh began to treat them as slaves and make them serve him *for naught*, or without compensation the Lord began his preparation for their deliverance; and when the time was fulfilled and the haughty oppressor had gone to an intolerable length in the severity of his treatment, Moses and Aaron, his accredited agents, were there ready and well prepared to act as their deliverers. Invested, as they were with ample authority and endowed with knowledge, wisdom and firmness, all the means of torment and destruction which Omnipotence had provided were at their command and the proud monarch of a great empire was soon cowering at the feet of his slaves. This was God's method of delivering his people from their bondage in Egypt, because such immediate interpositions or displays of his power were important for both the oppressor and the oppressed; but having made a full record of the transactions on the occasion, they will not be repeated any where else or in other ages.

The laws, customs, and occupations of the Greeks and Romans were so different from ours and the information which we have respecting the servile classes of the population is so scant and indefinite that we cannot tell precisely when *slavery*, in the proper sense of the term, commenced nor when it ceased. In Greece, the only portion of the servile class, of whom much is said in the histories of that country and to whom alone reference is made by writers of the present day, were the Helots of Sparta and both ancient and modern histories disagree about the time when they were subjected to a perpetual or entailed bondage as well as about the manner in which they were treated. According to the best writers on the subject they were reduced to a condition of what may be termed slavery when the Dorians conquered the Lacedemonian territory; but while they were occasionally subjected to great cruelties and indignities by the land holders or citizens, from their caprices and passions, their jealousies and apprehensions of danger, they never were reduced and never could be reduced to such a state of complete, absolute and entailed bondage as that to which our blacks have been reduced by the laws and usages of the country. They were required to cultivate the soil while the citizens, like the men among our Indian tribes, devoted themselves to war, hunting, and pleasure; but they were mostly *tenants;* for they paid but a moderate rent to the proprietors and the surplus was their own. As already noticed, they could accumulate and were allowed to possess a considerable amount in money and personal property. As many of them as were necessary were the teachers and companions of their masters' children and when they had satisfactorily performed the task assigned to them they were entitled to their freedom. They had their wives and children and could not be torn from them and sold under the hammer at the pleasure or for the interest of their masters. They were armed, trained and taken to war by thousands at a time; generally as light armed soldiers and attended their masters for the purpose of waiting on them and assisting them in an emergency; but on some occasions they were taken as heavy armed soldiers and fought in the ranks with the citizens. In such cases they had their freedom and were no longer subject to their masters. In addition to all this they could by an easy and not very tedious process obtain their freedom and become regular citizens; but, fired with indignation and resentment at those who exercised authority over them, they were often engaged in rebellion, in which they sometimes failed but at other times they were, to a considerable extent successful and finally triumphed in the desolation of that country. They had the instinctive love of freedom common to all men; and, we think, they never were long in subjugation at one time than the Israelites were in Egypt.

216

Similar remarks to those which have been made on Greece, especially on Sparta and the servile portion of its population might be made on the state of things in the Roman empire. We have met with no satisfactory and reliable account of the origin, progress, and continuance of slavery in Rome or its dependencies. It seems that when they conquered a people who were

217

civilized and pretty intelligent, they admitted them to the rights of citizenship or permitted them to retain their own laws and government. When they conquered a rude and barbarous tribe they sold them to the highest bidder or made them pass under the yoke, in either of which cases they were doomed to servitude for life. When they conquered a tribe or people who were but partially civilized, unless they had given them great provocation, they were placed somewhere between these extremes and occupied the place of servants, teachers of their children and personal attendants. In these troublous times , and for some special reasons, we have not access to all the sources of information that the country affords and write from early and imperfect recollections; but if we are not mistaken the institution of slavery in the proper sense, was not of very early origin and that it was not until they had attained their maximum of power that they formally adopted

218 the Jurus Partus sequitor ventrean. but however this may be, it is certain that they had some rights and privileges which are denied to our slaves. They were not only permitted to learn what they chose but were made the teachers of their masters; children. If masters at one time, had the power over their slaves they had the same power over their children but both these barbarous laws were soon repealed or substituted by others of a milder and more humane character. Masters could at anytime emancipate their slaves, as many did, the could often obtain their freedom by meritorious services; yet they never would remain long at a time in bondage; but would rise up and try to regain their freedom. Such attempts often cost them many lives; but, like our forefathers, they would rather die than be in subjection to mere human authority. The insurrection under Spartacus, about two generations before the Christian era, or a little more, so desolated the whole south of Italy that it never recovered and greatly weakened the powers of "the seven hilled city." After an immense destruction of life and property the slaves were eventually conquered; but it shows that they never would remain and never did remain long at a time in a state of bondage.

219 The Lord will not suffer a nation to hold their fellow beings in a state of perpetual bondage and to traffic in them as they do in any other property because he has given them no *right* to do so and they cannot elude his notice nor resist his power. If they are so ungrateful for what he has given them and so daring in their impiety as to employ the products of the soil, and everything included in the grant he has made them, to buy up the bones and sinews of the less favored portions of humanity and make them toil exclusively for the wealth and luxury and self indulgence he will either recall for a time the grant which he has made them or send on them other plagues, one after another as he did on Egypt until they feel their dependence and acknowledge their error. *The judge of all the earth will do right* and it is a well

attested fact that every nation which has ever undertaken to maintain the institution of slavery has lost far more in the end, by some means or other, than they gained by their labor. Such was certainly the fact with Egypt, Greece, and Rome; for, as to Egypt anyone who will be at the trouble of making a little calculation of the amount of gold and silver expended on the Tabernacle will find that, even at such an early age of the world, when one dollar was worth five or ten now, they must have carried away with them several millions of dollars worth in these metals besides a vast amount of such other property as could be taken on their journey. In Greece, where the number was comparatively small, the destruction of life and property, made by them at different times amounted to far more than the profits of their labor from first to last. In Rome besides their waste and pilferings all the times the destruction of life and property made by their different insurrections and especially in the one headed by Spartacus, which was the last one, amounted to incalculably more than the value of all their services up to that time and all they would then have sold for in the market.

Whether the Africans in their exodus from this country, are to go out, as the Israelites did from Egypt, quietly and well provided for, enriched and loaded with presents from their former masters; or with an immense destruction of life and property, remains to be seen. I have little or no apprehension that we shall ever witness here, from servile insurrection, such atrocities and deeds of wanton cruelty, such scenes of death and devastation as made the bloodiest picture in the history of that ambitious reckless and destructive empire; but the issue is known only to the Lord, and, *as he that heareth reproof is wise,* our part is to heed the warnings which he given us.

In the Mosaic institutions the Lord has shewn his abhorrence of all traffic in human beings by the law which he enacted on that subject and which is partially, very partially adopted in this country. See Exod 21:16: *And he that stealeth a man and selleth him or if he be found in his hand, he shall surely be put to death.* But one man could seldom steal another and carry him off to market as he would steal a piece of money or inert matter, nor even as he would steal a horse or any other domestic animal; for the object of such rapacity would not thus submit be clandestinely carried away and sold without making such resistance as he could and the thief, the man stealer, must either compel him by superior strength, or pretend that he was a run away servant or entice him by false promises to someplace where his accomplices were ready to secure him. By stealing a man must therefore be meant the act of getting another into his power, whether by force or falsehood, or in any way without the knowledge of those who might bring him to justice, and their making or aiming to make merchandise of him for if the unfortunate victim of his avarice and cruelty was only found

222 in his possession, though he had not yet offered him for sale, he was to suffer death without the benefit of clergy. No compensation in money or property could satisfy the penalty of the law; no promises of penitence or future amendment could be of any avail; and nothing but his life could atone for his crime. Judging from the penalty, the Lord seems to have estimated the guilt of bringing a man into a life-long bondage, or until the year of Jubilee, *for gain* and without any great offence against the peace and dignity of the state, as of equal enormity with that of murder and very justly; for men of any intelligence and understanding in regard to their rights would rather be dead than to be slaves. The old Greek and Roman maxim that "the day a man becomes a slave he ceases to be a man" is undoubtedly true, for he has neither the command of his own powers, nor the conscious dignity of a moral agent nor the intellectual and social enjoyment for which he was made and which if he did not have in a state of freedom it would be his own fault. God designed that the whole race of man, whom he created and has redeemed, should glorify him by the full and unimpeded exercise of all their powers and that they should have all the rational and social and religious enjoyment of which they are capable in this stage of their existence; but a slave could do very little more good and have very little more enjoyment than the lower orders of creation.

223 We believe it was a maxim of the old jurisprudence and has been adopted in the southern states that "a slave has no country" which implies that he has nothing of his own; no earthly inheritance, no civil rights, except to his miserable and degraded life and hardly to that; no right to his wife and children; for they belong to his masters who may sell them off at anytime to the highest bidder and they may never be permitted to see each other again; no right to employ his time and strength for his won improvement or for the extension of the Redeemer's kingdom in the world. He is placed just in the neighborhood of brutes and is forbidden to rise any higher. Then is not the crime of stealing a man or of apprehending him clandestinely, and of a selling him or doing all this with the design of selling him though not permitted to do it, of equal enormity with that of murder? And ought not the man catcher and the man enslaver to be put to death without any possibility of pardon or reprieve? But is not the purchaser a *particeps crimenis*? If there was no slave buyer there would be no slave catcher and if there was no body to receive stolen property there would be very little stolen. The purchasers were ready before the first slave ship sailed for the coast of

224 Africa or it would never have ventured on such an enterprise. But you say you continue the slave trade and are contented with what you have. We have about as many now as the country can well support and therefore you don't care about anymore; but are you not afraid to be a partaker in other men's

sins? A perpetuator in such enormous guilt? The length of time you have had possession does not cancel the guilt of the first transgression nor give you a valid right in the sight of heaven to hold them as property. Among men the undisputed possession of a freehold or tract of land for a certain number of years gives a valid claim because the imperfections all men; the inconvenience of being ousted, the loss of improvements made and of labor bestowed upon the premises in many other ways make some such regulation necessary; but with God *one day is as a thousand years and a thousand years as one day.* He is unchangeable and so are the great principles of his government. Persistence in crime for a thousand years cannot alter its nature or its desert. A *bribe blinds the eyes,* or the understanding, and so do gains in whatever way obtained. Custom, pride, and self indulgence also have their influence; but God will not suffer his churches and people to continue much longer in a state of so much indifference while the great interests of truth and freedom, humanity and religion are set at naught, or made subservient to their vanity, pride and worldliness.

Whatever individual enterprise or political measures makes it necessary to ignore and trample upon fundamental principles must be wrong and, if continued, ultimately ruinous to all concerned. The people of the South, in their blind zeal to perpetuate and extend the institution of slavery, have repudiated or set at naught, for the time being, two great principles, which had hitherto been regarded by all Americans and by the whole civilized world as essential to free and prosperous government, viz., that *a majority must rule;* and that, *the right of free discussion* must be allowed on all subjects of common interest.

In all associations, literary, civil, or religious, if a majority does not rule there can be no government or it must be an arbitrary one. A free or republican government is the only medium between anarchy and monarchy; but in a free, democratic or representative government the majority principle must be regard as indispensable; for if a minority may secede and resist the decisions of the majority at pleasure, that secession may go on until every man has seceded and the body is dissolved. Yet, for the sake of perpetuating and extending slavery we have commenced a course which, if carried out must end in the dissolution of all government.

No truth is more universally admitted in this country than that government originates with the people; that is designed for their safety and welfare; and that they have right to know whether the authority with which they have temporarily invested their rulers is in any respect perverted or used for their benefit. They give their rulers power; but cannot give them either wisdom or integrity; and it is therefore, on this account necessary that they should be left free to discuss the laws enacted and the measures adopted or proposed. It is often said that "wise men are not always wise" and we know well that good men are not perfectly good. The imperfections of all men render it indispensably necessary that they should be allowed freely to discuss every subject of interest, and especially every legislative act. Rulers are only men and all men are not only shortsighted, but are swayed by interest and are fond of power. All abuse of power is criminal, whether in individuals or in the appointed rulers of a nation. If a man, now were to overcome another by his superior strength, make him his slave for life and then transmit such to his children, everybody would exclaim against the injustice and cruelty of such conduct.

227 As political power originates from the will of the people it must in all cases be subject to that will or it becomes tyrannical. Legislative enactments, the injustice or evil tendency of which was not perceived at the time, owing to prejudice or the excitement of passion, may, after sober reflection and thorough discussion, be viewed in a very different light and may be found to be iniquitous and oppressive but if free discussion is prohibited nothing can be done. A certain length of time may give a valid right to property, because, in many cases, some limit must be fixed to prevent conflicting claims followed by vexatious lawsuits, and because it makes no difference with society in whose hands property may be lodged provided the right certain and the possession is secure; but it cannot be a matter of indifference to the community who are entrusted with power nor what use what use they make of it. The masses think slowly and are not capable of giving any important subject a thorough investigation at once. Besides in relation to many subjects, nearly if not quite the whole of the legislature are strongly tempted by their interest or their associations, to pass laws which will favor themselves but bear hard upon the mass of their constituents. The laws in

228 regard to slavery were passed by those who were interested and ought in all fairness, to be discussed by others, anywhere and everywhere with the utmost freedom. At least nine tenths of our legislators, we presume have been slave holders and legislated to suit themselves; but the slave owners are not now and never have been more than a fourth or a fifth part of the population nor even of the voters. These laws bear a little hard, in several respects, on the non slave holding part of the citizens who are three fourths or four fifths of the whole and, if they choose, they ought to have the privilege of making this appear in any way they can. The time and money spent on legislating on the subject is no small matter of which they have to bear not less than three fourths; and then they have to bear three fourths of the trouble and fatigue of patrolling. The military duties, especially in time of war, fall much heavier on them than if they whole population were free, and the laboring class of our citizens must generally work with them, however

unpleasant the association, or not get employment. The Quakers, a large and respectable part of our population, conscientiously believe slavery to be sinful and injurious to the best interests of the country; but besides the unpleasant feelings which it is all the time exciting in their minds, they have to bear their part of the expenses and trouble of keeping up, defending and quarreling against the dangers of such an institution.

We are not aware that any law has been passed in this state expressly prohibiting all discussion on the slavery question, either privately or publicly, by the voice or by the pen; but the enactments against incendiaries and incendiary publications has been practically made to have the same effect. For several years, no weekly paper in this state or anywhere in the south would have dared to publish even a mild and temperate communication, no matter from whom, male or female, on the "peculiar institution", and no man dared to say a word against it in private; or if he did it was whispered only in corners and to confidential friends. No preacher would have dared to utter from the pulpit even a doubt about its lawfulness and every man, no matter what might be his standing, his official or social position would have thought it as much as his life was worth to declare himself in favor of even a gradual emancipation. In some parts of the south, if reports be true, no man would undertake to defend slavery even in a common debating society and after a declaration that he would take the affirmation on the side in favor of slavery only for argument's sake and must not be understood as expressing his own sentiments. In the days of inquisition those who felt any preference at all for the Bible were not more cautious about giving utterance to their thoughts nor in greater dread of being overheard. All this is well known and needs no comment; but it was contended that such strong measures were necessary to guard against insurrections or any process for making the slaves dissatisfied with their condition. Then we say that, if this be true, or if it be necessary to trample on a fundamental principle of free government in order to maintain the institution, it is wrong and ought to be abandoned without delay; In this aspect of it alone, slavery is dangerous to the welfare of the state; for if interest in one quarter may be alleged as a sufficient reason for ignoring any elementary principle of free institutions a similar reason may be brought from department of business for suppressing some other fundamental principle and so on until they are all gone and government is at an end or is transformed into a stern iron handed despotism. No republic of any strength, consistency and duration was ever run into utter lawlessness and dissolution, nor changed into an absolute monarchy, at once. The strong foundation was gradually undermined; one column after another was prostrated until the whole was in ruins; for men cannot go to the extreme of wickedness and reckless daring at one bound.

231　　It may be asked if I would encourage incendiaries or leave the country unprotected against them? Emphatically I would answer *no*—no more than those who would so impertinently ask the question; and if it could be proved, clearly and dispassionately on any man, an intruder from abroad or a miscreant at home, that he was actually engaged in an effort to rouse up the blacks and produce an indiscriminate massacre let him be punished as he deserves; but in the name of truth and reason, freedom and humanity don't trample on the fundamental principles of republican government in doing it. There is far more danger to be apprehended to the country, sooner or later from this disregard of *principle* than from all the incendiaries that could come among us; for *if the foundations be destroyed*—if the foundations in religion, civil government or anything else, be ignored and trampled on—*what can the righteous do?* (Ps 11:2–3). It may be asked again if I would have the subject discussed everywhere and let the slaves know all about the hardships of their condition and the advantages of freedom? Why not? Can knowledge do any harm except to those who are engaged in wrong doing? For every one that *doeth evil hateth the light, neither cometh to the light lest his deeds should be reproved* (John 3:20).

232　　But would it not make them dissatisfied and unprofitable to their owners if not dangerous to the community? Suppose it did. Have they great reason to be dissatisfied? Would not *you* be dissatisfied were you in their place? But that it will make them dangerous to society is an utter mistake, for all their attempts at insurrection hitherto were made, not by the intelligent, but by the more ignorant portion of them. Ignorance is always to be dreaded and a large ignorant and degraded class in a community has in all ages and every where been a dangerous thing whither the Poet's sentiment that "a little learning is a dangerous thing," be true or not, there can be no danger in communicating to every class all the knowledge we have in the country. The most trusty and reliable servants I have ever known could read as well as the whites around them and were allowed to read everything, religious and secular, that was read in the family. If they should become sufficiently intelligent, or if they should be found to be so now, in spite of all the efforts that have been made to keep them in mutual darkness, then loosen their bonds and let them go, either give them land in America which they can call their own and where their power can be developed without or hindrance, or send them back to their fatherland with the blessings of salvation to this benighted race to maintain civilization and self government.

233　　The importance of this matter cannot be overrated; for fundamental principles in civil government are like fundamental doctrine in the Christian system, if one is removed or suppressed all the others are in danger; and, if the Lord has so constituted us and everything else that, in our present lapsed condition, the right of free discussion unimpaired and secured to all is indispensable to the maintenance of our free institutions, it will be infinitely better to give it full play and trust Him for the consequences. If it should occasion a little loss or inconvenience for the present it is only because we have gone wrong and when we get right all will move on far more pleasantly and profitably than it could otherwise do. Slaveholders generally seem to have little doubt that if the blacks should become sufficiently enlightened they must necessarily be emancipated and they will lose their value. Very well: Their freedom is just what ought to have been given them long ago; and as for the loss of their services or their value, that is not to be taken into the account. God did not consult Pharaoh's interest when he made the demand on him nor did he allow him to devise any plan by which he could save himself from such a heavy loss. As they have been made property by the constitutions and laws of the country, I always have been in favor of allowing the owners a moderate compensation but the southern people, if we mistake not have have haughtily and repeatedly rejected any proposal of that kind; and I am not sorry they did reject it; for, whether they will improve it or not, they have now the fine opportunity to make a noble and magnanimous sacrifice. Whether a sordid avarice or a generous liberality will prevail remains to be seen. *The liberal soul devises liberal things and by liberal things he shall stand* (Isa 32:8). God delights in mercy and so should we. He is no respecter of persons; but *makes the sun to shine and the rains to descend upon the evil and the good, upon the thankful and upon the unthankful. Therefore, be ye perfect as your father in heaven is perfect* (Matt 5:43). The brightest prosperity that is to be obtained in this life must be found in the way of a punctual and undeviating obedience to all the requirements of the Bible or by acting out the spirit of the gospel in all things and by a constant imitation of the example of Christ who, *though he was rich yet for our sakes became poor that we through his poverty might become rich* (2 Cor 8:9): for he designs our happiness in every thing and all things shall work together for good to them that love him; but apart from this and further than this we have no right to consult our interest where duty is concerned.

234

When Pharaoh issued the order that all the male children of the Hebrews should be put to death he had gone about as far as he could go, towards preventing their escape or their resistance, without exterminating the race, which would have been an impolitic excess of cruelty. Whether he intended the edict to be perpetual and by destroying all the young males, compel the Hebrews to amalgamate with the Egyptians, or only temporary for his own safety, is a matter of no consequence. He could go not farther towards making their bondage complete and perpetual but "man's extremity is God's opportunity"; and then it was that he interposed and broke the

235

rod of the oppressor. The people of the south advanced very gradually in completing the system and when they put down free discussion they had adopted the last measure they could well adopt towards making the possession of their slave property secure; but in a very short time the Lord brought upon us the terrible calamity of this civil war. Whether he will use this as the means of breaking the rod of the oppressor and letting the oppressed go free, we are not informed and we cannot penetrate the divine councils, nor is it at all necessary to my purpose; for the sacrifice of money and property, besides the unnumbered lives that have been and will yet be lost, is greater than the price of all the slaves in the southern states. It is a worse calamity even in a pecuniary point of view than the loss of all the slave property that could be paraded. The plagues sent upon the monarch of Egypt were successively solemn warnings which he ought to have heeded at the outset; but his unbelief and obstinacy proved his ruin. The loss of property and lives increased with every successive judgment and the last was the heaviest of all. If the abolition of slavery should not be the proximate result of this war we feel little doubt that it will be the final issue. This is a solemn warning which slave holders ought to take and which, if they do not harden their hearts, they will take; but if they will persist in their infatuated course, even amidst his judgments which are abroad in the land, and should become independent of the north, he can send much heavier plagues upon them and make them glad to let their bondmen go. We make no pretensions to prophecy or uncommon foresight, but are guided by the dictates of reason, conscience, and humanity, comfirmed, as we think by all the teachings of revelation, providence and history.

There are two or three historical facts, of a general kind, which are of much importance on this subject and which ought to be better understood and more attentively considered than they hitherto been. The first is that slavery has pretty much ruined, for a time at least, every nation in which it was ever established, on anything of a large scale and was continued long enough to work out its appropriate results. This has been already intimated, but it deserves a more distinct notice. The second is that no nation in which slavery was once fairly established ever gave it up except by force. The third is that, prior to the perilous experiment now making in this country, every nation in which it was ever established has been forced, by some means or other to give it up. After what has been already said we need not dwell upon these facts, nor attempt any proof of them by reference to authority for they are unquestionable; but they are very suggestive and should be made the subject of serious reflection. It is the part of wisdom to learn from the experience of others; but, if in any thing that concerns our duty or our welfare we give no heed to the lessons of the past, those have gone before have, so far, lived in vain for us.

It is manifest that the Lord has different ways and a variety of means always in readiness to punish the disobedient. *Power belongeth unto God* and no man and no set of men have any power at all except what he gives them. He has all power in heaven and on earth, and he exercises that power in such ways and by such means as he sees best. Every where and in all ages he employs the same means for accomplishing his purposes of wrath or of mercy, but varied in number and combination according to circumstances. Egypt was ruined by slavery in one way and Greece and Rome in another way. In dealing with Pharaoh and his servants he employed means and human agencies in such a way as to make his own power manifest. Both sides, the oppressors and the oppressed, must be convinced that he was Jehovah, the only living and true God; that he could do every thing; and that all his power was pledged for the protection and safety of the Israelites. Reptiles that crawled on the ground and were hated of all men; the insects that infest their bodies or floated in the air; darkness; ordinary diseases and the angel of death, accompanied by verbal admonitions and, to all appearance made effectual by human agency, were all employed to enforce the demand for the surrender of the Lord's people.

The same or similar means and agencies are still employed for the deliverance of the oppressed and for the destruction or punishment of their oppressors, sometimes with greater and sometimes with less effect as the case requires. The revelations of the last day will disclose a regular course of inflictions of wrath upon the disobedient and of relief to the poor and needy who cried unto him in secret in the usual occurrence of events, which are now overlooked or passed by unheeded, but which will them surprise even those who were sharers in them. Who thinks much about the Lord's design in sending an earthquake, a hurricane, or a hail storm, a war, a famine or a pestilence, a desolating swarm of Spanish flies, of army worms, or bugs in their harvest fields, of untimely frosts, of mill dew or of rust and blight? They cut off our anticipated gains and we regret the loss; but, who reflects as he ought on the sins of which they are the designed punishment and from a heart felt conviction of their ill dessert, breaks them off by righteousness? *The ox knows his owner and the ass his master's crib, but Israel doth not know, my people do not consider.* The orderings of Providence must be interpreted by the written revelation and to the sincere and Bible read Christian they are generally both intelligible and confirmatory of his faith; for they know that these inflictions were deserved and regards them as proofs of God's truth and faithfulness. We are too apt to think that Pharaoh's guilt was unusually great- far greater than ours; and that the plagues sent upon him were not designed to be repeated, but the god of this world is blinding the minds of them that believe not, and even Christians have yielded to the deceitful influence of worldly interest.

Usually, perhaps, the Lord leaves men to take their own course and to reap the fruit of their own doings. In Greece and Rome, the constitution and course of things was not interrupted by the Almighty yet slavery, by its appropriate and irresistible influence proved their ruin. Such a gross violation of justice and the claims of humanity could not be perpetrated on so large a scale and continued for many generations without working corruption in the departments of society and polluting the very fountains of social order and moral purity. Every reader of history knows that the Roman population, in all its grades, became awfully corrupt and that slavery was the most prominent means of producing that corruption. True, great wealth had been accumulated in the city and wealth usually produces luxury with its kindred vices; but that alone will not account for the sad and fatal results.

241 Their wealth enabled them to keep a large retinue of servile attendants probably of both sorts, servants and slaves; and that tended to foster pride, luxury and indolence, the parents of almost every other vice; but it was extremely corrupting to their children to be reared in the midst of such society or to be nursed and cared for and educated and trained by a set of such immoral, dissolute, and licentious men and women. Wealth seldom injures people provided they can be kept employed or have the resolution to keep themselves busily employed in some honest and gainful occupation; but children who very soon understand that they are born to an inheritance of wealth can seldom be kept thus employed and, giving themselves up to a life of ease and self indulgence become dissipated and worthless. We are inclined to think that the plagues inflicted upon Egypt, to effect the emancipation of their slaves did not produce half the permanent injury to the county that was produced by slavery in the ordinary course of things; and the influence, of a pernicious kind, thus exerted in these southern states has been immense. Thousands have been all the time living in idleness, luxury and sinful indulgence who would otherwise have been useful by employment, where pride, haughtiness, and an unusual sensitiveness in regard to what is falsely called honor and have been fallen by the pistol and the Bowie knife.

242 Improvements in agriculture, manufacturing and the useful arts generally have been neglected; the best lands have been cleared up and worn out; commerce has languished and literature of a high grade, has made little or no progress while those who might have distinguished themselves in science, philosophy, history and poetry have spent their time in reading newspapers and discussing the politics of the day.

It is astonishing what a bewitching or blinding and perverting influence a course of wrong doing has on the human mind. *The path of the just is as the shining light that shineth more and more unto the perfect day.* One who is in the way of duty and of eternal life has no tortuous or crooked course to pursue and needs no apology for doing what he knows to be right. It is not strange therefore that he should become more and more pleased with the practice of godliness; that familiarity and custom should render everything easy and pleasant to him; and that he should feel no need of labored arguments to satisfy himself or prove to others that he is not violating the rights of his fellow men or the claims of humanity; but it is strange that slave holders should persist in a practice which all others condemn and which all ingenuity of which they are capable has been enlisted in vain to justify.

In all sinful courses those who are engaged in them endeavor, by all the ingenuity and sophistry in their power to make others believe they are right and when that can't be done, as in the case of gambling, licentiousness and some other vices, they soon become so much under the power of temptation that resistance is out of the question; but, for one reason or another, they will not abandon the practice. It is not more strange that slave holders should endeavor to make others and themselves too believe in the lawfulness of slavery than that non slave holders, or any others, should seriously attempt to prove, as I have known them do, that it is positively right to get intoxicated occasionally, or that there is sound morality in the habitual use of tobacco. There is no justification of slavery in reason, or conscience or the light of nature, no sanction of it within the lids of the Bible, and no express grant from the Creator to hold slaves as property, yet those who have them will not give them up. No nation heretofore, in which slavery was unfairly established as a civil institution ever gave it up except by force and the people of the south are determined never to give up unless they are forced into the measure. They will fight while they can stand on their feet and "die in the last ditch before they will let their nigger property go. For this there are two reasons, neither of which is either valid or creditable to them as Christians: One is the fact that by the laws of the country, though without any grant from the Creator, or any sanction for it in his word, they hold them as *property* and they will fight to the death for their property. So will a man who has accumulated property by fraud, gambling, or any other iniquitous practice; and no property in the country has been acquired more unrighteously than that in slaves. The other reason is the influence of avarice, pride, and the love of power and self indulgence. The remark is made every where, by everybody and everyday of the year, the Lord's Day not excepted that all men desire power, physical, mental, moral political or any other kind, and when they once get it in their hands they will never let it be wrested from them except by a superior force. We long and fondly hoped to see the people of the south yield to justice, reason, Bible authority and the claims of humanity; but after what has already passed and in view of what is now passing before us, we see very little reason to hope any longer.

245   The great truth so clearly taught in the Bible and nowhere else, so alarming to the impenitent, so consolatory to the Christian and so essential to the welfare of the universe, that God is *unchangeable*, or that he is of one mind and no can turn him, secures the accomplishment of every purpose formed in the counsels of eternity and the fulfillment of every promise made to his people and of every threatening uttered against the wicked. He has by an express grant fixed the limits within which we may possess and improve and enjoy the things of this world: The grant includes al that we need and all that will be best for us. Here is ample room and abundant means for the full and harmonious development of all the powers we possess; but beyond these limits we may not go; for if we do, we go beyond our range and soon get into difficulty. We may go on without any assignable limit in subjecting the powers of nature to our control and in making them subservient to our comfort or our welfare but when we thus attempt to subjugate the intelligent creation, who feel that they belong to God and are accountable to Him alone we transcend our limits and attempt that in which we can never succeed; for we have neither the right nor the wisdom nor the power necessary to success.

246   The ways of Providence are always incomprehensible and often perplexing to us nor could it be otherwise, for we can judge only from very limited and distorted views. Why he should permit some nations to remain nearly two thousand years longer than others in the darkness of heathenism is a mystery which we cannot understand and perhaps it will be made plain to us only in the light of eternity but for the present we [must] believe and trust. He may permit a heathen nation, like that of the Hindus, for example, to be conquered by a more powerful one and be compelled to admit the Christian religion and the civilization attained by other portions of mankind; but not to be permanently enslaved; for that would in a great measure his beneficent design in their Christianization. Why he permits some portions of the human race to be enslaved even for a few generations is unaccountable to us, but not any more so than that despotism in any other form should be allowed for a long series of ages. He has his own ends to be accomplished, which we know are infinitely wise and good; but that does not dismiss the responsibility nor the guilt of the oppressor.

247   As already shown no religion has every been able to maintain the institution of slavery more than a very few generations and as it is directly opposed to God's revealed purposes in creation and redemption he never

will allow its permanent existence. Always when men in their greediness for the world, go beyond the limits which the creator has assigned them and encroach upon the spiritual temple which he is rearing out of our ruined race for the everlasting praise and glory of his grace, they will be driven back with shame and confusion. Every Christian is the temple of God through the Spirit and if any man will undertake to make that temple, the soul and body of a believer, subservient to his aggrandizement or his pleasures, he must take the consequences. *Let the potsherds strive with the potsherds of the earth; but let not man strive with his Maker.* The people of these southern states think that, although slavery has been a failure in all other nations, they can make it "a success" here and that "King cotton" and his Southern Confederacy are more powerful than Egypt, Greece or Rom because they have the influence of Christianity here of which those nations knew nothing. They can tell their slaves that they must be obedient to their masters; for the bible enjoins this upon them and they will make them believe it too. They must not be allowed to read it for themselves and become wise unto salvation through a knowledge of the Scriptures for they are an "inferior race" and, if they learned to read they would not be so profitable to their owners; but as the blacks are ignorant, weak minded and credulous they must believe just what the superior race tells them.

But whatever may be their views in regard to this matter, God's *thoughts are not as their thoughts, nor his ways as their ways.* Whatever may be their schemes and expectations of future greatness and however determined they may be to keep possession of their "nigger" property, the Lord's *counsel shall stand and he will do all his pleasure.* We think it just as certain that the southern states will, in a few years at most, be forced, in some way or other to give up their slaves as the nations of antiquity were forced and all the resistance they can make will be in vain.

The claim of the Southern people to their slave property rests, not on any origin or express grant from the Creator, but entirely on the constitutions and laws of the country; and the only reason offered in justification of those constitutions and laws in the pretended inferiority of the race. They are inferior in their attainments; for they have not made the progress in sciences, philosophy, and the arts, or in civilization generally, which has been made by the Anglosaxon and some other races. As already shown, for several hundred years after Noah's prediction they were the superior race; but, owing to a variety of secondary causes, which would require a volume to discuss and which would be out of place here, they gradually deteriorate and became dispersed and lost among the other tribes, as the larger portion of them appear to have sunk into a deplorable condition of ignorance, imbecility and of subjection to or of dependence upon the more advanced portions of mankind. A similar deterioration has come upon many of the nations which descended from Shem and Japheth and which were once the most flourishing and powerful in the world. What has become of the Babylonian empire,

250   What are the people of that country now compared with what they were in the time of Nebuchadnezzar and his immediate successors? What is the Persian Empire compared with its former extent and grandeur in the time of Cyrus, Xerxes, and others? What is modern Greece compared with the ancient country and people who bore that proud name in the days of Leonidas, Epaminondas, Aristides and Themosticles, of Aristotle, Socrates and Plato, of Phidias and Praxitites? What has Italy been for five hundred years compared with ancient Rome? The Lord rules among the nations and raises up one and puts down another at his pleasure; but he will suffer any nation to prohibit another nation, or millions of their fellow beings, for using the means of intellectual improvement and from such efforts as might enable them to raise themselves high in rank and social enjoyment among the surrounding communities. The Creator has made every planet and astroid in solar system the right size; so he has made the earth and every thing on it—every continent, sea, and river, every man and everything else of the right proportions; but he has given man no authority to meddle with his arrangements.

251   But to say that the Africans, as a race have naturally inferior minds and that they were made to be in a perpetual state of subjection to the authority of others is a slander upon them and a libel on the Creator. For some wise purpose he has permitted them to be long and deeply depressed, as he has suffered the Jews, for fifteen hundred years the most highly favored, prosperous and powerful nation in the world, to, for two thousand years, *a hissing and a byword* amongst the nations of the earth but this temporary depression is, in neither case, any proof of natural inferiority and give others no right to tyrannize over them and try to make this inferiority, which is owing merely to external and temporary circumstances a perpetual degradation. It gives occasion for the more favored race to shew their nobleness and magnanimity in elevating their condition and augmenting their enjoyment. True, in regard to the Africans especially it has also afforded the boasting Anglo Saxon an opportunity for gratifying their pride, avarice, and love of power; and they have thus far chosen the latter. Their

252   course has given them notoriety, but neither the honor nor the gratification of doing a great act. Since to my recollection, many Christian masters, in the middle and upper parts of this state, sent their black boys and girls to school with their own children and I never heard that the teachers thought them an inferior race or that they shewed any more want of capacity than

the white children. I have known them tried in Sunday School before any heathenish and unrighteous laws were made prohibiting such instruction, and I am sure that their progress was fully equal to that of poor white children in the neighborhood whose previous advantages had been very little if any better. In the Northern states quite a number of them have received a liberal education; and when their whole time has been devoted to that purpose and they have been furnished with competent instructors and all the requisite means, they have shown a capacity for learning everything in the course, equal to that of Anglo Saxon young men in any of our colleges. Notwithstanding all the disabilities under which they have been laid, the constant occupation of their time at hard labor and the enactments that have been made prohibiting the whites to teach them they appear to have, in this region where they are not numerous, as made good sense in their common business affair as their owners.

If it be true that the African race can bear to labor more in a very warm climate that the white race, it does not prove any natural inferiority of the intellectual powers; for the inherent vigor of the those powers is, of course, a natural endowment and their proper development depends on a variety of favorable circumstances with which climate has very little to do; nor does it authorize the other races to keep them in a condition of abject and degrading bondage; but it proves the wisdom and beneficence of the Creator in giving them a constitution adapted to such a climate while he has given to the other races a constitution adapted to the colder latitudes and it proves too the duty of all others to allow them the full liberty of cultivating the soil and of exercising their power, unimpeded and unmolested, in the climate for which they were made. If they have a "pigment," a layer of [adipose] matter under the skin of greater thickness than that of whites and consequently a more profuse perspiration, which, by its evaporation, enables them to endure the burning heats of a tropical sun, then given them exclusive possession of the soil and climate designed for them and, humanely and generously, give them every possible encouragement to elevate their character and improve their condition in life, so that the world, may have the full benefit of their capacity of enduring heart and of other peculiarities in their constitution under the genial influence of freedom and the stimulus afforded by the hope of reward.

In spite of all the prohibitory enactments that have been made, some thousands of them perhaps have learned to read and have acquired an amount of intelligence and refinement that commands the respect of their fancied superiors. Roberts, the first president of Liberia was until the middle or near the middle of life, as I have been told, a boatman on the Appomatox River and had very slender advantages for improvement, but he has shown himself fully equal to the duites of the station which he was called to fill. *Benson*, who now occupies the presidential chair, though a coal black megro and without the advantages of a liberal education, evidently possesses intellectual powers above the ordinary grade and is regarded with respect by most fo the governments in Europe. We think it highly probable that, in this country, a greater proportion of the negroes in spite of the depressing effects of bondage and of the constant occupation of their time in the most laborious employments of the country, have risen above their condition, as to intelligence, refinement of taste and elevation of character, than of the lower class of the white population, with all the advantages of common and Sunday schools and all the stimulating power of motives presented by the prospect of emolument and of a higher position in society. If so much has been done under every possible disadvantage it certainly gives assurance of what might be cone under more propitious circumstances.

255 By the favor of divine Providence or by the laws of nature, perhaps by both, the master portion of a community in which slavery exists have deteriorated or the slave portion have increased in numbers and in physical and moral power until they were able to triumph over their oppressors and to go out free. The more highly favored race have been treading down the slave population for generations and have been employing every means in their power to make them as degraded and as dependent as possible; but mortal man cannot chain down the immortal mind in darkness and degradation forever. Light of every kind is both stimulating and diffusive and the light of science is reaching them and rousing them up even in the low depths into which they have been sunk. Men cannot sleep when the sun is above the horizon unless they can get into some dark hole which the light cannot enter and where the hum of the busy crowd on the outside cannot be heard. You have not got the blacks sunk so low that they are entirely beyond the reach light and cannot hear the noise of the busy and buoyant crowd around them. You may tread them down and think you have them secure; but the waking energies of the undying and free born soul like subterranean or smoldering fires, will soon, and before you are aware of it, be bursting upon under your feet. They will suddenly come forth as

256 from their graves and commence the shout of defiance to their oppressors and the everlasting song of freedom. This is no fancy; for it is the unerring dictate of both reason and revelation and is confirmed by the generations and centuries that have been numbered with the years before the flood. The infatuated slave owners of the country may still say and try to believe that the slaves are contented and don't want to be free nor to leave their masters; but the truth is they are looking for their freedom as the result of this war with more confidence and on better ground than the leading secessionists

are looking for Southern independence. The time predicted that "Ethiopia shall stretch forth her hands unto God" and that all nations shall be given to Jesus Christ, so that they may become the Lord's freemen and be forced to call no man master on earth, will come and will not tarry. The time has come when the dead hear the voice of the Son of God and they that hear do live. The Lord has been demanding of the despotic governments in the old world to let the oppressed go free and they have been obeying his voice, slowly, and reluctantly, it may be, but certainly and without the power of retraction. The people of these Southern states, too, must hear them and yield to the demand, or refuse and take the consequences; and they must do it soon or not at all; for in a year or two more it will be too late. The country will be overrun and you will not have it in your power to make a voluntary surrender. They will go out free as the Israelites did go of Egypt and their former owners will gladly give them what they need in order to get their calamities removed.

257 ## III. *The reason* for the demand or the purpose for which it is made.

*L*ET MY PEOPLE GO *that they may serve me;* which implies that their service is indispensable to the accomplishment of his merciful designs for them and for the world, and that they *cannot* render such a service as he requires while in a state of servitude or absolute and perpetual bondage. This all important truth will be made plain we imagine, by the statement of a few facts and by such observations as they naturally suggest.

Their powers can never be developed while in condition of slavery.

The service which he requires consists in such a voluntary exercise of all their powers, mental, moral and physical, as will result in their increasing enjoyment and as will reflect increasing honor upon his wisdom, power and goodness in their creation. It belongs to the nature of all rational, finite, and dependent beings to be progressive and he had made ample provision, in nature and grace, for an everlasting progression in whatever is conducive to their well being. As such an employment of their powers is perfect freedom. The opposite of such employment, whether forced or voluntary, must be 258 bondage and hence according to the teachings of inspiration, all who have become reconciled with God through Jesus Christ are *free indeed,* , children of the household, sons and daughters of the Lord Almighty; but the unconverted and and unrenewed are represented as under bondage to the law and the servants of sin. Those who Christ has redeemed and disenthralled are in a condition to serve him with a perfect heart and a willing mind; and they are brought under such influences that their powers may be forever expanding in knowledge, purity, and love to the glory of his free and sovereign grace. No man has the shadow of a right to lay an arrest on this progress and to say that their whole time and bodily strength shall be devoted to his interests or his pleasures. Such an enslavement of those whom he has purchased with his own blood, whether actually converted or not, is a daring encroachment on his rights and a most unjust and cruel outrage on their privileges and enjoyments. The soul and body constitute only one person or percipient, intelligent, and accountable being; both were included in the great redemptive act on Calvary; both will share in the final results of that redemption and no man can prevent them without great guilt from sharing in the benefits here to the full extent of their capacity.

A mere glance at the condition of our slaves as it appears in the ordinary occupations and business transactions of every day life might satisfy any reflecting man that a regular cultivation of their minds, or any considerable progress in civilization is altogether impracticable. It was said on a former page that, in spite of all the prohibitory laws which had been passed, some thousands of them have learned to read and have acquired as much intelligence and refinement as a very large portion of our white population but a few thousands are no more to the whole mass than a drop from the bucket to the ocean. The comparatively few who have learned to read have lived in favored localities, having been kept as household servants in the towns, or in part of the country where they were few in number and belonged to Christian masters who encouraged if they did not assist them in learning; but the great mass of them are either entirely neglected or watched and guarded and effectually excluded from all the means and facilities by the free use of which they might rise above their conditions. If any man will notice the houses or dirty log cabins in which they are crowded together and the kind of bedding and other furniture which is allowed them, if he will observe the manner in which they are driven about late and early, and bought and sold without any regard to their social attachments or affections, he will se that they have neither time nor means nor inducements to learn.

But people have grown up with this institution among them and have become so familiar with all its horrid details that it makes very little impression on their minds. The thought hardly occurs to four fifths that their negroes deserve much better treatment than their horses or that they are not as much their property and may be bought and sold like any other property as suits their interests or their convenience. To understand the institution of slavery as it now exists and has long existed in the Southern states it is necessary to notice some of the laws that have been passed and are now in force on this subject. It was my design to give all our slave laws as they are found in the Revised Code of North Carolina, ed., 1855, chapter 107; but it soon become apparent that they would occupy entirely too much space. I must therefore limit myself with giving the substance of the most objectionable and refer the reader to the Code itself.

19. Slave Code of the South

Before we enter on the Code of North Carolina we will, partly as a matter of curiosity and partly as a proof of the cruelty which the slaves have been subjected ever since their first introduction into the country quote an act passed by the Colonial legislature of Maryland, which is in these words. "All negroes or other slaves within the province and all negroes and other slaves to be hereafter imported into the province, shall serve *durante vita*; and all children born of any negro or other slave, shall be slaves as their *fathers* were for the term of their lives" Sec. 1. "And forasmuch as divers free born *English* women, forgetful of their free condition and to the disgrace of our nation, do intermarry with negro slaves, by which also, divers suits may arise, touching the issue of such women, and a great damage doth befall the master of such negroes, for the prevention whereof, for deterring such freeborn women such shameful matches, be it enacted so that whatsoever freeborn women shall intermarry with any slave, from and after the last day of the present Assembly, shall serve the master of such slave during life of her husband; and that *all the issue of such free born women so married, shall be slaves as their fathers were.*"

262   This act was passed in 1663, and is the earliest of the Colonial enactments respecting slavery that has come under my notice. It was repealed in 1681, but as the repealing act contained *an express saving of the rights acquired under the Act of 1663, before the date of the repealing act, so far as concerned the enslavement of the woman and her issue,* it is not improbable that some of their d*escendants* are in bondage to this day (see Stroud's *Sketch*).

In the above enactment, however, there are two things which are vary remarkable and to which we call the reader's attention.

1st the adoption of the Common law doctrine, *partus sequitur pabrem* that the offspring follows the condition of *the father*.

2nd The slavery to which it subjected the *white freeborn English woman* This law was repealed about 1700 and there was no law on the subject in that state until 1715 when the following act was passed, "All negroes and other slaves already imported or hereafter to be imported into this province, and *all children now born or hereafter to be born of such negroes and slaves shall be slaves during their natural lives.*"

263   Here the legislature adopted the maxim of civil law, "partus sequitor ventrum" and from that day to the present the condition of the mother has determined the fate of the child. This maxim, which the advocates of universal freedom regard as "the genuine most degrading principle of slavery" was soon after adopted wherever slavery existed and we believe it has been enacted by all the slave states that the offspring shall follow the condition of the mother.

Before proceeding to the laws now in force in North Carolina, we feel tempted to give another act or two, in the "Olden Time" partly to gratify the curiosity of the reader but mainly to show the uneasiness of conscience and the crude notions which serious thinking people of that day had respecting the lawfulness of slavery, or of holding *Christians* in bondage. In 1715, the Colonial legislature of Maryland made the following enactment "For asmuch as many people have neglected to baptize their negroes, or *suffer them to be baptized*, on a vain apprehension that negroes, by receiving the sacrament of baptism, are manumitted and set free, *Be it enacted so that* no negroe or negress by receiving the holy sacrament of baptism, is thereby manumitted or set free, nor hath any right or title to freedom or manumission more than he or they had before any law, usage, or custom to the contrary notwithstanding." In 1711 the legislature of South Carolina passed the following act: "Since charity and the Christian religion which we profess oblige us to wish well to the souls of all men; and that religion may not be made a pretext to alter any man's property and right, and that no persons may neglect to baptize their negroes or slaves, or suffer them to be baptized; for fear that thereby they should be manumitted and set free, *Be it enacted* that it shall be, and is hereby declared lawful, for any negro or Indian slave, or any other slave or slaves whatsoever, to *receive and profess* the Christian religion and be thereunto baptized." The section then provides that such profession of religion and submission to baptism shall not be construed so as to entitle them to emancipation. At that time the impression seems to have been pretty generally on the minds of Christians that members of the Christian church, like those of the Jewish church could not be lawfully held in bondage and there was a conflict between their interest and their conscience.

Probably they had an idea that the negroes, before their conversion, were heathen and might be enslaved; but that, like the bondsmen of the Jews from among the heathen nations around, when they became proselytes to the Christian faith and were admitted to membership in the church, they were as free as any other members of the household of faith. In the notion that no members of the church have a right to hold other members in bondage they were not mistaken; but they did not recollect that they as well as the Africans were gentiles by nature and that all nations having been redeemed by Jesus Christ are entitled to the same rights and privileges. Christians in this state had to a great extent, the same notion and masters often presented the children of their slaves for baptism as they presented their own children and this had not ceased here entirely at the commencement of the present century; for although I never saw a case of the kind, I recollect to have heard in my early boyhood, of several such instances. They took it for granted that Abraham's servants were slaves and that as he had all his circumcised, so every Christian master ought to have all his household baptized.

But interest triumphed over conscience, as has been too often the case and the members of Christ's body were continued in bondage. It might and no doubt would have been alleged that if they were to be emancipated on their submission to baptism it would be too great a temptation to hypocrisy; but as their qualifications for the ordinance had to be judged of by ministers of the gospel, the extent to which false professions of religion might be carried, would depend upon *their* fidelity. In the Act of Assembly above quoted, the main and, in fact, the only reason assigned for continuing them in a state of bondage and degradation was *the interest of their masters*; and to that chiefly are to be ascribed all the atrocities and horrors of slavery and the slave trade. With a supreme desire for gain all the laws in all the slave codes of the southern states have been made and, unless Providence interfere in some effectual way, we fear that the god of this world will continue to hold dominion in this matter even over the church; but without further delay we now return to the Revised Code of North Carolina.

267   The first enactment in Chapter 107, relates to Africans brought into this state, surreptiously or without authority, from any foreign port, contrary to an act of congress, and, as we think, reflects very little credit on the legislative body by which it was passed. In the year 1807, the Federal Congress passed an act prohibiting the transportation of any more African slaves into the United States after the first day of January 1808; and, if we do not forget, for we have not the act at hand, declaring the slave trade piracy; In 1816, the legislature of North Carolina enacted that "Every negro or person of color, being a slave imported into this state from any foreign port, or place, for a slave or to be held to service or labor since the first day of January 1808, contrary to the provisions of the act of congress entitled; An Act to Prohibit the importation of Slaves *"shall be sold for the benefit of the state."* He was to be sold, after twenty days notice, by public practice at the court house door; and if he absconded, a reward was to be offered equal to one fifth part of his value when sold and search to be made for him until found.

268   This act, though virtually sanctioned by the 6th section of the Act passed by Congress, or might be so understood, was obviously in direct opposition to the benevolent spirit and design of the act and the advantages taken of the 6th section by several of the states, to get slaves imported into the territorial limits, soon made the adoption of very stringent measures necessary in order to maintain the law. But why this wanton and unprovoked and unmerited persecution of the African race? What enormous crime had they committed to justify or even to palliate such an outrage on justice, honor, and humanity? Was North Carolina so hard run for money? Or had her legislature such a rabid appetite for the bones and sinews of Africans that all their feelings of generosity and even of compassion were kept in abeyance? Would it not have been more magnanimous and more creditable to the name of the Old North State to send them back to their own country or

III. *THE REASON* FOR THE DEMAND OR THE PURPOSE FOR WHICH IT IS MADE

delivered them them up to the United States government? We simply state the facts and let the candid reader judge for himself.

As if the crime of being kidnapped in Africa and transported to this country against their will cold not be atoned for by a life time of bondages and hard labor, it was ordained in the act above quoted that their unborn posterity should be reduced to the same condition; but this was just placing them, without any other fault than their helplessness or the color of their skin, in the same degradation and wretchedness with the slaves already in the country.

When slave of any description ran away, either from severe treatment or oppressive labor, or from scanty provisions, or to avoid a separation, from their wives and children, any person may apprehend them and is stimulated to do so by the offer of a reward. He must be advertised and every possible effort made for his apprehension. When taken he must be lodged in jail until his owner comes for him and, if his owner cannot be found within a reasonable time, he must be sold to the highest bidder. When runaways pilfer poultry, pigs, or anything to satisfy their hunger they may be outlawed and taken dead or alive, especially if, when discovered they attempt either to resist or to escape from their pursuers.

Slaves are not allowed to hire their own time and of course have no encouragement to economy and enterprise. If a slave who has hired his time of his master is found going about no matter how unexceptionable may be his deportment, the master must be fined forty dollars, and the slave if found guilty, must be hired out for a year.

No person may grant permission for a meeting of the slaves of others at his house or on his premises for the purpose of dancing, no matter how orderly and civilly the meeting may be conducted, under a penalty of twenty dollars for every offense so that even those amusements which white people deem innocent and pleasurable and denied to the slaves.

They are not allowed to go off the plantation or premises where they are appointed to live, if it is only a mile, to see a husband or wife or a sick child, without a written permission from their master or overseer, under pain of a severe flogging if they are caught.

They are not allowed to raise any kind of stock for themselves; nor to traffic with other slaves or other persons except in such articles as are not bidden to be the subject of trade between white persons and slaves.

They are forbidden to preach or exhort, or in nay manner officiate as preacher or teacher, at any prayer meeting or other association for worship, where slaves of different families are collected together. Every slave is forbidden to teach, or *attempt* to teach any other slave or free negro to read or write.

We hold that a man must always be tried by his *peers* or equals and that this is the only guarantee we can get that justice will be done us; but slaves, in all jury cases, must be tried by a jury of *slave owners*.

272 "Any free person who shall teach or attempt to teach any slave to read or write, or shall give or sell to such slave any book or pamphlet, shall be deemed guilty of a misdemeanor and upon conviction thereof, if a white man or woman, shall be fined not less them one hundred dollars or more than two hundred dollars, or imprisoned; and if a freeperson of color, shall be fined imprisoned or whipped, not exceeding thirty nine nor less than twenty lashes."

If a human and benevolent master would emancipate a favorite slave, he must file a petition in writing, in any of the superior courts, setting forth, as near as may be, the name, sex and age of the slave and praying permission to emancipate the same, and the court shall grant the prayer on the following conditions; and not otherwise, namely,

(1) The petitioner shall show that he has given public notice of his intention to file the petition, at the court house of the county, and in the nearest gazette, for at least six weeks before the hearing of the petition; and (2) shall enter into bond with two able sureties payable to the State of North Carolina, in the sum of one thousand dollars for each slave named in the petition, conditioned that he shall honestly and correctly demean himself, while he shall remain within the state, and that he will within ninety days after granting the prayer for emancipation, leave the state and never afterwards come within the same. When a man directs in his will that one or more of his slaves shall be emancipated, the execution must go through essentially but is subject to a longer delay.

273 The above process is a attended with so many difficulties and with so much expense and trouble and responsibility that it amounts to a prohibition and was probably intended by the legislature to have that effect. As there were then and always have been many humane and generous masters in this state who would like to emancipate their slave, the representatives, no doubt felt that they must show some courtesy this portion of their constituents; but took care to make the act of emancipation so very onerous and difficult that it would never be put in practice.

No master is allowed to put his slave to work in certain swamps which are specified, until he has brought him to the clerk of the court of pleas and quarter sessions, who is required to enter on the records of court the names of the master and the slave and place of residence, with an exact description of the slave, stating his height complexion and every peculiarity by which he may be known. The clerk must then give the master for that slave, a certified copy of all this, and the slave must keep it about him when at work.

III. *THE REASON* FOR THE DEMAND OR THE PURPOSE FOR WHICH IT IS MADE

The master who puts his slaves to work in those swamps without procuring such a certificate for them is guilty of a *misdemeanor*; and if a free negro goes to work in either of the swamps specified without a similar certificate, he is guilty of a misdemeanor and may be punished at the discretion of the court, by fine, whipping or imprisonment, or all three of them. If a slave goes voluntarily to work then without his certificate he must, when the fact is ascertained, receive thirty nine lashes on his bare back and the person who arrests him shall receive a reward of twenty five dollars. We know not the reasons for this law but it must make the slave and free negroes feel mortified in the extreme.

Every slave is forbidden, not only to form any relation of affinity with any white person, but to intermarry or cohabit even with *free* negroes, which is declared to be a misdemeanor and the punishment, thirty nine lashes on the bare back. All these laws seem to be extremely severe when the slaves are not allowed to read and no pains are taken to inform them of the laws which relate especially to them. All masters, even though their interest requires it, are not considerate enough to give them the necessary information, and a large portion of them, belonging to minors are hired to men who care nothing for their safety or welfare.

A slave may be emancipated for meritorious services if he is over fifty years of age and if the meritorious services have been more than general duties; but it must be done by the superior court and on petition of the owner, or some other, the act does not say who. The owner, however, must prove on his own oath, or otherwise that said slave has performed such meritorious service; and the petitioner must swear that he has not received in money or otherwise, the price or value, or any part thereof, of said slave, or been induced to petition for his freedom in consideration of any price paid or to be paid thereafter. The petitioner must also give bond with good security, in the sum of five hundred dollars, that said slave shall honestly and correctly demean himself so long as remains in the state. Here we observe that the emancipation granted for meritorious services is not granted until the slave is of such an age that it can do him little or no good; and that few masters, especially such as are advanced in life, will be likely to issue the necessary expenses and assume the liabilities required by the act.

Every slave who has been emancipated according to the provisions made this chapter for other causes than meritorious services must leave the state within ninety days and never return; for if he does not leave in that time, or if he ever returns, he must be sold for a slave.

Free negroes are forbidden to migrate into this state and if any one do so, he shall be deemed guilty of a misdemeanor during all that time of his stay and may be indicted from time to time, until he removes out of the state; and on every conviction shall be fined five hundred dollars for the payment of which he may be hired out; *provided* that thirty days be allowed him to get away after one indictment before another is commenced.

Any person who shall bring into this state, by water or land, a free negro, shall forfeit and pay for every person so brought in, five hundred dollars; but there is an exception in favor of free negroes who are employed on board of ships and steam boats, or are traveling as servants with white gentlemen. Free negroes who are not now lawfully residing within the state cannot come into it and remain there free.

When a free negro, though a native of this state and a sober, peaceable and industrious in it all his life hitherto, goes into another state on a visit to his friends, or on business, no matter how urgent or difficult, and is absent over ninety days, unless he can prove that he was detained by sickness, forfeits his right to be a resident here and if he returns he be sold into bondage.

If any free person of color undertakes to preach or exhort in public, or to officiate as a preacher or teacher in any prayer meeting or association for worship where slaves of different families are collected together, he shall be guilty of a misdemeanor and shall receive not more than thirty nine lashes on his bare back. Free negroes are forbidden to intermarry or cohabit and live together as man and wife, with any slave; for any act of this kind is deemed a misdemeanor and he shall be fined, imprisoned, or have thirty nine lashes his bare back; unless such marriage or cohabitation took place with the consent of the master or mistress of the slave prior to Nov. 1, 1842. Free negroes are not allowed to hawk or peddle in any county of this state unless they have obtained a license from the court of pleas and quarter session within a year previous to the time when thus engaged; and for a violation of this law they shall be chargeable with a misdemeanor.

Every free negro is forbidden to wear or carry about his person or keep in his house any shotgun, musket, rifle, pistol, sword, dagger or bowie knife. And for every violation of this statute he shall be deemed guilty of a misdemeanor. All free negroes are forbidden by law directly or indirectly to sell or give to any person, bond or free, any spirituous liquors; and every act of this kind shall be deemed a misdemeanor. No captain of a steam boat or other vessel navigating the waters of this state, no conductor or agent of a railroad, and no driver a stage coach, is allowed to carry slaves in any of these public conveyances without a written permission from the owner.

It was finally ordained that all free persons descended from negro ancestors to the fourth generation inclusive, though one ancestor of each generation may have been a white person, shall be deemed free and persons of mixed blood.

Perhaps we ought to say here that when a white man kills a negro slave, with malice aforethought, he is deemed a murderer in law and some such have been executed in this state, but as negro testimony cannot be taken against a white man, it is extremely difficult to convict the criminal.

In the partial syllabus on the few preceding pages of our legislative enactments I have taken only such as seemed to be most important to my purpose and, with very few exceptions, these are not in the express words of the Revised Code, because space required brevity and because every intelligent reader had better turn to the Code itself. I recollect no express act of our legislature making the bondage of the Africans perpetual; but it is necessarily implied in some of which we have given; It is said, *No slave shall be set free but according to the provisions of this chapter.* It is enacted that the provisions of this chapter shall apply to every person of color and to the *issue* of every negro and person of color imported into this state after Jan 1st 1808. The fact that they are made *property* implies the permanence of the institution and very few slave owners think of anything else [than] that their property in slaves will be as permanent as their property in real estate. In some of the slave holding states laws were enacted which made them *de-facto* real estate, as in Louisiana "*Slaves though moveable by their nature are considered as immovable by the operation of law.*" That was by the *civil* law; but by an act of legislature, it was declared, June 7th 1816 that "Slaves shall always be reputed and considered *real estate*; they shall be as such subject to be mortgaged, according to the rules prescribed by law, and they shall be seized and sold as real estate" and shall pass, in consequence to heirs and to creditors (see Stroud's *Sketch*). If I do not forget such a law once existed in Virginia but was soon repealed—perhaps also in Kentucky—but they are considered now most of the states as *chattels*. In South Carolina the law reads thus. "Slaves shall be deemed, sold, taken, reputed, and adjudged in law to be *chattels personal* in the hands of their owners and possessors and their execution, administrations, and assigns; to all *intents, instructions and purposes whatsoever.*" We don't see how despotism could go any farther; and the practice of all the states is about the same. They are, everywhere, bought and sold, without any sort of regard to their feelings, their relationships or their welfare, just as if they were horses or mules.

From the foregoing syllabus of our legislative enactments on the subject of slavery we gather the following facts and present them in a condensed view to save our reader the trouble of bringing the items side by side, in regular form for themselves.

The master has power to say what the slave shall do, how much he shall do and when he shall do it. The slave may be so unwell that he ought to be in his bed but if he is able to go at all he must work and the command of an unfeeling master. An ungodly master may make a Christian work on the Sabbath, provided no white person is present or hear him give the order; and so with many other things the doing of which violates the laws of both God and man.

The master may furnish the slave with such food and clothing, as to quality and quantity, as he chooses and there is no remedy for; although by the laws of this state, if a man's slaves when starving and naked steal from his neighbors, he may be compelled to pay the damages, yet for various reasons which will readily occur to everyone, the law cannot be easily enforced; and although I have known a great many cases in which men were liable to the penalty, I have never known a single instance in which any attempt was made to enforce the law.

A man may subject his slave to any kind of amount of corporeal punishment he chooses and the sufferer has no redress. If a man kills his slave "right out" he may be prosecuted for murder, provided it can be proved on him, which for the want of white witnesses, can seldom be done but he may beat him so cruelly, once or repeatedly as *indirectly* to cause his death and he cannot be brought to account. Hundreds and probably thousands of such instances have occurred in the country. I have known a number myself in which nobody in the neighborhood had any doubt that the death of the slave was caused by the severity of his treatment, but no attempt was made to punish the cruel perpetrator of the deed. The master may delegate his power over the slave to an overseer or some other person who has no other thought or concern than to get as much work out of them as he can and thus they are often harder worked and worse treated than they would have been by avaricious master.

Slaves have no legal rights or can own no property in anything; but whatever they acquire, though it be by hard work when they ought to be asleep according to the law, belongs to their masters and I have known of several instances in which a faithful slave had, relying on the promise of emancipation, by extra services obtained enough or nearly enough to the pay the price fixed for his ransom, which, it was said he had paid, a part at a time, to their master or mistress, trusting to their word and honor; but just then that they were sold off to the speculators and the avaricious master or mistress pocketed the money.

Slaves being mere *chattels* may be at any time, sold, mortgaged, or leased at the will of their owners or they be sold by process of law to satisfy the debts of their masters, either while living or after their death. All this is passing before us every day and most people have been so accustomed to it from their childhood that they don't seem ever to reflect on its enormity.

III. *THE REASON* FOR THE DEMAND OR THE PURPOSE FOR WHICH IT IS MADE

No slave can be a party before any judicial tribunal, against his master no matter how cruel may have been the treatment which he has received or how great the injuries that may have been done him. If anything is done to obtain redress or prevent the like atrocities in future, others must do it for him, and I have never known a cause of such interference.

Slaves cannot purchase their own freedom nor even obtain a change of masters, no matter how harsh and persistent may have been their treatment. *Property* cannot purchase itself nor change hands at pleasure.

As slaves are property, unrighteously made so by the laws of the country if they are injured by a third person the owner may bring suit and recover damages as he would for a horse or any other species of property ; but the slaves can do nothing themselves. Slaves can, of course, make no contracts, with white or black, that are binding in law.

Even the *domestic* relations are denied them, in any form that will be obligatory as a civil transaction, or that will make them permanent. Their marriages are nothing more than what the Romans termed a *contubernium*, a temporary concubinage, which can last no longer the parties choose, or until their masters from interest, convenience, or caprice sells them off separately to the highest bidder.

Slavery is made perpetual and is entailed, without reason, necessity, or humanity, upon their unborn and unoffending offspring down to the end of line. This is the worst part of the institution; for, if there was to be a termination of the evil, at no great distance, it could be bore, but *hope deferred makes the heart sick*.

It seems as if human cupidity and ingenuity had been exhausted in the way of legislation to make the bondage of the Africans absolute, complete, and perpetual; for we can think of nothing more and if anything could be added to the slave code now in force to make their fetters stronger, their yoke more galling, we have no doubt it would be done.

Under such laws and with such an abject and general submission to the god of this world; is it possible that their intellectual and social powers can ever be developed? Does any sane man expect it? Is it not the determined purpose of legislatures and all slave holders, with perhaps a chance exception here and there, that they never shall advance in knowledge and civilization? In 1821 if my recollection serves me, when the law was passed (see Rev. Code, chap. 34, sec. 82) making it a penal offense, a misdemeanor in law for any free person—white or black, of course—to teach the slaves the use of letters, as I well recollect, they only argument I ever heard used in or out of the legislature in favor of the law was that if they learned the use of letters they would read the Declaration of the Independence, newspapers, speeches on the subject, by which they would become acquainted with their rights, dissatisfied with their condition and less *profitable* as slaves.

It seems strange that a protestant people, a Christian people, nominally such at least were not ashamed to use such an argument in their halls of legislation and at their firesides; but so powerful is the influence of that "cursed lust of gold" that it makes people too often give up their interest both worlds.

286   The development of the powers is education and in the present lapsed, depraved, and erring condition of mankind it must be carried forward, if successful under a variety of agencies, means, and influences such as the instruction and example of parents, and the kindly and stimulating influence of the whole household; the instructions of teachers in schools, academics, and colleges and the all controlling power of providential circumstance which more than anything and everything else, give impulse and direction to the mind; or, to change the language, test not the sense, education consists in rightly developing all the original instincts of our nature and this should be regarded by every man and every woman as the great end of life for on the full and harmonious gratification of all these instincts or tendencies of our nature, depends the purest most perfect and every increasing enjoyment of which we are capable, but each one of these original instincts, or as they are often called, laws of our nature can be developed only by the conscious possession of the object of which it tends as the needle to the pole. Conditioned as we now are, the *possessory* instinct or its appropriate development lies at the formulation of all progress and of almost every thing else that is good and desireable.

287   The posessory instinct in its widest range includes everything that we can justly obtain and rightfully hold as a permanent possession, such as knowledge of every kind, and an interest in Christ; a pure and unalloyed friendship with God and man, which constitute a large portion of the future and eternal inheritance, but, as we are only making a passing remark or two on the subject, we shall consider it no farther in this place than the possession of its present objects is necessary to procure the time and means requisite for further progress. Of all the instincts that belong to us as intelligent beings this is the first that is decidedly manifested and, though not, subsequently, the strongest in Christians it continues through life the strongest in mere men of the world. You see its outworkings from the cradle to the grave. Before it has learned the word, *meum* and *tuum* or mine and yours; the child becomes furious if it toys are taken from it; and the savage in the wildernesss, few and simple as are his acquisitions, has the sense of possession or the *right* to possess what he has honestly obtained as strong as any man in the most civilized community upon earth.

288 The slave has not an hour of time more a dime of money that he can legally call his own; for he has no rights. He himself is as much property as a horse or a mule. A few masters of more humane feelings than others give their slaves a half or quarter of an acre, which they may cultivate for themselves, while they ought to be asleep or when they can, and make what disposal of the products they please; but that is such a pitiful act of generosity that it is hardly worthy of a notice. The spirit and character of a nation is always judged abroad, not by little acts of humanity on the part of individuals, but by their laws and general usages. Slaves here, as the civilized world is well aware are mere chattels and have no civil right more than any other stock except that when charged with a capital crime they are allowed a trial by jury, but it must be a packed jury; they are not allowed to be tried by their peers or equals, so that this pretended right is little more than a mockery, but the main point here is that the slaves instinctive desire of possession can neither be developed nor gratified nor made subservient to his higher and more important attainments.

289 Fallen from God, as we are, and under the power of sin, all men, until renewed by grace, make this world their portion and grasp as much of it as they can get. Obviously this is as sad perversion of an original and noble instinct of our nature, but the Bible give us instructions in regard to this matter which would be just right if we were as sinless and as little prone to sin as Adam was when he came from the hands of his Creator; for, be it remembered that the Bible makes no allowance for human imperfection. Its language to all is *Sin not, but if any man sin,* no matter what may have been his frailties or his temptations, *we have an Advocate with the Father.* The simple direction in regard to this world is, *Give me neither poverty nor riches* but a *competency,* a medium between two fatal extremes—not a destitution for then there would be neither time nor means for further progress in all that makes existence comfortable or desirable—not so much as to occupy the whole attention and bring a burden of care on the mind and foster pride and enervate the powers. Some have a greater tact for business than others

290 and could soon become rich, while many around them who have quite as much native intellect and would show it in other things if they had the means of culture, remain in straitened circumstances if not in absolute poverty; but there is a sufficiency in the world to furnish all with a *quantum sufficit* for every desirable purpose and the liberality which the gospel requires, if it is so practiced as it ought to be and will be someday, would furnish every human being with the means for the full development of all his powers; but are adequate portion of this world is indispensable to the enjoyment of life and to such advancement in knowledge and the general intelligence and refinement of taste as are essential to our well being; and when, by an unjust,

avaricious and cruel despotism, a man cannot, legally claim one hour as his won nor the value of one dime out of all his toils and sufferings, it is impossible, in the nature of the case that this instinctive desire of possession can every be gratified, or that his powers can every be developed. This is a constant and most distressing wear and tear on the sensibilities, a daring encroachment on the prerogative of God and a robbing him of the glory which would otherwise redound to the his creative wisdom and power; and no reason has been given or can be given for it, except the pride and avarice of the dominant race.

291   The desire of *immortality* is an original instinct of the soul and however much it may be overborne and perverted by the carnal passions of a depraved heart, it is neither extinct nor inactive. Man was made an immortal being and that law of his existence was, at the creation, stamped upon his nature. Even the most barbarous tribes give proofs of its existence; for although their notions of the future may be crude and in many respects, very erroneous, because they have had nothing to give it strength and direction but they dread the idea of ceasing to and, in fact, the thought of *annihilation* seems never to enter their minds. It has not been a mooted question among them and they have no apprehension lest they should cease at death to feel, to think, to or hate and to enjoy such pleasures as they now have if not far better. It is essential to our comfort and progress, and even to the safety and well being of society, that this original law or instinct of our nature should be maintained in its full force; for if men once believe in annihilation—if they every do really believe such a lie—they degenerate fast in every moral attribute and they don't care what they do. *Let us eat and drink for tomorrow we die*. Men never believe in annihilation unless their crimes, secret or open, of the flesh or of the mind, make it desirable as the only way to escape an awful doom.

292   Guilty and depraved as we are, having lost the favor of God and unable to regain it by anything we can do, "this dread of falling into naught," this strong and imperishable desire of immortality, can be fully assured only by the gospel; for by that Christ has brought life and immortality to light; but in all ordinary cases a man must be able to read the Bible for himself and not be compelled to take what he knows about it upon trust and from those of whose honesty he feels that he has great reason to be suspicious. To say that many whites cannot read it for themselves; that until within half a generation, more or less, thousands of the poorer class over the country never went to school and never learned to read—all this is mere quibbling and unworthy of honest men. For, as to a large portion of them, if they never learned to read it was their own fault. There was no law forbidding others, under a heavy penalty, to teach them the use of letters. They were

not compelled to labor hard as long as they could labor at all, exclusively for the benefit of others, were never liable to be bought and sold for the interest or convenience of interested and avaricious masters. Their depression, so far as it was not their own fault, was produced by the unjust and cruel power of man, but more directly by the agency of divine Providence, and was designed to be only temporary.

The temporary changes which are everywhere and all the time taking place, by the agency of Providence, in families and communities are, as we have shown on a former page, for wise and beneficent ends. They act as a powerful stimulus on the faculties and energies of mankind, at least of those who are now, or at any given time, in a condition which makes exertion necessary; and to that class the world is indebted for all the great improvements which have been made in civilization; but the conduct of men in dooming millions of their fellow beings, with their unborn generations, by penal statutes, to a most degrading bondage and to an eternal ignorance of the Bible, except what little they can occasionally gather from others and that little they don't know half the time whether to believe or disbelieve. It is often said that many of them become very pious people and, although we can't know the heart, charity would lead us to believe or hope so, but no thanks to slavery or the slave laws of the South for such a result. The Lord is all the time overruling the most selfish plans and the most atrocious deeds of man for the glory of his name and for the furtherance of his cause in the world; but is that any excuse for them or will it make their future doom less terrible? If Jesus Christ in his abounding grace, converts and saves many of them in every successive generation, to show men that their unrighteous laws cannot prevent the accomplishment of his merciful purposes and to have a seed among them ready to maintain his cause in their own land when the set time for their deliverance shall come it neither lessens the guilt nor the reproach of their oppressors. Among the Israelites under Pharaoh there were some of the brightest examples of piety that the world has ever known; but that neither lessened the guilt nor mitigated the doom of the tyrants who ruled over them. The pious men and women among our blacks, as far as I have seen, were not the intelligent large minded and influential men and women that they would have been if their powers had been properly developed. They knew by the operations of the Holy Spirit on their hearts that they had experienced a great change in their feelings, that Jesus Christ had atoned for their sins and that they might now hope for eternal life through him; but there was none of those enlarged views, nor that expansion of soul which is always imparted by scriptural and enlightened sentiments of immortality sustained by a full view of the truth as there is in Jesus.

295	The desire of knowledge is an original instinct of our nature which is strongly manifested in childhood and with few exceptions, increases through life. The inquisitiveness of children is notorious and they often ask questions which the wisest men cannot answer. The kind of knowledge which people seek to gain depends, in general, upon the circumstances of early life and on the direction which is then given to their powers. If they have advantages of education and if their attention is then confined to trifles they seldom, afterwards, aspire to the knowledge of more lofty and ennobling subjects. A knowledge of God and of his works has many advantages in the business of life and is a great source of pure, high and lasting enjoyment. It raises men up from the neighborhood of the brutes and prepares them to rank with angels. Ever since the time of Bacon, the maxim has been in everybody's mouth that "knowledge is power" and it is true; for the extent of a man's influence is measured by that of his knowledge. By his increasing acquisitions of knowledge, in a state of freedom, all his other powers are developed and there is a harmonious and delightful progress throughout; but in ignorance nothing is developed except the depravity of the heart. An inspired oracle has said, *That the soul be without knowledge it is not good;* and how dare you,

296	by your impious enactments, doom millions of your fellow beings to such a gross and perpetual ignorance? How dare you say that neither they nor their unborn generations shall ever be taught to read the glorious revelation that God has given and designed for them as much as for you? Neither the time nor the means necessary for the purpose are allowed them and that is but the smaller part of the enormity; for if any free person, white or black, shall attempt to teach them the use of letters, or shall sell or *give* them a book of pamphlet of any kind, he shall be found guilty of a misdemeanor in law; and if they shall undertake to teach one another they shall be severely punished. If there were no such heathenish laws, as they have neither the means nor the time necessary to learn, they could not make much progress in knowledge and their powers could not be developed while in a state of bondage; but the slave code of this country would shame ancient Greece and Rome or the dark ages of Christianity. If slaves become dangerous as they become intelligent, it is only because they are *slaves* and their knowledge of God and his government can make them dangerous in no other way than by compelling their masters to *respect* them and consequently to treat them as human beings, or in other words, to give them their freedom as a result devoutly to be wished; but the lawmakers and slave owners of this country have surely assumed a tremendous weight of moral responsibility.

297	That veneration which all finite or dependent beings feel for a superior being, of real or imaginary excellence, and that supreme veneration which they feel for the Supreme Being when he becomes known to them, is an original and therefore an imperishable instinct or tendency of our nature; but *worship*, taken in its widest sense, does not consist merely in feelings of adoration, love, and praise. It includes the employment of our time or portions of it in ways which will express the homage of the heart, and free will offerings from the fruit of our labors. Much of all this is not in the power of the slave; for all his time is occupied and all the fruits of this toils are taken to gratify the avarice of his master.

The slave may feel, as every one ought to feel, intensely thankful that his is out of hell and, if he has a well founded hope of heaven, he may feel more gratitude than he can express for that and he may feel as thankful as any others for what few temporary comforts are allowed him—his health and the exercise of his reason, for his food and rainment; for the sympathy of such black friends as he has and for the little dirty cabin which protects him from "the peltings of the pitiless storm"; but he cannot feel grateful for what he does not possess or enjoy. *Liberty* is regarded by white men as the greatest of all earthly blessings; and while they are riveting the fetters of the slave upon him with on hand and holding the scourge over him with the other, they are jubilating and thanking the Almighty that they are the freest people on earth. I speak of slavery, not as it is in a few indulgent families or neighborhoods; but as it is seen in the slave codes of the south and as it is now viewed by the protestant world. The slave in his devotions, cannot thank God for the greatest of all earthly blessings. The slave's instinct or natural tendency to worship and honor the infinite Being who made him cannot be properly developed while in a state of such ignorance and degradation because his knowledge of God and divine things is so very limited and because the richest of all earthly blessings are denied to him.

For what the Lord does by the agency of his Providence we are not answerable; but for what *we* do while he looks on and hinders not, we must give an account at his bar. By favoring circumstances alone we have become for a time, the dominant race and he has thus given us an opportunity to elevate the character and increase the enjoyments of the African race among us a hundred fold or to keep them in ignorance, degradation and wretchedness. To have done the former would have been acting nobly and in a manner worthy of a free people whom the Lord has so highly favored; but to our everlasting reproach we have done the latter and while we have been embittering their life we have been robbing God, so far as we could do it, of the honor which would otherwise have been given him.

The *conjugal* and *parental* instincts, which may be regarded pretty much as the source of all that is good or bad in society cannot be developed at all among our slaves. The fact is they are, all the time, ignored, trampled on, and set at naught. The husband, if such he may be called, has no legal right to his wife nor the wife to her husband, the parent to affections and services of their children, nor the children to the protection and kindness of their parents. Their marriages are nothing more than what the old Romans called a *Concubernium*, a kind of temporary *concubinage*, without sacredness, without durability and without the beneficial results which usually attend legal and regular marriages. There are many instances of very strong attachment between those who call themselves husband and wife and many a sad tragedy of broken hearts and ruined hopes has been the result. I have known some instances in which they have been permitted to live on in great harmony and affection to an advanced age; but such instances, so far as my observations have gone, have been "like angel visits" few and far between." Generally, in a few years at most, they have been separated, sold off under the hammer like other stock and borne away to returnless distance. God say that man shall not put asunder those whom he has joined together; but our laws ignore the laws of God on this subject, so far as the slaves are concerned, and their affections and conjugal rights are trampled on with as much indifference as if they were dumb brutes.

300   A free man considers his wife and children as his richest treasure; but a slave has neither wife nor children, by any legal right; for they are all the property of his master and may be sold at anytime, like other stock, as his convenience or necessities require. The family of a free man is a nursery for church and for the country. The family of a slave, so long as he is permitted to have one is a nursery for the slave market. The charges made by northern people that the slaves states are "slave breeders" has produced a great deal of angry recrimination and to a sober thinking man the idea is certainly disagreeable; but the charge must be admitted, at least to some extent; for even in the cotton states where, as they are sooner killed or die of disease, they depend more on buying, the *children* of their slaves are regarded as slaves in law and as really an addition to their estate as their colts or young mules; and in the border states I have heard many a slave owner remark that their labor was not profitable in this upper country, but that their *increase* would be worth something, i.e., in a more southern market. If an Englishman or a Frenchman could be made to believe or was assured, that this was not "slave breeding" in the northern sense of the expression, he would probably be at a loss for some term or phrase to designate the practice. We do no wish either to wrong or to irritate our countrymen; for we love the south and if the slaves were all removed, we would greatly prefer it ot any other country in the world, but facts are stubborn things.

301   About the time that slavery was first introduced in the British Colonies in the West Indies and North America it was introduced in the colonies of Spain, Portugal, and France, in the gulf of Mexico and on the South

III. *THE REASON* FOR THE DEMAND OR THE PURPOSE FOR WHICH IT IS MADE

American coast, but somewhat modified in its form; for being employed in the cultivation of the soil they cannot be detached from by sale and consequently husbands and wives and parents and children cannot be separated. The Code Noir, Art. 47, prohibits the selling of the husband without the wife, the parents without the children, or *vice versa*. In voluntary sales made contrary to this regulation, the wife or husband, children or parents through expressly reserved by the seller, pass by the same conveyance to the purchaser and may be claimed by him without any additional price. This law, says the compiler of the Annals of the Sovereign Council of Martinique, "has always been rigidly executed, whenever a claim has been set up on the part of the purchaser. I have known slaves who have been sent to Guadeloupe or St. Domingo, to be expatriated and sold, to reclaim their children remaining in our colony, with success, through the action of the purchasers in the colonies to which they were sent" (see Stroud's *Sketch*).

In all the countries mentioned above, Popery is the established religion and the French gov't has long boasted that it is the protector of the Roman Catholic Church, yet they have shown a humanity in their slave laws which ought to make us Protestants blush with shame. More than a generation ago England abolished slavery in all her possessions; in the Spanish West Indies, especially in the large island of Cuba, it still tolerated buy whether France has practically abolished the institution in her colonies or still retains it in a mild form I am not informed and have at hand no means of ascertaining. All European writers, even such as were slave holders and advocates of the slavery when they wrote, seem to regard the practice in this country of selling them by process of laws, like their horses or mules, as one of the greatest and most wanton cruelties to which they are subjected. Bryan Edwards, a zealous champion of slavery and the slave trade in his history of the West Indies, vol. 2, book 4, after speaking of certain regulations which had been proposed for the amelioration of slavery, uses the following language, "But these and all other regulations which can be devised for the protection and improvement of this unfortunate class of people, will be of little avail, unless, as a *preliminary measure,* they shall be exempted from the *cruel hardships* to which they are frequently liable of being *sold by creditors,* and made subject in course of administration by executors, to the payment of all debts, both of simple contract and speciality." This he stigmatizes as a *"grievance remorseless and tyrannical in its principles,* and dreadful in *its effects"*—the revival in a country which pretends to Christianity of the odious severity of Roman law, which declared sentient beings to be *inter res*—"a practice injurious to national character and disgraceful to humanity." "A good negro with his wife and young family rising about him, is seized by the sheriff's officer, forcibly separated from his wife and children, dragged to public auction, purchased by a stranger, and perhaps sent to terminate his miserable existence in the mines of Mexico; and all this without any crime or demerit on his part, real or pretended. He is punished because his master is unfortunate." To the above description so vivid and touching, nothing need be added. To read it is enough to make one's blood run cold and yet the horrid scenes so feelingly described are witnessed everywhere everyday, Sunday not excepted by thousands of Christians, without a blush or a shudder, but to *our* shame be it spoken, such scenes of hard hearted cruelty are now witnessed, as we believe, only in this land of boasted freedom, intelligence, and Christian influence. Mr. Stephens, another British writer says, "Of the liability of slaves to be seized and sold separately from the land they cultivated by their master's creditors, for the payment of his debts, it may safely, I believe, be pronounced that a precedent of such cruel injustice is not to be found in any part of the old world." Plantation slaves, not only the Spanish Portugese, but in the French colonies also, are *real estate* and attached to the soil they cultivate, partaking therewith all the restraints upon voluntary alienation to which the possessor of the land is their liable, and they cannot be seized or sold by creditors for satisfaction of the debts of the owner." By the *Code Noir* as already stated, the husband cannot be sold without wife nor the parents without the children—sales made contrary to this regulation, by process of law, under seizure *for debts,* are declared void (see Stroud's *Sketch*, 53).

As the first settlers of Louisiana were chiefly French, they seem to have adopted the common law and the *Code Noir*, substantially in relation to their slaves. It has been already remarked that by the laws of that state slaves are regarded as *real estate- immoveable* property; so that when the owner of a slave is also a *bona fide* land holder, as is almost uniformly the case, the slave cannot be separated from it by process of law. In accordance with this humane—*comparatively* humane regulation, there are, as might be expected some others which deserve our attention—"If, at a public sale of slaves, there happen to be some who are disabled through old age or otherwise, and who have children such slaves shall not be sold but with such of his or her children whom he or she may think proper to go with."

"Every person is expressly prohibited from selling separately from their mother, the children who shall not have attained the full age of ten years." It is refreshing to find even this much humanity amidst such a wide spread, unmitigated and unparalleled scene of injustice and oppression. It is like a little oasis in the arid waste which however small, is reviving and we notice it with pleasure. Some three or four years ago I was told that a law had been recently passed in Georgia, relative to the separation of husband and wife, and of parents and children, similar to the one above noticed in Louisiana, but if such a law has been enacted there, I have not met with it and do not know whether my information was reliable; but the scenes of anguish and distress occasioned by such separations in most of the states are heart rending. I have seen gang after gang driven through the streets of Greensboro, the village where I live, apparently about middle age, or near it, and ten or a dozen in a gang, every one of whom was hand cuffed to a long heavy chain like a log chain which was just the length of their line, carried by them day after day, while the "speculator" and one or two others rode along armed with whips, sticks, and pistols. These men, I was told, had been torn from their wives and children and could not trusted. As one of these gangs was driven by the courthouse one autumn evening, they were singing "Hail Columbia, happy land." The severest irony on this boasted land of freedom that I have ever read or heard. Most of the Spectators felt it keenly and some of them even dropped a tear of pity.

306

Many a parent and many a widow made such *defacto* by the unfeeling avarice of men, have been thus brought down to an untimely grave. Some have contended that owing to their ignorance and degradation their feelings are more of an *animal* kind than those of the whites and consequently that they do not suffer so much from the separations of which we are speaking. Jefferson, in his notes on Virginia, says, "In general their existence appears to participate more of sensation than reflection. To this must be ascribed their disposition to sleep when abstracted from their diversions and unemployed in labor. An *animal* whose body is at rest and who does not reflect must be disposed to sleep of course." To some this may appear a very philosophical explanation but it is not satisfactory. The fact that they have no apprehension of losing what they already possess; their freedom from anxious thought about the future, and their hard toil in the sun from morning till night and from day to day are much better reasons for their sleepiness. As far as we have observed, white men who thus labor can go to sleep with about as much facility as the blacks, and they have about as little reflection.

As already shown there can be no such thing as marriage among them; for the laws by making them personal property and liable to be sold to the highest bidder like any other chattels, as the convenience or interests or necessities of the master require, render any effort or desire on their part to cherish the sacredness of the relation or to maintain its permanence, utterly unavailing. Theirs is no religious ceremony, no obligation taken, nothing done to make the contract binding. The majority of them regard any connection of the kind which they form as a mere temporary cohabitation and, of course, they separate whenever they feel disposed to do so. A man often has a number of children by different women and the same woman has a number of children by different men. In such cases there cannot be the same conjugal and parental attachments which might otherwise be expected. For

307

all this the whites are to blame and must answer for it at a higher tribunal. You talk about their licentiousness and immoralities but in the mane of conscience, reason, and common honesty, how can they be chaste and continent and moral when you trample on and pollute the very fountains of all virtue and morality. Some Christian owners do what they can to prevent the separation of their married slaves; but it amounts to very little for after their death, if not before, they are either sold to pay his debts or seized and carried off by avaricious heirs; If then there are not as many strong attachments of a conjugal and parental kind, nor as many heart rending scenes occasioned by their separations as would otherwise be; it is owing to the abominable laws and usages of the country: but when a couple have got a serious [turn] of mind and have been tolerably well instructed in their Christian and social duties and have fortunately lived long enough in wedlock, or as a husband and wife, to raise a family of children and to mature their mutual affections, their conjugal and parental attachments become very strong. A number of years ago there was a black man in my congregation whose history, in this respect, was sad and painful in the extreme. He was a man of as good natural mind and as good judgment in covenant matters as most the white men in the neighborhood. He could read quite well and always carried his hymnbook to church. A more trusty and reliable servant could not be found in the land and no money could have bought him from his master. I had no doubt of his piety for his very countenance seemed to indicate the Christian serenity of his mind and no white member of the church was more consistent in his life and deportment but I never could prevail on him to join the church. He cheerfully acknowledged his hopes for eternity; but he said that he saw too many inconsistencies in many of the members and did not wish to go where he too might dishonor the cause.

This faithful servant had a most estimable woman for a wife, belonging to the same master, and they raised a remarkably fine family of sons and daughters. He taught them all to read and took great pains in training them to habits of sobriety and virtue; and there was not a family, of white or black, in the congregation who conducted with more decorum and propriety, at home, at church, or anywhere else; but at length the master died, somewhat enthralled, and there had to be a separation. The oldest daughter, a fine looking young woman of her race, about grown, and, if I do not forget, a profession of religion, having recently made a profession, was the first one sold and some time before any of the others. She was bought by a speculator and immediately carried off to the southwest and nobody here ever knew into whose hands she had thus fallen. Soon after probably the next Sabbath at church, I saw her father, when he came, after service, as usual to harness my horse in the buggy for me and he appeared to be in great trouble. On may asking him, in a kind and sympathizing manner—for I felt towards him as a Christian—what was the matter, "O," said he, "my oldest daughter, my first born, was sold off the other day before my eyes, and my heart is *crushed*." Here, with his hands laid across his breast and his hymnbook in one of them, his emotions choked his utterance and the big tears chased each other down his manly cheeks. In some two or three weeks, before he could be sold, he died of a broken heart and so did his wife. Which of them died first I do not recollect, but their separation was a very short one. Their children were then all sold and, if I do not forget, were mostly bought by the merciless speculators and taken off to the cotton or sugar states. I could fill a volume with similar cases hardly less interesting, or less sad in their issue or less reproachable to the Christian name; but one may suffice as a specimen of the whole. In the name of high heaven, "is there no flesh in man's obdurate heart?" How shall such scenes of injustice and cruelty, such sorrow and distress, be enacted almost daily before the eyes of a Christian community and too often by their voluntary doings, without stirring up the compassion of the soul to its lowest depths and without calling forth a united and determined effort to drive this intolerable scourge of humanity from the land? How much longer can we expect that justice will slumber and that the divine forbearance will hold out? Or how much more must yet be added before the measure of our iniquity is full? A man, if permitted to have his wife and children about him can bear a great deal of wrong and oppression; but must sink when bereft of the sympathy and consolation which alone could sustain him under his heaviest burdens and cheer him in his deepest sorrows.

From what has been said it is manifest that our slaves can make little or no improvement and that their intellectual and moral powers can never be developed, because the time, the means, the motives necessary to improvement have been denied them. The dominant race have, moreover, made it a penal offence for the whites to teach them and for them to teach one another. Legislature and slave owners have done everything in their power to keep the slaves in perfect ignorance and in the lowest degradation. The little attempts which have been made in some few places to preach to them occasionally and to teach them a sort of child's catechism *orally*, is only a salve to conscience and little more than a solemn mockery of the whole business. It amounts to almost nothing and never can develop their powers. The whites, instead of doing a magnanimous act by elevating their condition as they ought to have done long ago, have most ignobly determined to keep them in as much ignorance and degradation as possible. For this they are accountable; and, when the illusions of time shall have vanished and when the gratification of avarice will be no longer possible, they many find it a more serious matter than they now suppose. We leave them to answer for the past and for the future, too, if they choose to persist in their inhuman practice; but while we have the cause of truth and justice, of honor and humanity we advocate the claims of Jesus Christ to a service as full, free, and unrestricted from the African race as from the Anglo Saxon race. Both were given him in the covenant of redemption and he has redeemed both by the same price. He designs the happiness of both without partiality and he ought to be honored as much by the one as by the other. It is very convenient for slave owners, especially for such as are serious minded or have a conscience, to talk about the wonderful providence of God in bringing so many of the Africans to this Christian land where they may be converted to the faith of the gospel and, in due time, be sent back to Christianize their benighted countrymen, while they are doing everything in their power to keep them in ignorance and make them subservient to their interests when, under the present laws and the absolute reign of mammon, do you think they will be prepared to become missionaries to their fatherland? And when, do you think you will have made so much money by their labors that you will be willing to let them go? Do be consistent: If you are determined to hold them as long as you can and to make as much out of them or by them as you can, say at once and go on; but if believe, as you pretend, that the Lord's design in permitting them to be brought here was that they might be converted and prepared to carry the gospel back to Africa, repeal your law, forbidding them to be taught, give them the time, means, and motives necessary to improvement and then send them back full handed and well instructed to the land of their fathers.

20. According to the present laws and usages of the land, slaves cannot make that entire surrender of themselves to the Lord which the gospel requires and to which the renewed nature prompts them.

Under this head we shall not trouble the reader with many references; for two or three will be amply sufficient. In Rom 12:1, 2, we read thus: *I beseech you therefore brethren, by the mercies of God, that ye present your bodies a living sacrifice, holy, acceptable unto God, which is your reasonable (or rational) service.* The terms here employed have all as reference to the Jewish sacrifices and this fact ought to be distinctly noticed. In their sacrifices for sin the offerer selected the best of his flock, brought it before the altar and presented it to God as an atonement for his sins. So all believers are required to give themselves up to the Lord, in the spirit of sacrifice, to be as wholly devoted to Him as the whole burnt offering, no part of which was allowed to be reserved or put to any other use; but while the sacrifices required by the law were slain at the altar, the Christian sacrifice or offering of himself must be *living* sacrifice; and as that was to be without blemish, so this must be *holy*, free from such moral defects as would render vice and therefore cause the whole to be rejected with indignation.

Surely no one will undertake to assert that our slaves an thus present their *bodies* a living sacrifice, holy and acceptable unto God, as the free will offering of rational beings and moral agents; for they have no command of their time nor their actions, plans, and pursuits. Their avaricious masters claim their bodies as a living sacrifice to them and then the Lord may have just such service from them as he can get or as they can render him. A servant, in the sense in which we use the term, in which it is given in the lexicons and in which it ought to be taken by everyone who would use language with precision, *can* thus consecrate himself to the Lord and Savior, because he acts voluntarily in what he does; because he receives wages or compensation for his services, of which he can dispose as he pleases; and because, if he has unwittingly engaged in the employment of a man who would require him to violate the Sabbath, or to do anything which is forbidden in the Bible and the doing of which we destroy or disturb his peace of mind, he can leave him and seek employment elsewhere. Servitude in that sense is recognized all through the Bible and is a necessity; nor could there be much progress without it, but on God's plan the term of service is seldom for more than a lifetime and often not half so long; but slaves when required by an ungodly master to violate the Sabbath or to do other things which their consciences condemn, they cannot change masters and they have no redress. The master must be obeyed though God is dishonored and his claims ignored. They have not an hour they can employ specially in the service of their heavenly master and not a dime that they can appropriate to the relief of suffering saints or to the spread of the gospel. What little favors may be shown them by one or a few humane masters here and there is not worth noticing in comparison with the loss of liberty; but we mean that by the laws and the general practice of the country they can do nothing for the Lord who made them and redeemed them, but in their hearts to thank him for the past and trust him for the future. Their masters, from pride or vanity and the love of gain, interpose their sordid claims, regardless of the authority and power of Jesus Christ who bought them with his own blood, and put a stern veto upon the promptings of the renewed nature. It was perhaps thought by many an act of great condescension in the legislatures of South Carolina and one or two other states when they permitted the slaves to profess the Christian religion; but they made no provision for them to enjoy the benefit of Christian ordinances. They might attend the church of their masters or perhaps, some other with his written "permission"; but if they went to hear the unsearchable riches of Christ preached to a lost world, whether one, five, or ten miles, they must toil along on foot when they ought to be resting themselves for the labors of the next week. The Apostle says, *Jesus Christ loved us and gave himself for us that he might redeem us from iniquity and purify unto himself a peculiar people, zealous of good works;* but their peculiarities seem to consist entirely in the hardships of their lot, their wrongs and oppressions; for they have neither time nor opportunity to show themselves zealous of good works. It was predicted that Jesus Christ would proclaim deliverance to the captives, in its unlimited sense, of course, and that he should set the prisoners free; but his professed following rivet the chains of their bondage and drive them to market, like as many cattle, often loaded with fetters of iron. The slavery of this country is manifestly at war with justice, humanity, and the strongest claims of the Christian religion. The claim of their masters on the whole time and strength, together with enactments for keeping them in gross ignorance, render the claims of the gospel in a great measure nugatory and are inconsistent with a Christian profession.

The verse following the one first quoted is as follows: *And be not conformed to this world; but be ye transformed by the renewing of your minds, that ye may prove what is the good and acceptable and perfect will of God* , can have in some respects no application to slaves; for they have neither the time nor the means of becoming conformed to it; but in other respects, they are compelled by the authority of their master to be conformed to it, externally, at least. Not having an hour of time at their disposal nor a dime that they can legally call their own they cannot conform to the world by gay clothing and costly equipage nor by drinking and gambling and attending dancing parties and other fashionable amusements; but, if house servants, they must cook a rich dinner on the Sabbath and if guests are entertained they must go through all the useless parade and ceremony that are common with the gay and fashionable world on such occasions. Whatever may be their peculiar circumstances whether they are subject to religious or ungodly masters, to the good and gentle or *to the forward*—the morose, the infidel or the profane, they cannot comply with the injunction, *Be not conformed to this world* in its spirit and intent, as they might do if their powers were developed and their time and strength were all at their own disposal.

In 1Cor 6:20 the Apostle says, *For ye were bought with a price; therefore glorify god in your body and in your spirit which are God's.* The import of this verse is nearly the same with that of the one which we first quoted from Romans; but both *body and spirit* are here severally and distinctly mentioned

III. *THE REASON* FOR THE DEMAND OR THE PURPOSE FOR WHICH IT IS MADE

and the two include the whole man, so that since Christ redeemed the body as well as the soul and both together constitute but one accountable being he claims the entire services of the whole man, soul, and body.

In Eph 5:20-21, we have an injunction of a very different kind, but one which is quite as inconsistent with slavery. *Giving thanks always for all things unto God the Father in the name of our Lord Jesus Christ submitting yourselves one to another in the fear of God.* Can any Christian slave in these southern states feel like thanking God all the time for such an unjust and degrading bondage as that which he is held and which is with such wanton cruelty entailed upon his unborn and unoffending offspring—a bondage so derogatory to his nature, so destructive of his peace, so incompatible with his improvement, so much at war with the full discharge of his Christian duties and so utterly destitute of hope? We can pray for nothing that is not the subject of promise; but surely no one will say that such abject servitude can be the subject of promise.

No one can be always giving thanks to God for the greatest temporal evil which can befall him and which can be productive of no possible good to him, except by a special act of sovereign grace, as a man is sometimes made to feel shocked at his own wickedness and is thus turned from his iniquities. In itself slavery is evil and only evil continually; and if—the Lord ever does, in any instance, bring good out of it to the slave, it very rarely and by a special act of his sovereign power and goodness as he brought the greatest of all blessings out of the avarice and treachery of Judas. Many slaveholders whose conscience is not altogether easy appear to console themselves with the idea that the Lord will yet bring great good out of this enormous evil and thus go on in their iniquity: So Judas might have consoled himself while engaged in the act of betraying his master; but be it remembered that if the Lord does overrule the selfish, ambitious, and unrighteous agency of those who are actors in the drama, so as to advance his own glory and the cause of truth and righteousness in the earth, that does not cancel their guilt and will not avert the punishment which they deserve. It is preposterous to talk of a slave always thanking God for a condition which positively forbids his intellectual improvement, which wrests from him all the fruits of his labor, which precludes the possibility of his enjoying the ordinary comforts of life, which leaves him no means or power of usefulness and which places him and his unborn posterity beside the beasts of the field; for as the Lord has said that the he is the avenger of all who wrong their fellow men and that he will deliver the poor and needy when cry unto him, he is authorized to pray always and earnestly for deliverance from such cruel oppression.

But the Apostle says, *Submit yourselves one to another in the fear of God.* The language is general and as the church to which he was writing had, no doubt, a number in it who were servants in the world and perhaps some who were slaves, it must have been applicable to all alike; but, although slave here are condescendingly "allowed to profess the Christian religion," would the prejudices of masters suffer them to place themselves so far on an equality with their slaves? And how can slaves, who have no rights or privileges whatever in the church except that of partaking of the elements when the Lord's Supper is administered, in the gallery or in some corner by themselves, be said, in the spirit of the text, to submit themselves to their brethren in the fear of God? *Submitting yourselves to one another* implies equal rights and privileges; but have our slaves equal rights and privileges in the church with the white members? Or would such a thing be tolerated any where in this slave holding country? We do not say that it would be proper; but we say that an institution which makes such an invidious distinction necessary in the church of Christ is wrong.

321 We have no very minute information respecting the regulation of affairs in the church, during the Apostolic age and not a word about the position occupied by either servants or slaves in the household of faith. For anything that appears to the contrary the members all had equal rights and privileges, and there was no distinction between bond and free. The Apostle told all servants to be honest, trusty, and obedient to their masters as he told all others to labor with their own hands and to submit to the existing government of the Roman empire though a most despotic, cruel, and persecuting government. As we have no express information we can affirm nothing respecting the manner in which servants and slaves were regarded as members of the primitive church; but from the fact that the Apostle advised them by all means to prefer freedom, if they could get it and from the endearing way in which he spoke of Onesimus we might infer that they enjoyed all the rights and privileges of other members and that their bondage to heathen masters was regarded in the same light with the persecutions which Christians of every grade had then to endure. But slaves then and now, there and here, could not and cannot possibly make that entire surrender of themselves which the gospel and the promptings of the renewed nature require, and the human laws and institutions which hold them in bondage, ignorance, and degradation are unjust, cruel, and impious.

322 Everything, or nearly everything in the Bible was, in the first instance, addressed to individuals or communities in particular circumstances, but it was intended just as much for us and for the whole world. Hence the command of the Savior to the Jews, *Search the Scriptures; for in them ye think ye have eternal life, and they are they which testify of me,* is as binding upon us and upon all who know anything of the Bible as it was upon them; but slaves cannot obey this command; and they are unable to do it, just because

III. *THE REASON* FOR THE DEMAND OR THE PURPOSE FOR WHICH IT IS MADE

our laws make it a penal offence in any man, white or black, bond or free to teach them the use of letters. Had it not been for these impious enactments, so directly in conflict with the authority of Jesus Christ and so wantonly opposed to all the best interests of humanity, we imagine they would all have been able to read the Bible long ago. This we regard as irrational and wicked in the extreme; for no man in his sober senses can suppose that teaching people their duty will make them worse, whatever may be their relation in life; and if, as slave holders pretend, the Bible sanctions slavery, why not teach them to read the Bible and learn their duty from it themselves? This fact proves, as we think, their insincerity and at least a strong impression on their minds if not a full conviction that the Bible does not justify slavery and tends to indiscriminate and universal freedom.

Either the advocates of slavery do not believe that the Bible sanctions the institution, or they have no confidence in its teachings, or their love of gain is stronger than their convictions of duty; but if mankind are indebted to the Bible for whatever freedom they enjoy, as all Protestant Christians admit, then the Bible is in favor of liberty and against slavery. The Pope of Rome says and has long said that common Christians shall not read the word of god for themselves, the alleged reason for which is that they will misunderstand what they read, but the true reason for such an impious, heaven daring prohibition is that they will then obey God rather than him. Slave holding Christians, like the Pope, forbid a certain class of persons, men and women, many of whom have been brought to the knowledge of their sins and admitted to full membership in the church, to read the Bible, because, if they learned to read that they would want to be free like other people and would not be so profitable as slaves. The Christian communities, of all denominations are to blame for these unchristian laws; for they have sufficient influence to have them altered; but it is to be apprehended that a large portion would even go against any material alteration. If they were not more than a fourth part as numerous and influential as they are, it would be their duty to remonstrate or petition against acts so dishonorable to Christianity and to Protestant freedom.

American Christians who send off their money mostly the earnings of their slaves, by thousands of dollars every year, not only to teach the heathen orally as they do their black population at home, but to teach the science and everything we know ourselves ought to be ashamed of their inconsistency. Many Christians, we know, would be glad to have their servants taught to read; but we speak of the mass of professors and even those who have some better views and feelings than the generality, do not seem to be at all apprized of the great responsibility that is resting upon them. Let them keep their money at home or cease to hold four millions of their fellow beings in all the ignorance and degradation of heathens here at home at the own doors and right in their own houses. Don't say that they can hear preaching every Sunday; for not one half of them can attend the church of the whites without walking six or eight miles, which, in winter season, is too hard, and then, most of the preaching they hear "shouting over their heads." If you will give them only a moderate share of English education and develop their powers a little, the preaching of educated ministers, such as we have generally in this country might be of some advantage to them; but the fact is that they cannot feel confidence in the sincerity of the dominant class and one half of them would rather be visiting or amusing themselves in some way than going to a "white folks meeting."

325 **21. Under the existing laws and in the present state of society slaves cannot have that equality of rights and privileges which is in the New Testament accorded to all true believers.**

It has been frequently remarked that the laws of a country are an unerring index to the intelligence, the sentiments and the moral principles of its people; and this is especially the case in a country like ours where they indirectly make the laws and where they can, at any time, have them repealed or modified, if they find, on reflection, that they are not conformable to truth and equity; If they find that a law is positively injurious in its operations they have it repealed; if they think it is simply not beneficial so many disregard it that it becomes a dead letter; If it accords with their sentiments or feelings and interests they inquire no further into its moral character. Our laws on the subject of slavery are denounced by most other nations and by a pretty large and respectable portion of the people here at home, even in the Southern state, as violative of all those inalienable rights which the Creator has given to all alike and as hostile to the best interests of humanity and the great principles of Christianity, yet the majority think these laws favorable to their interests as slave holders and without troubling themselves with any inquiry in to their Christian or unchristian character. They give them a steady support and act out their spirit in all the business and intercourse of life.

326   The condition of our slaves is very little better in an ecclesiastical than in a civil point of view; for their place in the church is barely recognized and nothing more; but that, in the present state of things they cannot enjoy the rights and privileges to which as believers and members of Christ's spiritual

III. *THE REASON* FOR THE DEMAND OR THE PURPOSE FOR WHICH IT IS MADE

family, they are entitled and consequently cannot serve him as he requires, will appear with more clearness by a little attention to one or two passages.

In Col 3:11 we read thus: *Where, that is in the new creation, there is neither Greek nor Jew, circumcision nor uncircumcision, Barbarian, Scythian, bond nor free; but Christ is all and in all.* From this it appears that the distinction here mentioned are disregarded in the work of grace and should not be made or regarded by the followers of Christ. As they are all the result of depravity- of pride, ambition, avarice, and the love of power, they are wrong and should be abandoned. All classes and conditions, all nations and kindreds and tongues and people were ransomed by the same price and are regenerated by the same spirit. They all compose our family here and are all heirs to the source of glorious and eternal inheritance. You ask me if I would admit slaves to hold offices in the church, to occupy the same seats with their masters and to be in an equality with them in every respect? I answer, no; not as slaves; for I would have no such thing as slavery known in the church. I would have no slave holders in the church for I would have the unchristian institution abolished forthright and then all could stand on the same level.

In 1Cor 12:13 we have a similar statement, but more explicit in regard to the matter under discussion. *For by one Spirit are we all baptized into one body, whether we be Jews or Gentiles, whether we are bond or free; and have been all made to drink into one Spirit.* From this verse and the context it appears that the only differences then found in the membership and the only differences which should be no recognized are those which consist in mental endowments by nature and in the gifts of the Spirit, fitting them for the duties which they had respectively to perform. The diversified and important gifts mentioned in vv. 1–11 seem to have been bestowed upon all, without any distinction between bond and free; for by one Spirit they had all been baptized into one body. The *bond* here mentioned or alluded to, were either servants or slaves, probably the latter belonging to heathen masters whom the Apostle advised, in another place, to their liberty if they could, but if not, to submit with equanimity and cheerfulness to the orderings of Providence. In his Epistles to the different churches this Apostle intimates no distinction of rank or grade among the members, but addresses all, including those, of course, who were servants or slaves to men of the world; with equal respect and affection. They were all children of the same father, they were all brethren in Christ and had all been baptized by the same Spirit into one body, or into one great and rejoicing and ever increasing household of faith and love.

In Gal 3:26–29 he says: *For ye are all, circumcised and uncircumcised, Jews and Greeks bond and free, the children of God by faith; for as many of* you as have been baptized into Christ, have put on Christ. *There is neither Jew nor Greek, there is neither bond nor free; there is neither male nor female; but ye are all one in Christ Jesus. And if ye be Christ's then are ye Abraham's seed and heirs according to the promise.* Does this language intimate any such distinctions as are man made between the slaves and the white population? Either slavery is wrong, radically and grievously wrong or the language of the Apostles is very strange. The slaves in our country have no such standing and recognition in the church now and the "bond" had the days of the Apostles. Slave members no have no voice in anything that is done; their names stand on the sessional records by themselves; they are barely permitted to partake of the elements, in some by corner of the church, by the themselves, when the Lord's supper is administered; and even old men and women who are worn out in their master's service and ought to be favored at least on the Sabbath, if they got to the communion at all or to preaching at anytime, have to walk five or six miles and home again in the same day. How much better are they treated than the horses or mules which they work? In the whole their treatment and in the feelings with which they are regarded, even in the church and on it most sacred festivals, we see nothing of the liberal, kind, and generous spirit manifested towards themthat was universal in the primitive church.

329   When the Apostle says, Rom 15:7, *Wherefore receive ye one another, as Christ also received us to the glory of God the Father,* he must have included those whom the world held in bondage and stigmatized and treated with contempt as a servile class; and we can't understand him as meaning anything else than that they should receive others and that others should receive them, or that they should all receive one another with the freedom and kindness with which Christ had received every one of them alike to the glory of God the Father. If the Apostle included those who were employed as servants by a portion of the Christian community and those who were held as slaves by the heathen population there must have been a very different state of things in the church then from anything we witness in it at the present day; for it was not sufficient that they should receive one another with freedom and with kindly feelings, but it should be done in such a way as to convince each other that it was done with such feelings. There must be a *reciprocity* of such feelings and of all those kindly acts by which they are naturally expressed. There should be the utmost sincerity and nothing in the deportment and tones of voice; in the expressions of countenance and style of address and manner of intercourse which would make anyone feel that the was disparaged, or that any invidious distinctions were made, on account of poverty, family descent, comeliness of

III. *THE REASON* FOR THE DEMAND OR THE PURPOSE FOR WHICH IT IS MADE

person, want of education or any other circumstance which make such a wide difference in men of the world.

Our slaves who are members in our churches are not only denied a voice in all ecclesiastical matters, but they hardly ever have any benefit from pastoral visitation. The watchful care of the pastor and elders is seldom if ever extended to them. If they do anything grossly inconsistent with their profession they are often disciplined as severely as the white members, perhaps more so; but nothing is done to prevent them from going astray and bringing a reproach on the cause. As slaves they are severely punished by the laws of the land; but nothing is done to make them acquainted with the laws and often they do not know that they are violating any law until they are brought to trial and to the whipping post. It is made a penal offence in anyone, white or black, bond or free to teach them the use of letters, or to *give* them a Bible, pamphlet, or book of any description yet they are punished with more severity for every little petty offence than those who have every opportunity of knowing their duty. In the church so far as my observation has gone, no sort of pains are taken to instruct them in the doctrines and duties of religion. Often they are neglected entirely and not even brought to account for their aberrations. It is surely as gross inconsistency, in the office bearers of the church to receive them within the fold and then pay no more attention to them than if they belonged to the world.

When sick, I have known only one or two instances in which they asked that the pastor of the church might be sent for, or in which they expressed a desire to see him. With some exceptions, their funerals are without religious services; and I do not now recollect an instance in which a pastor made it his business to visit a bereaved family of colored people under his charge, whenever a case of the kind occurred, as he would visit a white family in similar circumstances to pray with them and administer to them the consolations of religion. There is evidently a want of that sympathy and mutual confidence which ought to exist among all the members of a church, that *family* affection and reciprocal kindness which is always characteristic of true Christians where not permitted by untoward circumstance. The oppressed never can have confidence in their oppressors; and so long as the blacks are designedly kept in gross ignorance and they are kept toiling all their life to foster the pride or pamper the vices or increase the wealth of their masters and find this cruel bondage entailed upon their unborn generations, they never will- perhaps we might say, they never *can* feel confidence in the sincerity and good intentions of those who are thus lording it over them. It is not in human nature; and to be satisfied of this we have only to consult our own feelings, or what would be our feelings in an exchange of circumstances. Perhaps few men in the country have had a

332 better opportunity of knowing or have taken more pains to find out what is the real state of their minds in regard to their condition and I am sure that there are very few white preachers, especially if they are slave holders of whose Christian honesty and goodwill they have no suspicions. There is not a race of people in the world who are more accessible to the gospel when it is brought to them under favorable circumstances and if a *slave* who was at all qualified for the work, or if he could only read and had good natural sense, were allowed to make appointments over the country, they would flock to hear him in crowds, though they had to walk eight or ten miles in the dead of winter, and would drink in his preaching as the thirsty traveler drinks of a cooling stream in a burning desert. I have seen this repeatedly tried and speak from observation. It is so, just because there is then a full tide of sympathy between the speaker and the hearers. He feels for them and his feeling catches and spreads among them like fire in a prairie. No speaker, white or black, can do his hearers much good if there is no sympathy between them; or if he is not in earnest and if they have not full confidence in his sincerity and his good intentions. There are no doubt, many exceptions among them but we speak of them in general and we are willing that any should test the truth of the above statements by a thorough and impartial inquiry.

333 Slaves, in this country, an effectually prevented from rendering a full obedience to the requirements of the gospel and they are just as effectually prevented from enjoying the full extent of its privileges. The Apostle Peter enjoins it upon all believers alike, To grow in grace and in the *knowledge of the Lord and Savior Jesus Christ;* but as slaves are not allowed to read or to be taught, nor to have any printed matter, not even a Bible or a religious tract, and have the whole of their time occupied in hard labor, how are they to grow in knowledge? Their owners know that it is impracticable and are determined that they shall not be able to obey the command; but for their inability, of this kind, to comply with every requirement in the Bible, these owners must be responsible.

The Apostle says of the church members at Rome among them whom there must have been many servants, and slaves too, that they were *filled with all knowledge and able also to admonish one another* (Rom 15:14). This ought to be true of all the members belonging to every church or believing community; and it was true, we presume, of the servants and slaves who were the members of the church in Rome, for they were mostly educated and became the teachers of their masters children. Of course, many of them were more intelligent than half of the three members; but the foolish pride and cupidity of their masters have doomed our slaves to ignorance, toil, and

334 drudgery. They are debarred both by their ignorance and by the prejudices of the white from taking their share in the mutual admonitions spoken of in

the passage quoted and they are debarred by the laws from even becoming qualified to occupy a position even of common respectability, usefulness, and Christian enjoyment in the church.

We deprecate anything like fanaticism or sophistry; for we plead the cause of truth and justice, of humanity and religion. We advocate the sacred and inalienable rights of four millions of human beings with their rapidly increasing generations and we contend for the claims of God to their services in opposition to the tyrannical and cruel usurpations of a dominant race. We stand up as we have ever done for the poor and afflicted, the oppressed and the downtrodden against their civilized and nominally Christian oppressors. There are a great many sincere Christians, we feel well assured, in the southern states; but they are not a majority and they have not made the laws and many of them are so much under the influence of interest that they overlook the enormity of the institution. The heart of man, every man, is deceitful above all things and desperately wicked; and he that trusts his own heart, though he be indeed and in truth, a Christian, Solomon says, is a fool. The slavery of the south is now the most absolute despotism in the world and should not be any longer tolerated in a Christian and protestant country.

Of slavery as it existed in Egypt, Greece and Rome, and we may add in Ancient Germany, where slave were not prohibited from learning, but were pretty generally educated, where they were permitted to possess and enjoy property of their own to a considerable amount, where their masters could set them free whenever they chose and where they could by a very simple process obtain their own freedom, we have already said enough and need not occupy further space with the repetition. In Poland, though inhabited by a rude and warlike people, and before the recent alleviations of their lot were made, slaves were not only allowed to hold property, but were endowed with it by their lords or masters. In the Spanish and Portugese colonies, the money and effects which a slave acquires by his labor at times set apart for his own use, or by other honest means are *legally* his won and could not be seized by his master as in the these southern states though slavery was introduced there by the British government and subject to the same general laws which prevailed in the other colonies, the harsh features of the institution were never known. In Massachussettes, so early as 1641, the following law was made. "It is ordered by this court and the authority there of, that there shall never be any bond slavery, villainage or captivity among us, unless it be lawful captives taken in just war, such as willingly sell themselves or are sold to us, and such shall have *the liberties and Christian usage which the law of God established in Israel concerning such persons doth require.*" That law was not a dead letter we learn from an opinion delivered in a certain case, by

Chief Justice Parsons. "Slavery," says he, "was introduced into this country soon after its first settlement. The slave was the property of his master, subject to his orders, and to reasonable correction for misbehavior. If the master was guilty of a cruel or unreasonable castigation of his slave, he was liable to be punished *for the breach of peace*" and, I believe the slave was allowed to demand sureties of the peace against a violent and barbarous master under these regulations, the treatment of slaves was in general mild and humane, and they suffered hardships not greater than hired servants.

In Connecticut, Judge Reeve, speaking of slavery there, uses the following language, "The law as heretofore practiced in this state, respecting slaves, must now be uninteresting. I will however, lest the slavery which prevailed in this should be forgotten, mention some things which show that slavery here was very far from being of the absolute, rigid kind. The master had not control over the life of his slave. If he killed him, he was liable to the same punishment as if he killed a freeman. The master was as liable to be sued by the slave in an action for beating, or wounding, or for immoderate chastisement as he would be if he thus treated an apprentice. A slave was capable of holding property, in character of devisee or legatee. If the master should take away such property, his slave would be entitled to an action against him by his *prochin ami* (next friend). From the whole, we see that slaves had the same right of life and property as apprentices; and that the difference betwixt them was this: an apprentice is servant for time and the slave is a servant for life" (see Stroud's *Sketch*).

Everyone can now see the difference between the slavery that has been in other countries and in these southern states and how much worse it is here than anywhere else in the known world. We speak, not of the kindness which individual masters may show their slaves, but of the laws; for when the best of masters die or become enthralled the slaves are subject to the operation of law. Besides the majority of masters are not indulgent and care for nothing except their gains or their pleasures but if all were as humane and as kind in their treatment of their slaves as some are it would be nothing compared with the injustice and hardships of the bondage itself. What, after all, can the most kind hearted and sympathizing masters do for their slaves? Nothing more than afford some *mitigation* of the wretchedness which they would have to endure under other masters; but the great calamity remains. All the comforts bestowed upon their slaves by the most humane and indulgent masters, while they continue to hold them as slaves and not only as slaves, but as property, is like the partial relief afforded by the physician to his suffering patient when he can't remove the *cause* of his sufferings, or a few kind acts done a despot on the throne to his subjects, while the despotic government remains and his successor may be a Nero for cruelty.

III. *THE REASON* FOR THE DEMAND OR THE PURPOSE FOR WHICH IT IS MADE

From what has been hitherto said, the attentive reader will perceive that the slavery question should be considered and must be discussed too, before long, with more general honesty and thoroughness than it has hitherto been discussed, in three aspects: The causeless, unprovoked, and immense wrong which is done to the slaves; the injury which slavery does to the welfare of society at large, or to the cause of truth and freedom in the world; and the claims of God to their services, which can be neither denied, evaded, nor resisted are really alarming.

That slavery is an unprovoked, unjustifiable, and grievous wrong to the slaves no candid and fair minded man can deny. The advocates of slavery say that their condition here, with all its hardships and grievances is better than it was in Africa, for there they were sunk in the grossest ignorance and superstition and tyrannized over by petty kings or chieftains; but here they are brought under the ameliorating and elevating influence of Christianity and civilization. This may be true to some extent, but it is no justification of slavery for the gospel, with its institutions would have elevated their condition in Africa and it was our duty to give it to them as we have been endeavoring to send it to all other heathen nations without enslaving them. Besides their extreme degradation on the coast of Africa is owing to that abominable traffic, the slave trade, which is instituted and upheld by slavery.

The horrors of the "middle passage" have long been proverbial as the *chef d su eve* of human cruelty, not surpassed even by the Inquisition, and have certainly not been half equaled by that diabolical institution in number of its victims. Why such untold sufferings and such an immense sacrifice of human life to get a few slaves? Why generously and magnanimously send them the gospel at once? It is said that white people can not live in Africa and consequently cannot go there to Christianize them. Be it so; but there were other ways of giving them the blessing which we enjoy without going there to live among them and with very little expense or trouble. We have brought young men from modern Greece, from China, and from other countries to be educated and sent back to their benighted countrymen with the *unsearchable riches of Christ* and with all the inestimable blessings of science and civilization. Why not do the same with Africa? But the great plea urged by the advocates of slavery, especially by ministers of the gospel who are slave holders is the *Providence* has permitted them to be brought here that they might be Christianized and sent back to their "fatherland" as missionaries of the cross and as pioneers in the great work of civilization. Very well; but when are you going to engage in the godlike enterprise of returning them to the law which God gave to their fathers? Or even of preparing them for such a mission?

340   Has it not hitherto been, and is it not still, the great object of all slaveholders to get as much labor out of them as they can and thus add as much as possible to their gains?

Do we hear a word said, even by the most zealous of our southern advocates of foreign missions, about sending them back to the unnumbered millions there who are calling for the "white man's religion"? Or has any man yet suggested an immediate and efficient course of preparation for the work? We have no sort of confidence in the sincerity of those who are always talking but do nothing. As time is short and life is uncertain, a man who would accomplish anything for the welfare of mankind must go to work at once and work in earnest. Look at the unchristian, unjust, and odious enactments on your statute books, making them *property*, mere chattels, like your horses or any other stock and subjecting them to all the consequences of such a condition, disregarding the most sacred and endearing relations of life, punishing them with severity for their violation of laws of which they are kept in ignorance, except as they may hear of them by chance and dooming them and their posterity to a life long drudgery for the sole benefit of others—then break off your sins by righteousness, undo what is wrong in your legislation as you do on all other subjects, and take some prompt and efficient course to compensate them, in whatever way and by whatever means you can, for the injustice and the cruelties inflicted on them during a series of generations.

341   The enslavement and degradation of four millions of Africans in this country where they do not properly belong, with their increasing generations, is a great injury to the cause of religion and of civilization in the world; for, if the other races cannot live in that country, they are the only people in Christendom that can spread the Christian religion and all the blessings of science, and the arts, literature, and civilization over that vast continent. If therefore, from avarice and the love of power in sordid consideration of worldly gains and profits, we refuse to give them up and send the exiles home, in the fullness of *the blessings of the gospel of Christ,* we show to the whole world, Christian and heathen, that all our boasted zeal for liberty and human progress is mere pretence, or that, like Rosseau, who talked like a saint but lived like a reprobate, we see and approve what is right, but condemn and yet pursue what is wrong. Since the Apostles, after having suffered the loss of all things for Christ went forth, amidst scoffs and persecutions, with the blessing of salvation to a *world lying in wickedness* and sinking down by millions every year to perdition no people have ever had such a glorious opportunity of doing a work of beneficence, at which suffering humanity from the rising to the setting of

342   the sun and through all future ages will rejoice; but be it remembered that

III. *THE REASON* FOR THE DEMAND OR THE PURPOSE FOR WHICH IT IS MADE   151

if we ignominiously refuse, the scorn the civilized world, or at least of the Protestant world will rest upon us and the cry of untold millions whom we now have it in our power to elevate and bless and save will call down the wrath of heaven upon us and upon our posterity, perhaps to the third and the fourth generation. Must a hundred and fifty millions in Africa be suffered to remain in the region and [show] of death and pass into eternity unblessed and unsaved because a few slave holders here are so avaricious and sordid that they will not make the sacrifice which justice, honor, and humanity require? So much injustice and cruelty cannot be practiced, from generation to generation, on four millions of human beings, *in this land which the Lord hath blessed,* without spreading a tide of deadly influence over the benighted, debased, and oppressed nations of the earth. We are a city set upon a hill which cannot be hid! We have been entrusted with the richest bounties of heaven for the hitherto unvisited, unreclaimed and perishing nations of the world, who must be saved by the people of these slaveholding states or be unblessed and die in their sins.

But as humanity, in its widest sense is the cause of God, his claim is paramount to all others and his demand will in due times, be enforced, whether men will comply or refuse and regardless of the factitious rights. Slaveholders say that, as their slaves are their property, the will not give them up unless they are payed for them and they have got a large portion of non slaveholders to adopt the maxim that "the rights of property must be respected." As already stated, since the slaves have been made property by the constitutions and laws of the country, however unjustly, I have always been in favor of allowing them a reasonable compensation, a wholesale and moderate price; but they are not disposed to take less than they could have got, by retail, three or four years ago and previous to that time. If I do not forget, the northern people proposed many years ago and perhaps more than once, that the general government should buy them at a wholesale price and they would cheerfully pay their part, which would be three fourths of the whole; but the south rather contemptuously rejected the proposal. Whether, by that rejection they have forfeited all right to expect any compensation whatever the Lord must now decide; for since they have appealed to arms there is no other tribunal where a decision can be had. The Lord may grant them temporary success and give them some respite, as he did to Pharaoh a number of tiems, that he may prove them or make it manifest whether they will obey or refuse; but that he will urge his demand until we let them go, I think there is little doubt. The Lord made no compensation to Pharaoh nor the Greeks and Romans, and he may not make any to slave owners here. If the pretended right by which they are held is, de facto, a usurpation, strict justice will not allow them any remuneration and, for aught any man can now tell, they many be an entire loss; for as all men are by nature equally free, no man can acquire a right over another except by his consent. All the world over "involuntary servitude, unless inflicted by society as the punishment of crime, is a usurpation of power." and it would be strange indeed if society could not at any time and in whatever way it deemed but with or without remuneration to individuals, undo is won wrong. The British parliament allowed the slave owners in their West India colonies a wholesale price; but so far as I am aware the north America states that have heretofore emancipated their slaves said nothing about compensation to the owners. In most of those states however, emancipation was a gradual process and the owners had the service of those slaves which were then born or over a certain age during life.

22. Progress of Emancipation.

Many of our readers would probably like to know when and how the North American states which are now free become such and what is the prospect, humanly speaking of further emancipation. Most of the northern states gae freedom to their slaves or passes acts of emancipation, during the revolutionary war and the others followed soon after. It is well known that Great Britain introduced negro slavery into all her American colonies by means of the African slave trade, that most iniquitous, but gainful traffic and that it was protected by the colonial laws until the Declaration of Independence and for some years afterwards. The Commonwealth of Pennsylvania led the way by a noble act of her legislature for its abolition, passed March 1st 1780, and entitled *An act for the gradual abolition of slavery.* The preamble to the act is one of the finest productions of that great era in American history and is worthy of being transmitted beside the Declaration of Independence. It is fraught with so much truth, clothed in such elegance of language and portrays so vividly the sorrows of slavery, and presents the arguments for its abolition with so much force and clearness, that we deem no apology necessary for transcribing its entirety; for we are sure that every man of liberal sentiments and human feelings will be gratified by its perusal.

"When we contemplate our abhorrence of that condition to which the arms of tyranny of Great Britain were exerted to reduce us, when we look back on the variety of dangers to which we have been exposed, and how miraculously our wants in many instances have been supplied, and our deliverance wrought, when even hope and human fortitude have unequal to the conflict, we are unavoidably led to a serious and grateful sense of the manifold blessings which we have undeservedly received from the hand of that Being from whom every good and perfect gift cometh. Impressed with these ideas we conceive that it is our duty, and we rejoice that it is in our power to give a portion of that freedom to others which hath been extended to us, and release them from that state of thralldom to which we ourselves were tyrannically doomed and from which we have now every prospect of being delivered. It is not for us to inquire why in the creation of mankind, the inhabitants of the several parts of the earth were distinguished by a difference in features or complexion. It is sufficient to know that all are the work of an Almighty hand. We find in the distribution of the human species that the most fertile as well as the most barren parts of the earth are inhabited by men of complexions different from ours and from each other; from whence we may reasonably as well as religiously infer, that He, who placed them in their various situations hath extended equally his care and protection to all, and that it becometh not us to counteract his mercies. We esteem it a particular blessing granted to us, that we are enabled this day to add one more step to universal civilization, by removing, as much as possible, the sorrows of those who have lived in undeserved bondage, and from which, by the assumed authority of the kings of Great Britain, no effectual relief could be obtained. Weaned by a long course of experience from those narrow prejudices and particularities we had imbibed we find our hearts enlarged with kindness and benevolence towards men of all conditions and nations; and we conceive ourselves at this particular period extraordinarily called upon, by the blessings which we have received to manifest the sincerity of our profession, and to give a substantial proof of our gratitude. And whereas the condition of those persons who have heretofore been denominated negro and mulatto slaves, has been attended with circumstances which not only deprived them of the common blessings that they were by nature entitled to, but has cast them into the deepest afflictions by an unnatural separation and sale of husband and wife from each other and from their children, an injury, the greatness of which can only be conceived by supposing that we were in the same unhappy case. In justice, therefore, to persons so unhappily circumstanced, and who, having no prospect before them whereon they may rest their sorrows and their hopes, have no reasonable inducement to render their services to society, which they otherwise might do and also in grateful commemoration of our own happy deliverance from that state of unconditional submission to which we were doomed by the tyranny of Britain, Be it enacted, That all persons as well as negroes and mulattos as others, who shall be born within this state from and after the passing of this act, shall not be deemed and considered servants for life or slaves; and that all servitude for life or slavery of children in consequence of the slavery of their mothers, in the case of all children born within this state from and after the passing of this act as aforesaid, shall be and hereby is, utterly taken away, *extinguished and forever abolished.*"

All who might be born after the date of the act should be born free; but all who were then living and held as slaves might be retained as slaves for life, provided the owner would cause such slave, whether male or female, to be registered at a place particularly designated, the registry to contain the name, age and sex of the slave, and the name, surname, occupation or profession of the master and the name of the county wherein the master resided on or before the 1st day of Nov., but if such an entry was not duly made all such slaves should be free.

349   It is altogether unnecessary to go into any further details as to the provisions of this act; but we ought to add in justice to that noble state that it was sufficiently guarded against any infringement of the rights of slave holders in other states; for it was deemed in consistent with the duty, which as a member of the Union, Pennsylvania owed to her sister states, to interfere with what in those states were regarded as *rights of property* and, on this account, it was expressly provided, that nothing contained in the act, "should give protection to any slave, absconding from his or her owner so residing in any other state and coming into this state" (see Stroud's *Sketch*). The Act, which was, on the whole well drawn up, was liberal in its provisions and, as far as possible, guarded the interests of all concerned. Delegates in Congress from the other American states, foreign ministers and consuls, and persons passing through or sojourning in the state and not becoming resident therein, were allowed to retain their slaves unmolested, provided they did not reside in the state more than six months; but if a man went with his slaves from any one of the other American states or from any other part of the world to become a citizen of that state or if he resided there more than six months, his slaves must be subject to the same laws with those of the native citizens.

350   So early as June 7th 1712, the colonial legislature of Pennsylvania passed an act entitled "An act to prevent the importation of negroes and Indians into this province" which it is said, though it never became a law, may still be found on record in the office of the Secretary of the Commonwealth of Harrisburg; but on the 20th of Feb. 1713, Queen Anne put her veto on it and it was consequently repealed. Had the act become a law, the example would probably have been followed, in a short time by all the other colonies, and the whole territory since included within the limits of the United States, when we got our independence, would have been free soil; but as soon as it became pretty certain that the thirteen colonies would be successful in their struggle for freedom. Pennsylvania, in her sovereign capacity as a state, disregarding the authority and the power of Great Britain, passed the act of

March 1st 1780, the preamble to which with its fine Anglosaxon style and its human and patriotic sentiments we have given above. It is certainly right that we should give honor to whom honor is due; and, although southern politicians have reviled that good old state for harboring their runaway "niggers" her name will be honored and her wise, firm, and magnanimous leadership in the cause of universal freedom will be praised by coming generations until generations shall cease on earth.

On the 2nd day of March 1780, one day after the famous abolition act of Pennsylvania, Massachusetts adopted her state constitution, the first article in the Declaration of rights prefixed to which was as follows: "All men are born free and equal, and have certain certain natural, essential, and unalienable rights; among which may be reckoned the right of enjoying and defending their lives and liberties; that of acquiring, possessing and protecting property; in fine, that of seeking and obtaining their safety and happiness." The abolition of slavery in Massachusetts was not therefore effected by a specific act of the legislature, but resulted as a consequence from this primary article in their *bill of rights* prefixed to the constitution. Some attempts were made perhaps to dispute the constitutional validity of the article, but without success. The enslavement of one part of the human family by another was admitted by all sober-minded men and women to be unjust and cruel; yet there were some, mere money lovers, who were so much under the power of avarice that they cared little for the welfare of others; but it was soon determined by a solemn adjudication of the courts that *slavery was by this means forever abolished* in Massachusetts and was thenceforth admitted to be so in practice.

351

Other states soon followed with less energy and decision in the cause of universal freedom. In Connecticut, at a special meeting of the legislature held in January 1784, for the purpose of revising and amending he code of laws, that body agreed to incorporate this section: "No negro or mulatto child, that shall after the first day of March, 1784, be born within this state, shall be held in servitude longer than until they arrive to the age of twenty five years; notwithstanding the mother or parents of such child was held in servitude at the time of its birth, but such child, at the age aforesaid, shall be free."

352

About the same time Rhode Island enacted the following law on the same subject: "No person born within this state on or after the first day of March A.D.1784, shall be deemed or considered a servant for life or a slave, and all servitude for life or slavery of children to born as aforesaid, in consequence of the condition of their mothers, be and the same is hereby taken away, extinguished, and forever abolished." The *importation* of slaves into Connecticut having been prohibited in October 1774, and in

Rhode Island about the same time, the entire abolition of slavery in these states, as well as in Pennsylvania was in due time accomplished and they have long since been free from the shame and reproach which yet rest upon the southern states.

In a very few years Vermont followed in the march of freedom and took a noble stand beside Massachusetts and Rhode Island. On the 4th of July 1793, her state constitution was adopted and in it was contained the following Article: "That all men are born equally free and independent, and have certain natural, inherent and unalienable rights, amongst which are the enjoying and defending life and liberty; acquiring, possessing and protecting property; and pursuing and obtaining happiness and safety; therefore no male from over sea, ought to beholden by law to serve any person as a servant, slave, or apprentice, after he arrives at the age of twenty one years, nor female in like manner, after she arrives to the age of eighteen years, unless they are bound by their own consent after they arrive at such age, or bound by law, for the payment of debts, damages, fines, costs or the like." The constitution is dated, July 4th 1793; and, I presume that must be considered as the date of its adoption.

On the 29th day of March 1799 an act of gradual emancipation was passed by the legislative of New York, which provides, "That all children born of slaves after the 4th of July 1799, should be held by the owner of the mother of the same only until they should respectively attain the age of twenty eight years, if males and if females, until the age of twenty five years." On the 8th of April 1801, another act was passed which did not differ materially from the first one; but on the 31st of March 1817, the legislature passed an act which finally put an end to the domination of slaveholders. The 4th section of this Act says that "Every child born of a slave within the state after the fourth day of July, in the year of our Lord one thousand seven hundred and ninety nine, shall be free, but shall remain the servant of the owner of his or her master, and the executors, administrators or assigns of such owner, in the same manner as if such child had been bound to service, by the overseers of the poor, and shall continue in such service, if a male until the age of twenty eight years, and if a female, until the age of twenty five years; and every child born of a slave within this state, after the passing of this act, shall remain a servant as aforesaid, until the age of twenty one years, and no longer."

And by the thirty second section of the same act it was declared that "Every negro, mulatto or mustee within this state born before the fourth of July, 1799, should from and after the fourth of July, 1827, *be free.*" Since that date a vestige of slavery within its borders and in a career of unparalleled prosperity and happiness. Not the clanking of a chain, nor a crack

III. *THE REASON* FOR THE DEMAND OR THE PURPOSE FOR WHICH IT IS MADE

of the master's whip, nor a groan of anguish for the loss of near and dear relatives sold under the hammer has been learned or will be heard, we hope till time is no more.

New Hampshire inserted in her constitution, which was finally ratified on the eighth day of February, 1792, a provision of similar import and in nearly the same words with that of Massachusetts by which slavery was at once abolished and from that time she became a free state.

The state of New Jersey did not act with quite as much promptness and decision as Pennsylvania or New England, but eventually took her position beside them on the firm and broad basis of universal freedom. After several ineffectual efforts by the friends of abolition, an act was finally passed by the legislature on the 14th day of February, 1804, entitled, "An act for the gradual abolition of slavery," which did not differ materially from that of Rhode Island, except that white male children born of slaves, after the 4th of July, 1804, might be retained *as servants* by the owners of their mothers, until the age of twenty five years only, and female children, in like manner, until the age of twenty one years only. Of course a little remnant of slavery might be found in that state longer than in most of the northern states; but it is now some years since the last vestige of such despotism and cruelty disappeared entirely from her borders.

The states of Ohio; Indiana and Illinois, to which may be now added, Michigan, Iowa, and Minnesota, become states from their organization, by the "ordinance for the government of the territory of the United States northwest of the river Ohio" which was ratified by Congress July 13th, 1787. Our readers are aware we presume, that the above named territory, was ceded to the United States by Massachusetts, Connecticut, New York and Virginia; and the articles by which the cession was made, were [styled], "Articles of compact between the original states and the people and states within the said territory, *forever to remain unalterable, unless by common consent* the sixth of which articles provides that "There shall be neither slavery nor involuntary servitude in said territory, otherwise than in the punishment of crimes whereof the party shall have been duly convicted."

To prevent any disputes afterwards and to give a practical proof at the outset of their belief in the great principle of universal freedom the people of Ohio embodied in their constitution the following provision: "Nor shall any indenture of any negro or mulatto hereafter made and executed out of this state or, if made *in* the state, where the term of service exceeds one year, be of the least validity except those given in the case of apprentices." Illinois inserted in her constitution a provision of the same import and very nearly in the same words. So did Indiana with the omission of the clause, "or if made in the state," and hence these north western states have been, from their first organization, as free and their people have been as much opposed to slavery as those of New England.

During the revolutionary war and for many years after, the present state of Maine was a part of Massachusetts and, consequently, as a sovereign state never had the curse of slavery fixed upon it; but her constitution which was adopted October 1829ᵗʰ 1819 by a convention chosen for the purpose and ratified by Congress on the 2ⁿᵈ of March 1821, contains the same noble and Christian declaration of unalienable rights which gave immediate and unconditional freedom to all slaves within the territorial limits of the parent state.

From the above facts it appears that in some of the northern states abolition was *gradual* and in others it was *immediate*. By *gradual* abolition is meant the extinction of slavery by confining it to the existing generation or depriving it of its hereditary character. Such were the abolition acts of Pennsylvania, Connecticut, Rhode Island, New Jersey and the first two abolition acts passed by the legislature of New York. By *immediate* abolition is meant an act which gives freedom to all that are in bondage at the time of its adoption, as will as to their posterity, whether their actual emancipation follows immediately on the passing of the act or not until they attain a certain age.

Such were the constitutional provisions of Massachusetts, New Hampshire, and Vermont. The last abolition act of New York and the sixth article of the ordinance of congress of 1787, for the government of the territories northwest of the Ohio river.

In those states where abolition was gradual, especially in Pennsylvania, there was, for a time, as might have been expected, some inconsistencies in the legislative enactments or rather in their judicial proceedings. Prejudice, the rickety offspring of ignorance and depravity, pride and the lust of gain kept up in some degree, the invidious distinctions which formerly existed and, in some instances perhaps caused decisions to be made from the Bench which were not in harmony with their legislative enactments; but, in the course of a few years, experience and reflection adjusted the balance and set all right.

In the Constitutions of the slaveholding states, perhaps without an exception, are contained general principles of free government which, if carried out, would banish slavery from the domain; but, strangely enough, it is asserted that they are designed to protect the rights of *freemen* alone. Thus the state of Delaware, though a slave holding state, has, in its constitution the following declaration of universal and equal rights: "Through Divine goodness, *all* men have, by nature, the rights of worshipping and serving their Creator according to the dictates of their consciences; *of enjoying and defending life and liberty; of acquiring and protecting reputation and*

III. *THE REASON* FOR THE DEMAND OR THE PURPOSE FOR WHICH IT IS MADE

property; and in general of attaining objects suitable to their condition without injury by one to another."

We could not ask a more ample charter of liberty, and yet, unaccountable as it may seem, they have added no explicit qualification.

These facts or others of a similar kind and the inferences and reflections which they suggest might be extended to a much greater length, but our limits will not admit of further detail and perhaps enough has been said for the satisfaction of the reader. In writing the above account of the rise and progress of the abolition movement in the United States, I have had before me the first Constitutions of all "the old Thirteen"; but most of the legislative enactments and several other facts of a historical kind, I have taken, some of them in substance and others verbatim or nearly so, though not always with quotation marks from Stroud's *Sketch*. The work was prepared by the author, who was then a young lawyer of Eastern Pennsylvania, with great care and accuracy; and I take pleasure in recommending it to all who have a desire for that kind of information. Mr. Stroud had been a college mate of the present writer and as then regarded as a young man of much promise—if the legislation of a country, especially of a free country like ours is always an index to the sentiments of the people, it is certain that their prosperity and welfare depend, to a very great extent, on the wise and equitable and generous laws which they adopt.

Consistency, duty, and interest all required that slavery should be immediately abolished throughout the nation when we got our independence, for then the love of liberty was strong; the community at large felt grateful, in some measure, to the infinite source of all blessing and happiness for the independence which he had granted them; and serious people, of every grade, had, at that time strong doubts about the lawfulness of slavery; but they deferred a compliance with the dictates of conscience and humanity to a more convenient season and avarice or the desire of gain soon overcame their sense of justice. By the power of habit, the strong inducements of worldly interest and the influence of aspiring and ambitious politicians, the sentiments of the southern people have, within half a generation, undergone an almost entire change. Familiarity with injustice, cruelty or evil of any kind transforms it into a virtue or blinds us to its odious nature and its ruinous tendency. Hence the people of this country denounce the despotisms of the old world in no measured terms, while they are every day practicing a more absolute despotism here at home, and yet will be ready to shoot you or knock you down if you insinuate that they are stern and merciless tyrants.

For half a century no actual or legislative progress has been made in the cause of abolition; but the subject has been discussed with increasing earnestness and acrimony, by men of all professions and all grades of ability.

The free states have been increasing rapidly in population and making unparalleled progress in wealth and in the arts and sciences, while the slave states have been almost stationary. Thus matters have been working on to a crisis; and a disinterested spectator did not need a prophets' ken to foresee the calamity that is now upon us. While slave holders have been taking ground in regard to the lawfulness of slavery which their revolutionary forefathers would have spurned and, like Pharaoh, have been doing everything in their power to make their property in human beings secure, by putting it on the same ground with their horses and mules and by pressing them down to the lowest possible degree of ignorance and degradation. The way has been preparing for a radical and general change in that species of property. Whether this change is to be produced gradually or in the course of a few months by the present war, is a matter of little importance but the Lord has not permitted a dissection of our glorious union which was cemented with the blood of our forefather and ought to have been regarded as sacred and perpetual, nor left us to become involved in such a bloody and destructive war to maintain and extend the "peculiar institution." This we know is the design of southern politicians and slave holders, especially in the cotton states; but the Lord's thoughts are not as their thoughts nor his ways as their ways; and the whole history of nations and of individuals proves that they are oftener than otherwise accomplishing purposes which had not entered into their minds. No enlightened and reflecting slaveholder now believes that the Lord will permit four millions of human beings with their increasing generations to be always kept in such ignorance and degradation,—at least a number of slave holders in this region have of late so expressed themselves to me; and the impression on the minds of the community at large seems to be increasing that an entire abolition of slavery will be the final issue of these secession movements. Such an expectation is evident by increasing among the blacks themselves and although the issue of many conflicts may have been in favor of these south, the general aspect and progress of affairs appears now to indicate a different result; but however this may be, the Lord is, in many ways, urging his claim to the African race, as well as to all other unchristianized races, and is enforcing his demand for their release from bondage. In the plagues inflicted upon Pharaoh no one was so decisive as to make him willing to give up his "property" and let the oppressed go free until the tenth and last; it has been so in other instances without number and it may be so in this unnatural war.

We can have no access to the archives of heaven, no can we penetrate far into the future; but whatever may be the proximate results of the present conflict, much will be gained for the cause of abolition. Many thousands of slaves have already been rescued from bondage and set free by the northern armies and the states lying along Mason and Dixon's line, Delaware, Maryland, Kentucky and Missouri, which, as I have always understood, determined, by a majority of about two thirds, to remain in the Union, it is generally expected will soon become free states. This will be a great curtailment of the slave territory and as the free soil extends south the progress of abolition will still keep ahead of it. This may *possibly* be the plan which the Lord designs to have carried out in our case; for, according to our imperfect views, it would not be best for them to turn them loose and let them remain here among the whites, where they would have no certain means of support; and their transportation to Africa or any where else would require considerable time. Often within the last thirty years when urging upon slaveholders the duty of emancipating their slaves, the question has been asked, what would we do with them? Would you have them remain here among us? Or where would you send them? and when told that they should be sent back to Africa their "father land," where a refuge has been provided for them, the reply has generally been that their transportation could never be effected or not in a hundred years and that the attempt would be useless; but this was only the suggestion of avarice and could not be meant as a serious objection. "Where there's a will there's a way"; and people can always accomplish anything in the world that they ought to do. The money expended and the property already destroyed in this war would pay for every "nigger" in the south, at a moderate wholesale price, and then pay for his transportation to the shores of Africa. The Lord has manifestly a great work for them to do on that widely extended continent. He claims them and he will have them. His demand for the emancipation of the slaves in these southern states is just as positive and as explicit as it was for the release of the Israelites from their bondage in Egypt; and Pharaoh, if Moses had been allowed to reason with him might have made substantially every plea for retaining them which is now made by slave holders in this country; but God did not ask him for any reasons and he did not allow his accredited agents to parley with him. When he takes from us anything, friends or property to which he has given a claim so long as it will be best for us, he does not sk for our consent, and when he takes that to which has given us no sort of right, he does it without making any compensation and in a way which manifests his displeasure.

In a former section the following questions were asked and answered so far as was deemed necessary: What is property? How do we get the right to hold anything as property and what is the extent of that right? It was there remarked in substance that we can have no valid right to hold anything as property without an express grant from the Creator; that in all governmental transactions human and divine, what is not expressly granted is reserved; and that if he has given any one portion of the human family a right to enslave another portion they are bound to produce the record. If such an express grant is to found within the lids of the Bible we have not been able to find it, and if they have any other accredited revelation from heaven it ought to be produced. In a matter so deeply affecting the welfare and happiness of millions, born and unborn, we must have a "thus saith the Lord," or regard those who keep their fellow beings toiling for them, like brute beasts, in ignorance and degradation as impiously daring to usurp the prerogative of the Almighty. That he has permitted them, in his Providence to do this is no justification; for he has permitted all the cruelties and abominations that have been done in the world; but that did not lessen the guilt nor avert the doom of those concerned. When the measure of iniquity is full judgment will come, suddenly and in full measure: It will not tarry.

366 We profess to be a Christian and protestant people; and, as such, we avowedly take the Bible for the rule of our faith and practice in everything; but I have long believed that there were radical errors in our political constitutions and in our legislative enactments, especially on the subject of property which would sooner or later bring ruin on the country, because fundamental principles were not understood or not duly regarded and consequently, because a latitude was thus given to the insatiable desire of men for wealth and power which must eventually prove dangerous to the peace of society. The limits which the Creator has fixed on this subject are just those which are best for us; and this has been amply demonstrated in the experience of mankind. That "God is seen in history" by every serious and attentive observer there can be no question; for all history, so far as it is true, is just a record of what he has done in his government of the world. It is full of the errors and delusions, the sufferings and sorrows of men; and, if it is the part of wisdom to learn from the experience of those who have gone before us on the path way of life it behooves us to contemplate the ruin or the calamities sent upon those who were pursuing the same iniquitous course on which we have ventured. The principles of God's moral government are immutable and those principles he will maintain forever.

367 The Lord has given us a full and complete revelation of all we need to know; and it has been stereotyped and made so plain that he who *runs made read*. The perceptive and prohibitory code is so minute and explicit that there is nothing more to be desired; and the *minatory* communications, or the warnings and threatenings are amply sufficient to guard us against all aberrations and dangers. Of course, no special messenger, furnished with credentials well attested and clothed with power adequate to every purpose of his mission will be now commissioned to tell us what God would have us do or what judgments he will send on the disobedient. We must consult the record and render a prompt obedience, or be speedily and unexpectedly

III. *THE REASON* FOR THE DEMAND OR THE PURPOSE FOR WHICH IT IS MADE

overtaken by the ministers of his displeasure. Every refusal of Pharaoh to comply with demand made upon him for the surrender of his bondsmen, was immediately followed by a visitation of the divine wrath.

When Nebuchadnezzar was walking in his palace and congratulating himself on the extent of his dominions and the stability of his throne, the commandment came for his banishment and he was forthwith driven from the society of men. While Beltashezzar was reveling with his lords and concubines and not dreaming of any danger the handwriting appeared on the wall of the palace where he was and while Daniel was interpreting the mysterious words, the enemy was entering the gates of his capital. Alexander was permitted to conquer the world and then was suddenly taken off by an excess of indulgence in his sensual pleasures. Caesar attained the zenith of human power, the mastery of the great Roman empire and was soon after assassinated by those who had formerly been his friends. Bonaparte went on conquering and to conquer until he was likely to bring all the nations of Europe into one consolidated empire; but, most unexpectedly to him, his army was overwhelmed by the snows of the north and he was soon after driven into perpetual exile. Here is a man who is every year adding thousands of thousands he had already accumulated; but the flames break out in his dwelling or store or manufacturing establishment and the fruits of his hard and anxious toils for many years are all gone. There was a man yesterday in the vigor of life and the bloom of health; but today he is gone and for him the mourners go about the streets, when men are crying, *Peace and safety then sudden destruction cometh upon them and they cannot escape.* Warnings of every kind have been given and if we will not heed them nor observe the signs of the times, but continue in the willful or thoughtless neglect of the instructions which have been given us, we must take the consequences.

With such facts before us, we ought to be, in all the transactions of this life, very certain that we are right and, most assuredly, there is nothing about which we ought to more solicitous to know that our course is justifiable than that of slavery; for there is no other subject of human legislation in which great principles, essential to human progress and individual happiness are so grossly and so recklessly violated. Before we doom four millions of our fellow beings, with their unborn and unoffending offspring, to a condition of ignorance, degradation, and laborious servitude we must have an express grant from the creator to do so, or be chargeable before high heaven with wholesale injustice and oppression. It is strange that a Christian and a protestant people, who profess to value liberty above every other consideration on earth and to regard it as indispensable to the welfare of mankind should exhibit to the world such a legalized and systematized course of downright despotism. The plea is a pitiful one that they are better off here

370 than in their own country and that their bondage is therefore a blessing to them. Are those who talk thus sincere and consistent with themselves? When not thinking of slavery they tell you that liberty is above all *price* and that slavery is worse than death; but when their *property in human beings is concerned* they "eat their own words" in making the plea. If the condition of the negroes is worse anywhere in Africa than in a state of bondage here, it is only on the coast and it made worse there by slavery, or by the slave trade, which is about the same thing, but does any man know that God so regards it? Or that their condition in that arid and sunburnt land is not, apart from the degradation and wretchedness produced by that abominable traffic, the slave trade, the very one in which he would have them to be like all other heathen nations, that we might have the honor and the gratification of sending them the gospel with all its humanizing and saving influences? We regard it as indisputable that He who assigned to all the other nations of the earth their inheritance designed Africa for the black race; and it is presumption in us or any other nation to interfere with his arrangements. The advocates of slavery, when pressed on this subject, commonly say that we are not to blame for the introduction of slavery into this country and that may be so; but we are to blame for *keeping* it in the country; for if England did wrong in bringing them over and forcing them upon the colonies, that is no reason why we should continue this wrong. England has long since abolished slavery in her other colonies and so ought we to have done in our own land, which is otherwise, so free and so prosperous.

371 With a small but increasing number of exceptions, all slaveholders, not thinking of or caring for any higher law than that of the land, insist upon it that as they have bought their slaves with their money, or raised them like other stock on the farm, they are their property and they will not let tem go without an equivalent. So Pharaoh determined and we know the consequences. He contended with the Almighty and was overcome. If God reigns and governs the world in righteousness, our interest must not be suffered to violate great moral and fundamental principles or sore calamities if not utter ruin will certainly ensue. It will be far better for the owners to lose the price of them, if that be necessary, than to incur the displeasure of Jehovah. While the Israelites were honestly and strictly obedient to all his commands, even those who seemed to militate against their success in the world, such as that which required them to let their land lie uncultivated every seventh year, the one which required them to pay a tenth, or as many say, a fifth of their income to the support of religion, they were the most prosperous people on the face of the earth; but when they disobeyed his commands and yielded to the suggestions of avarice, when they cultivated their land every year, oppressed their servants by keeping them in bondage beyond the seventh

III. *THE REASON* FOR THE DEMAND OR THE PURPOSE FOR WHICH IT IS MADE

year and withheld their offerings from the altar and from the treasury of the Lord, they were visited by the locust and caterpillar, by war, famine, and pestilence; their enemies overcome them on every side and ruled them with a tyrant until they confessed their sins, repented of their folly and returned to their obedience. It is as true now as it was in the days of Solomon, king of Israel, that the *blessing of the Lord maketh rich and he addeth no sorrow with it.* Without his favor and benediction we cannot prosper; but he can and, if we make the sacrifice willingly and for the glory of his name, he will increase our stores of every thing desirable to an extent that would more than compensate the country and their owners too of the loss of the slaves. The question of loss or gain, however, ought never to be discussed in such a case; for even if slavery were right and the Lord required the sacrifice, as he now demands their unconditional surrender for the Christianization of Africa, we ought not to reluctate or parley one moment; but if slavery is unjust, oppressive and cruel as the whole protestant world, except a portion of the people in their southern states, say it is, then the owners can have no rightful claim for indemnity. If the governments which made them property will or can make them any compensation, very well; but if the Lord, in His Providence should order it otherwise, he could not be charged with injustice and if he should demand an additional sacrifice no man would have any right to complain.

That slavery will be abolished in this country and before very long, we think there is little room to doubt; but precisely when and in what way, is yet among the secret purposes of infinite wisdom and goodness. A judicious commander in the field of conflict keeps his plans and contemplated movements a profound secret, because if they were made public the enemy would guard against them; or his own men, not liking the hardships and perils to which they would be exposed, might rebel or abscond; and if the Lord were to make all the operations of his Providence known beforehand, though all the combinations that could be formed against him could not disappoint him in his designs, it would assuredly be attended with unhappy consequences to all concerned. It is *possible* that the present war may result immediately in the entire emancipation of all who are now held in bondage; but, judging from the relative strength of the contending parties and from the progress hitherto made, the stronger probability is that it may require half a generation or more. With that, however, as it depends on a higher power, we have nothing to do and should be concerned only to know and be enabled to discharge our duty. Although a terrible calamity is now upon us and still heavier judgments seem to threaten us, the uplifted scourge may, through the divine mercy be stayed by repentance and a speedy return to the earnest and free discharge of our duty.

374   The first thing that ought to be done and done with promptness and a ready mind is to repeal all the unjust, unchristian, and oppressive acts which now disgrace our statute books; such as, that which perpetuates their bondage by subjecting the offspring to the condition of the mother; that which makes them mere *chattels,* to be bought and sold like cattle in the market regardless of the natural attachments and relationships of life; that which forbids them to be taught the use of letters; that which deprives humane masters of the privilege and the gratification of emancipating their slaves, except at such expence and under such responsibilities as amount to a positive prohibition and that which forbids them to be liberated for meritorious services, no matter how numerous and important, except at such an age and by a process so expensive and difficult that it is a little more than a mockery. This would soon prepare them for a return to Africa with all the inestimable blessings of Christianity and civilization; and it would be simply complying with the obvious demands of justice and humanity, reason and religion. We speak directly and mainly to those who profess to be Christians; and we would appeal to their conscience, their love of Christ, and their acknowledged obligations to bring all nations into the fold of the great Shepherd and to do good unto all men as they have opportunity.

375   In addition to all this, every possible encouragement ought be given them to cultivate their minds, to become more thoroughly acquainted with the arts of civilized life and to form a moral and religious character which would make them respectable in society. They should be regularly married, as nature and the Bible require and they should be taught to regard the relations as sacred and as bindings for life. At the proper age they should have some advantages of the common school system which is supported as much by their labor as by that of the whites, and in whatever way might be deemed most expedient. The children and youth should be taken into Sunday Schools established expressly for them, where they would be greatly assisted in learning to read and where their minds, in the formative period of life, would be brought more under the influence of gospel truth. Those of them whom the proper authorities in the respective churches or denominations to which they belong might judge to be duly qualified for the work should be allowed to preach, at least to their own color and we see no serious evil that could possibly arise from this course; for, in view of all the past and present and future circumstances, the judicatories which had the licensing power would even more on their guard against licensing any who were not found to be intelligent, pious, and discreet than they would be or have been

376   generally in licensing those of their own color. The credit and success of the denomination would then be more at stake than heretofore and that would necessarily produce more care and circumspection. As they are to be free

III. *THE REASON* FOR THE DEMAND OR THE PURPOSE FOR WHICH IT IS MADE

and must be free and will be free before very long, reason and humanity, conscience, and religion require that some such course should be taken to give them the speediest and best preparation that can be given, under all the circumstances, for such a change in their condition. It is, moreover, something like what ought to be done for them whether the day of their emancipation is at hand or not; for, as their intellectual and moral improvement it would be just giving them advantages similar though still inferior to those which are afforded to all of the heathen people by the missionaries of the gospel. In this the latter half of the nineteenth century and when the nations of the old world are bursting the fetters of despotism in which they had been so long held, it cannot be that four millions of human beings in this land of boasted freedom and of protestant Christianity can be kept much longer in such a condition of ignorance and degradation. Jesus Christ came *to preach liberty to the captive and the opening of the prison to them that are bound* and he will deliver his people who are so unjustly and so cruelly held in bondage here, either by the power of his grace on their hearts of their owners or by such judgments as will make them learn righteousness.

The palaver which we so often hear from slave holders about the mild and humane treatment of their slaves is nothing to the purpose, for it amounts to very little and the truth, so far as there is any in it, proceeds from self interest. Few of them are now left to go entirely naked or to perish with hunger and they are not very often whipped until they die, under the lash which was formerly the case in hundreds and probably in thousands of instances. Men have learned that it is for their interest not to starve them beyond the endurance of mature or to overwork them until they sink under their tasks, as they have learned that it is not for their interest to starve or overstrain their horses or working beasts of any kind. In some states laws have been made limiting the time of labor; but as negro testimony can't be taken against white persons such laws are nugatory. In South Carolina, by an Act passed in 1840, which I presume is still in force, they may be kept at hard labor for *fifteen* hours out of the twenty four and every day in the year except Sundays. In Louisiana, by an Act passed in 1866, they are allowed a specified time for breakfast and dinner; but excepting this time, they may be kept at hard labor, so far as appears to the contrary, during the whole twenty four hours, or as long as the master pleases. In the island of Jamaica, while slavery existed there, many holidays were accorded by law to the slaves and on the other days they could not be compelled to labor more than ten hours in the twenty four. In the penitentiaries of Maryland, Virginia, and Georgia, as well as in those of Pennsylvania and New Jersey, where the *punishment* was designed to consist chiefly in hard labor, *convicted felons* are required to labor only eight hours during a part of the year, nine hours during another part and not more than ten hours in the twenty four during the long days in summer; but in South Carolina they may be kept hard at work during *fifteen* hours in the twenty four, half as much more as *convicted felons*; while in most of the slave states, where no such acts have been past it depends on the will of the master. Do you call that mild and human treatment? As to provisions, the legislature of Louisiana passed an Act, July 7th 1806, requiring every owner of slaves to give each of them one barrel of Indian corn per month or its equivalent in rice, beans, or other grain, and a pint of salt, but no meat nor anything else. The corn, we suppose, they might take to mill and the pay the toll of grinding, or beat it into hominy when the ought to be asleep, or parch and eat it like the hogs. In North Carolina the allowance was still less; for by a law passed in 1753, every master was required to give each of his slaves *one quart* of corn per day, but no meat nor anything else; and they were punished severely for even catching *fish* in certain streams! The corn alone they might prepare and eat in any way they could, but with that they must be contented or suffer the consequences; for they dare not complain. And that was kind and humane treatment?

379   So far as has come under my notice, the legislature of Louisiana is the only one which has attempted to specify the kind and quantity of clothing which would be deemed sufficient and that is certainly a very scanty allowance. In Martin's Digest, as quoted by Stroud, we find the following: The slaves who shall not have from their owners a lot of ground to cultivate on their own account, shall be entitled to receive from said owner, *one* linen shirt and pantaloons for the summer, and linen shirt and woolen great coat and pantaloons for the winter. If the slave was allowed to cultivate a lot for himself, though only a quarter of an acre, he must, of course, find his own clothing. Then he was allowed only *one* linen shirt and one pair of linen pantaloons, for the vernal to the autumnal equinox, which he must wear without washing until they were worn out, or go naked while they were in the wash, and if they did not last him six months, he must do without any until the next suit came. Nothing is said about the women; but a similar provision was probably made for them. As the other states have not, by any legislative enactment, specified the kind and amount of clothing which would be necessary, it must depend upon their masters whether they are made comfortable in this respect, or left to go in all kinds of weather, with a few old tatters or dirty rags hanging about them which are insufficient to conceal their nakedness, much less to keep them warm. These laws, where they exist, respecting food, clothing and oppressive labor are, moreover,

380   never put in force. Negro testimony can't be taken; a slave cannot make complaint against his master before any tribunal of justice nor summon witnesses, and when there is not white testimony enough at hand, the owner is

allowed to clear himself, as in Louisiana by an *"expurgatory oath."* All this is mild and humane treatment!! In some sections when the number of slaves is comparatively small and where Christianity has a more general influence than in others, they may be better cared for; but such Christian and humane masters are not more than two thirds of the entire slave holding population and their general treatment must be judged of by the laws.

Slaves are much more severely punished, in all the slaveholding states than white persons, for the same or similar offences. The number of *capital* offences is much greater in their case than in that of the white, and many acts, for which the laws inflict no punishment whatever on a white man or only a small fine, are punished there with great severity. Stroud enumerates 38 crimes or acts for which, by the laws of Mississippi, slaves are punished by *death;* but for which white men are subject only to a moderate fine or a short imprisonment. In Tennessee the number of *capital* felonies with which slaves may be chargeable are reduced to five, viz.: *Murder, arson, burglary, rape, and robbery.* In Missouri there is only a slight variation; but while a slave must suffer death for anyone of these crimes only a *part* of them are regarded as capital offences when committed by white persons.

The same author referred to above says that in Virginia there are *seventy one* crimes punishable with death if committed by slaves while the worst of them, if committed by white men are punished only by imprisonment in the penitentiary. It was once enacted by the legislature of Maryland that, "if any negro or other slave, shall be convicted by confession or verdict of a jury of any political treason or murder or willful burning of dwelling houses, it shall and may be lawful for the justices before whom such conviction shall be, to give judgment against such negro or other slave, *To have the right hand cut off, to be hanged in the usual manner, the head severed from the body, the body divided into four quarters, and the head and the quarters set up in the most public places of the county where such fact was committed."* Whether this cruel act has been repealed or changed in its character, I am not informed; but if not repealed, we imagine, it has become a dead letter. In North Carolina, though the crimes for which slaves may be executed are not so definitively settled as in some other states, a slave who runs away and hides in the swamps , if he resists or attempts to escape when pursued, may be outlawed, and anyone who can may shoot him, or knock him in the head with a bludgeon or kill him in whatever way he finds most convenient; but we need not go into any further details for what has been said furnishes sufficient proof of their mild and humane treatment!

Every white man is, to a considerable extent the master of every slave; for no slave is allowed to strike any white man not even in his own defense. No matter how worthless, unprincipled and insulting the white man may be, he shall for the *first* offence, according to the laws in most of the states, be subject to such punishment as the justices may appoint, which is generally *whipping* on the bare back, and *death* for the second offense. In some states, if not all, when a slave is found off his master's premises without a written permission *any person* may apprehend him and, without judge or jury, give him twenty lashes on his bark back. In some of the states the intervention of a magistrate is required; but, we believe, in very few. In one or two states, if a slave shall be found off his master's premises without some white person in company and shall refuse to submit to an examination of *any white person*, such white person may seize and correct him on the spot, and if he assault and strike such white person he may be lawfully *killed*. In Virginia, Mississippi, Missouri, and in some other states if a slave comes on the plantation of any person without a written permission from his master, employer, or overseer, the owner of the plantation may give him ten lashes for every such offence. In some of the southwestern states, if *any person* shall see more than seven men slaves without some white person with them, traveling or assembled together in any high road, such person may apprehend them and give them twenty lashes apiece. If a slave or Indian shall *take away or let loose a boat* or canoe from the place where the owner fastened it, shall for the first offense receive thirty nine lashes on his bare back, and for the second offense, *forfeit and have cut off from his head one ear*. No slave is allowed to carry a gun, or powder, or shot, or a club or any other weapon whatsoever, offensive or defensive, under a penalty, in some states, of thirty nine lashes to be inflicted by a justice of the peace, and, in other states, of twenty lashes to be inflicted by nearest constable, without the intervention of a magistrate, for every offense. In most of the states a slave is not allowed to have *any article* of property for sale, without a written permission from his master, particularly specifying the same and authorizing its sale by the slave, under a penalty of ten lashes to be given by order of the Captain of the patrollers, or, if taken before a magistrate, thirty nine lashes may be given. If a slave is found at an *unlawful* assembly, and such assemblies are numerous here as they are under all despotic governments, the captain of the patrollers may give him ten lashes, and if the offender is taken before a magistrate, thirty nine lashes may be ordered. If a slave in going from his master's plantation leaves the usual and most accustomed road, the owner, of the land on which he is found may give him forty lashes. If he travels by night without a pass, the penalty is forty lashes; or if he is found in another person's negro quarter or kitchen; and if such a vagrant slave is by chance found in the company of another, the one in whose company he is found must have twenty lashes. Such was and, I believe, is still the law in this state. According to the Revised Code of N. Carolina, as we have seen, a slave may be *outlawed* and then killed by anyone who pleases, for merely running away and lurking in the swamps, a most barbarous law which ought to be abolished in other states where it once existed, or rather, it is a burning shame that such a barbarous law was ever made. If a slave hunts in the woods, even on his master's plantation, he is subject to a penalty of thirty nine lashes. In some states, if a slave entice, or endeavor to entice another slave to run away, or aid him with provisions he incurs the penalty of death; and if a slave aid and abed the slave who is endeavoring to entice another slave to run away, he too must suffer *death*. In South Carolina and Georgia, if a slave conceal or entertain a runaway slave, he is liable to any amount of corporeal punishment, not extending to life or limb; and, in Maryland, for harboring the runaway only *one hour*, to thirty nine lashes. If a slave is found on *horseback* in Louisiana, without a written permission from his master, he incurs twenty five lashes; in Mississippi, for *keeping a dog*: twenty five lashes for *killing a deer*, though by the command of his master or overseer, unless he can produce their *written* permission he must have *twenty lashes;* and, by an Act of Maryland, in 1757, if a slave *rambles, rides or goes abroad in the night, or rides horses in the daytime without leave,* he may be whipped *cropt,* or *branded on the cheek with the letter R,* or otherwise punished, not extending to life or so as to render him unfit for labor. In this state, Maryland, if a slave who is half starved at home, beat the Patuxent river, for the purpose of catching fish; and if he place a *siene* across a certain creek, which are named, a justice of the peace may order thirty nine lashes to be given him. In 1824, the legislature of Mississippi attempted to revise and to condense into one all its acts relating to runaway slaves, which is too long to be copied here; but we may remark that it is one of great cruelty. The legislature of N. Carolina, after enacting that the willful murder of a slave should receive the same punishment as if he had killed a free man say *"Provided always, this act shall not extend to the person killing a slave outlawed by virtue of an Act of Assembly of the state, or to any slave in the act of resistance to his lawful owner or master, or to any slave dying under moderate correction."* In Georgia, it is, I believe, a constitutional law that "Any person who shall maliciously dismember or deprive a slave of life, shall suffer such punishment as would be inflicted in case the like offence had been committed on a free white person, and on the like proof, except less *such death should happen by accident in giving such slave moderate correction."*

If the constitution of one state, Georgia, and the legislative enactments of the at least two other states, N. Carolina and Tennessee, regard that as *moderate connection,* which may result in the death of the slave, or while enduring when he may expire under the lash, I can not conceive what they would regard as *immoderate* correction. Such laws are an outrage on humanity and an ever lasting reproach to a protestant people but all these *croppings* and cruel whippings, not for any violations of the moral law, for such offenses are seldom punished in slaves; but for their violations of positive laws, little petty offenses, for a large proportion of which a white man would be subject to no punishment whatever, are deemed a *mild and humane treatment* for Africans who are chargeable with the "atrocious crime" of having a dark skin. They must not be taught the use of letters and nothing is done to make them acquainted with laws to which they are answerable. No one is required to give them the necessary information and of course nobody will take the trouble consequently they often do things which subject them to heavy punishment without being aware that they are violating any precept and the first information they get in regard to the law is by thirty nine or twenty lashes on the bare back. All is included in their mild and humane treatment; but in all reason and conscience, law missionaries ought to be sent among them to read the law to them and give them "oral instruction."

387   When on trial for capital offences, slaves have not the rights of humanity accorded to them as whites men have when tried for the same offences. In South Carolina and Louisiana they are denied the right of trial by a jury of any description and are not allowed even to have counsel; but are tried by what is styled "the justices and freeholders court," which is composed of two justices of the peace and any number of freeholders, not less than three nor more than five who shall hear the accusation and defense such as the poor ignorant slaves can make then examine witnesses such of course as they choose to cite and determine the matter before them in the most *summary and expeditious* manner. This is the law in South Carolina and was adopted, in 1806, by the legislature of Louisiana, without any other alteration than that a judge of the court if present may act instead of the two magistrates. Any one who will reflect a moment can see what little chance that slave has, in many cases at least, when arraignment before such a tribunal to get justice done him for, although many magistrates in all the states are upright and trustworthy men, others, we know, are profane, drunken heartless wretches, who neither fear God nor regard man, or if they were not so when appointed, they become so afterward. The slave cannot summon witnesses nor manage his own cause and the life of a slave is little valued by slaveholders generally unless they are strongly under the influence of Christian principle.

388   In Virginia, slaves are denied the right of trial by jury; but they have two little advantages which they do not have in the states just mentioned: they are allowed the benefit of counsel, and the decision of the justices must be unanimous. Trial by jury has always been regarded as the *palladium* of

liberty and is, in fact, the only guarantee we have for the due administration of justice; but here this security is denied to the slave. In most of the other states perhaps in all of them, slaves can be condemned only by the verdict of a jury; but that jury is composed entirely of slave holders and a slave who had, accidentally or designedly, killed a white man, though allowed the benefit of counsel, could have very little hope of a fair trial. Even in the case of white men, a jury does not always give an impartial verdict; for, although they are acting under the solemnity of an oath and are passing sentence on a fellow citizen, they are often influenced by the excitement of the community and many an innocent man has been thus condemned to death. Now consider the prejudices of the white man against the negro, the contempt with which the latter is treated and the little value put upon his life and happiness compared with that of a white man and judge of the wrong to which he is liable; but all this is "mild and humane treatment" for human beings, made of the same flesh and blood with ourselves; redeemed by the same sacrifice, regenerated by the same grace and entitled to the same inheritance of everlasting glory and blessedness—because they are of a different color.

In all wrong doing which can't be justified and the love of gain is too strong to give up the practice, people smooth things over as much as possible; and for some years the advocates of slavery have been using a kind of hokeyed expression which sounds very prettily and is quite convenient. It is that slavery is a *domestic* institution, a very beneficent arrangement and that nobody in Yankydom, in Europe, or anywhere else in the "round world" has a right to meddle with it. So the heathen tell your missionaries that hey have their religion which suits them and nobody has a right to interfere with their institutions; but you do not allow your missionaries to be put off in that way. Their commission from the Head of the Church requires them to preach the gospel to all men whether they will hear or whether they will forbear, and to pull down the strongholds of sin and Satan. In the law of Moses it was enjoined upon every Israelite *not to suffer sin upon his neighbor; but in any wise to reprove him;* and it is the *duty* of all who think slavery wrong to make every reasonable effort in their power for its abolition. While the people of the north, in their endeavors to accomplish the emancipation of our slaves, confined themselves to reason and Bible authority, no prohibition ought to have been laid upon them; for it is by the collision of earnest minds that truth is brought to light and truth is or ought to be the great object of pursuit and inquiry with all human beings. Important error ruins those who are under its influence but a knowledge of the truth saves those that have it from calamity here and from perdition hereafter. We should listen to the reproofs of those who think we are wrong and attend to the admonitions even of our enemies; for we hear more truth from them than from our friends.

Yes, but you must let our domestic institution alone—not at all; no more than any other institutions that are wrong, for whatever hinders the progress of the gospel and of civilization must be assaulted by the friends of truth and of human weal until it gives way; but what sort of a domestic and beneficent institution is that which ignores and tramples on all the natural relations of life and all the strongest and tenderest affections of the human heart? The sacredness of the domestic relations and the endearments of home and kindred are no more regarded in them than if they were dumb brutes. Some Christians think they do what they can to prevent the separation of husband and wife, parents and children; but as soon as they are gone if not before it, the laws take their course and they are bought and sold under the hammer as circumstances seem to require and without pity or remorse. People have been accustomed to see whole families, affectionate and happy families—as happy as their condition of servitude would allow, sold off separately, at our courthouse doors, and other places until they have ceased to feel either remorse or compassion. All the satisfaction a poor slave has in this world is in his wife and children and when they are torn from him, his last hope expires and his wretchedness is complete. Hundreds and thousands, thus ruthlessly torn asunder by the stern mandates of law or by the gripping hand of avarice, have died of broken hearts and no monument, or novel or tale of romance has told the sad story; but their record is on high and the day of recompense and of retribution too will come.

But why talk about *domestic institutions* and *mild and humane treatment*? It is a mockery of human wretchedness and satisfies no man of sense who is not under the dominion of avarice or hardened by familiarity with suffering. Is not slavery itself, at least such slavery as we have in these southern states, the most absolute despotism, the lowest degradation and the most unmitigated cruelty to which human beings can be subjected? Preachers and Christian slaveholders sometimes talk about doing their *duty* to their slaves; but it is all a sham; for no master can possibly do his duty to them while he holds them in bondage; and many slave owners have frankly confessed that to me. The only way in which any slave holder on earth can do his *duty* to his slaves is to give them their freedom, with such compensation as he can make them for their services or for the wrong he had done them, and the sooner he does it the better it will be for him and for them and for the cause of truth and freedom and justice and of suffering humanity in the world.

The Lord did not authorize Moses and Aaron to charge Pharaoh with his cruelty to the Israelites nor to urge upon him the necessity of a mild and humane treatment, but positively and absolutely *to demand their release*. *Let them go* was reiterated to him with the annunciation of every plague from first to last and as nothing more was required nothing less would exempt him from the terrible inflictions of God's displeasure. This is his demand now upon all slave holders in this country and nothing else will exempt us from the penalty of his disobedience. After every plague he gave Pharaoh a little respite and so he may do with southern slave holders, every one of whom is as responsible in this matter as if he were monarch of the land. Don't be afraid that half the world will go naked if you do not raise cotton for them by slave labor; for if the slaves were all taken away tomorrow there would soon be more cotton raised here *per annum* than has been raised heretofore. Besides, large portions of the earth elsewhere are well adapted to cotton and mankind could in a little time, be supplied from them if the states on the Gulf of Mexico were all sunk in the ocean; and you may therefore let your charity be first extended to your ignorant, oppressed, and degraded slaves. If your horses had capacity and could get the knowledge you have they would be of no use; but it would then be your duty to let them go free. You have been *brutifying* your slaves in order to make them serviceable; but as they have the capacity and lack only the means and the opportunity to acquire all that you could teach them; you have no right to retain them; for the demand of God, expressly is upon you, *Let my people go that they may serve me*.

23. The influence which the abolition slavery in these southern states would probably have upon the African slave trade, upon slavery in other parts of the world and upon the future destiny of the whole African race.

That slavery and the slave trade are parts of the same system; that they originated in and as maintained by the same principle, the inordinate love of riches; and that they must stand or fall together, can hardly admit of a doubt. No respectable or plausible reason has ever been assigned for the slave trade except the love of money and without contradiction, that alone has maintained slavery in our country to the present time. The burden of all, or nearly all the speeches made by southern members in congress for the last ten years has been the *profit* of slave labor in the cotton states and it is the reason assigned by every slave holder from Mason and Dixon's line to the Gulf, when you are not troubling his *conscience* on the subject. The slave trade and slavery stand, therefore, to each other very much in the same relation in which distilling and retailing spirits, in larger or smaller quantities, stand to each other, so that if you could put down either the other would go down of course. True, there are now slaves enough in this country to keep up the institution by their increase and, if some change is not made, they will in a little time, more than supply the "home market"; but slave holders here are as intent on buying and selling, or making gain of them in some way, as the slaver is on getting his cargo along the coast of Africa. Some other countries, such as the large island of Cuba, where they do not live so long as here and the intensive empire of Brazil, which is not yet stocked are supplied by the slave trade; but there are probably more slaves in the slaveholding states of this country than in all other parts of Christendom put together.

This is, therefore, the greatest slave holding country in the world or at least in the Catholic and Protestant portions of it; and as slavery and the slave trade confessedly originated in and are maintained by the same principle, the love of money, and as mankind in their ideas of things, make no radical distinction between them, this country actually does more indirectly, to keep up the slave trade than all other nations. This may seem a heavy charge, when the slave trade has here been declared *piracy;* but example is always more forcible than precept and if we say one thing while we practice another our professions will be believed. We are certainly viewed in this light by the principle nations of Europe; and within a very few years some cargoes of Africans have been landed upon shores in open violation of the laws which we profess to revere; yet no adequate punishment was visited upon the perpetrators of the crime and they seemed even to glory in having it known to the world that such a thing was done. The proximity of the cotton states to Cuba and the slave holding portions of South America enables the unprincipled and reckless at almost anytime to commit such outrages on humanity; and, while the friends of the African race can only mourn over such deeds of atrocity, the wretched slaver, the very dregs of society, desire no greater encouragement.

The abolition of slavery here would then, have a powerful influence, both directly and indirectly in putting an end to the slave trade. *Directly,* because we should give no encouragement to the lawless and unprincipled men who engage in that traffic; and *indirectly,* because the abolition of slavery in these southern states would soon be followed by its abolition in all other portions of the world. As already stated, the only countries of any note that are now supplied with slaves from Africa are, the island of Cuba, in the Gulf of Mexico, and the empire of Brazil, on the eastern side of South America. As already stated, slavery in the Spanish territories never did assume that despotic and cruel character which it had in the British West India and North American colonies. It does not exist there now on such a large scale as here and the government at home could at any time put an end to its existence. Its proximity to our shores and the influence

III. *THE REASON* FOR THE DEMAND OR THE PURPOSE FOR WHICH IT IS MADE

of our exampled, combined with that of England and France would soon banish it from the soil. The same remarks will apply and perhaps with still greater force, to the empire of Brazil; for, as the emperor is descended from the royal house of Harpsburg and is connected with other royal families in Europe, he could not resist their united influence. Of the one who occupies the throne I know nothing, as our papers, since these troublous times commenced, have taken no notice of foreign affairs, but I presume he is a son or brother of the late emperor. All the slavery existing in other portions of Christendom is a mere nothing and would soon fade away like a mountain mist before the rising sun.

If the Union had remained entire it would soon have exerted a more powerful influence than any other nation on the globe; not by its physical resources, but by its moral and political associations. It is regarded by all other nations as the birth place of free institutions. Here liberty, invigorated by the uncontaminated atmosphere of the new world and taught wisdom by a long experience and sustained by a pure Christianity, first unfurled her banner to the breezes of heaven and gained a complete triumph over the minions of despotism. Her Declaration of Independence, so fraught with the noblest sentiments and written in the finest style of our good old mother tongue alarmed the monarchs of Europe for their safety and awakened in the masses an earnest desire and an imperishable hope of freedom. Here was exhibited to an admiring world the unexampled progress of a free people in population, in science and literature, in arts and arms, in commerce and in everything which constitutes a high state of civilization. To this unparalleled prosperity there appeared to be no assignable limit—and if no disruption had taken place, and slavery were abolished, the United States might soon have ruled the world, by their moral power alone, and made our free institutions the inheritance of all mankind; but there may yet await us, in the mysterious and comprehensive designs of infinite wisdom, a more thorough comprehension of the great principles which lie at the foundation of a free and Christian government, and a still greater and more desirable prosperity than any we have hitherto realized or been able, by any effort of imagination to conceive.

From the alternations of defeat and victory which have thus far attended the present conflict, no man can foresee the issue; but so far as the abolition of slavery is concerned, it will neither be retarded by southern independence nor hastened by a reestablishment of the Union; for slave holders will be forced in some way or other to resign the power which they have usurped and to part with a species of property to which the Creator has given them no right. As already remarked, he will not allow a perpetual ownership of anything to which he has given no express grant, but which he has reserved exclusively for himself. Men are not adequate to the task of ruling beyond their prescribed limits and when they attempt to extend their power into the domain of immortal beings who are accountable to God alone they make as bad work as Pharaoh did when he undertook to drive the chariot of the sun; but God, who is jealous of his won honor, never has suffered and never will suffer such daring impiety to proceed very far nor to continue very long. We have always advocated a voluntary and gradual emancipation. Our feelings have hitherto revolted at anything like force; but it *may* have become necessary and, if so, we must submit; but it is not yet too late to make a voluntary surrender and we would rejoice to see it made, not from cowardice in what we believe to be a good cause; but ever since sober reflection took the place of youthful levity, we have not felt disposed to fight against God. Whether we are right or not in our views of slavery we leave others to judge under a full sense of their accountability; but our convictions on the subject are the result of much investigation and unalterable.

At the present we are under no compulsion nor is it by any means certain that the Federal government will succeed in subduing the south; and a voluntary act of general emancipation either immediately or gradual, would, probably, at this time, have a greater moral power in arresting the slave trade and impressing mankind with the immense value of liberty than if the Union had remained entire. We are neither a craven nor a fanatic; we are neither advising nor importuning; but merely stating what we think justice, humanity, and religion require; and what would be the effect of such a generous and magnanimous sacrifice on the part of our southern slave holders. It would be one of the noblest acts and one of the greatest events of the nineteenth century. Then, it would be rolling off an immense amount of responsibility, which has been voluntarily assumed and which will be crushing in its weight; for the country has assumed the responsibility of saying by their legislative enactments that four millions of human beings shall not be allowed to read the Bible nor anything else; that their powers shall not be developed; and that they shall not be developed; and that they shall not make an entire consecration of themselves, soul and body, to the service of their divine Master. Set them free and the responsibility of their improvement will rest upon themselves; but while you hold them in bondage under the present laws and as you now have them, with their whole time and strength employed for your emolument, you are accountable for the improvement which they might otherwise make and for all the good which they might otherwise do. It would, moreover, be a candid and honorable acknowledgement of past error, which all the world could not but admire, applaud, and imitate; but the most commendable thing about it and the most impressive aspect in which it could be viewed by the world would be the nobleness of the deed, the generosity of the sacrifice made, and the beneficent effect which it would have upon the wronged oppressed and down trodden race of Africans here and in their own land. Never once think about the diminution of your gains or your pleasures; for such considerations should, in no case, be suffered to conflict with the claims of justice, humanity, and religion; for the path of duty is always the path of safety and of progress. Christians profess to belong, not to themselves but to the Lord and to have made such a consecration of everything to his service that they can call nothing their own; that their powers of body and mind must be all employed for his glory in the salvation of men; and that, in the things of this world, they are only stewards for him. *Godliness,* or vital and consistent piety, *has* the promise of the life that now is as well as of that which is to come; and his blessing on your future efforts will more than compensate you for the sacrifices you make for him, or for the present and eternal welfare of those whom he has bought with his own blood. Pride goes before a fall; but humility before exaltation Jesus Christ made far greater sacrifices than we have it in our power to make for, though, he was rich, yet for our sakes he become poor that we through his poverty might become rich. He took upon him the form of a servant and became obedient even unto death. He not only suffered the torments and the ignominy of the cross, but went down into the cold and silent tomb and was thence raised to infinite exaltation and to boundless glory. The greater the sacrifice and the deeper the humiliation, the richer will be the reward nad the higher will be the promotion. As all history proves this is true of both individuals and communities; for it seems to be a settled principle of the divine government and necessary in our fallen and depraved condition. It is, in many respects , *more blessed to give than to receive;* and he that denies himself for the purpose of promoting the present and future welfare of others shall be blessed in his deeds; but there is neither Christian self denial nor Christian liberality in giving a few dollars, earned by your slaves, to Christianize the heathen on the opposite side of the globe when you have four millions here among you held in such ignorance, degradation, and cruel bondage. *The liberal soul deviseth liberal things* said the prophet *and by liberal things he shall stand.* If I had it in my power, as I have not to ensure the future prosperity of these southern states, I would certainly never engage to while slavery exists, nor until a majority of the people were so much under the liberalizing, self denying and generous spirit of the gospel that they would, in all circumstances and at all times, stand by their convictions and follow out the truth as it is in Jesus, leaving the results of whatever self denial or present sacrifices it might require to the awards of the master whom they serve. Christians cannot do their duty nor have the rejoicing which they might have from the testimony of their consciences without a whole hearted devotion to the cause of Christ and an implicit trust in his providential care.

401   If voluntary emancipation, whether immediate or gradual, were once determined on, a great change of feeling towards them would take place and everything would become easy. Such enactments as are most objectionable, for example, such as those which forbid them to be taught the use of letters; those which make them mere chattels and liable to be sold off like other stock on the farm, as the interest or the convenience or the necessities of the master require, with no more regard to the most endearing relations and the most tender and sacred attachments than if they were dumb brutes. Those which forbid them to claim anything as their own, and some others would be instantly repealed or disregarded in practice. Three or four days ago a neighbor told me that if his information was correct, some minister of the gospel in the south, has commenced preaching with considerable earnestness on the duty, expediency, and importance of educating the whole of our black population; and, if this be true, we would hail it as the dawn of better times. Had this been done from the first or only for the last two or three generations, we should now have a very different and a much more desirable state of things; but whether they are emancipated just now or not, we do hope that, for the sake of humanity and for the honor of protestant Christianity, the enactments mentioned above will soon be repealed, or, at least that the Christian feelings and good sense of the community will cause them to become a dead letter, a mere *brutum fulmen*, and that the world will not have it much longer to say that we forbid four millions of people, human beings like ourselves, to read the word of God, the gospel of their salvation.

402   Whether right or wrong the impression on the minds of people, slaveholders as well as others seems to be increasing that a train of events has commenced which will sooner or later, issue in the entire and final abolition of slavery. Such is the fact, at least within the sphere of my acquaintance or observation, which is not very extensive; but precisely when or how and what disposition shall be made of them—whether they to become the dominant population round the Gulf of Mexico and gradually amalgamate with the whites, as the Spaniards did to a great extent with the Moors and with the natives of South America, or be transported to Africa, as all admit to be probable, are things which lie beyond the ken of mortals. The more prevalent opinion is that the larger portion of them will be returned to Africa and be the means of producing a moral reformation in that ill fated country; but emancipation whenever and however it may be effected, will be like a resurrection to the slaves here, raising them up from the very lowest depths of degradation and setting them forth, with the invigorated powers of a new and ever increasing life, on the vast theatre of activity, of

III. *THE REASON* FOR THE DEMAND OR THE PURPOSE FOR WHICH IT IS MADE

enjoyment and of progress, while their return to the land of their forefathers, carrying with them their inestimable boon of a pure Christianity and all the blessings of civilization, would be hailed, by a hundred and fifty millions of a down trodden race, with a triumph in which angels would join and at which all nature would assume an aspect of gladness. This is neither a reverie of enthusiasm nor a picture of poetic fancy, but the truthful enunciation of rapt and high prophetic inspiration.

That the African race, so long oppressed and wronged and down trodden by those who call themselves Christians, will be "redeemed, regenerated and disenthralled," there can be no doubt; for the mouth of the Lord hath spoken it. They are, of course, included in the general predictions that all nations and kindreds and tongues and people shall serve Jesus Christ; and although there is only one specific promise relating to them it is a very comprehensive one: *Ethiopia shall stretch forth her hands unto God*, by which is generally understood to be meant that the colored race shall receive the Christian religion, be brought under the protection of Jehovah and incorporated into the visible church. Of course they will be civilized, respected and treated with kindness by all who belong to that kingdom which is righteousness and peace and joy in the Holy Ghost. A Christian and enlightened people cannot be long enslaved for neither the moral power of the renewed nature nor the faithfulness of God will long permit such a wrong. The persecuting emperors of Rome with all the civil and military force they could command were, in about six generations, a little more or less, perhaps, overcome by the increasing numbers and morale of the persecuted, and the wicked shall not triumph over the righteous. That the Africans or any other race are of an inferior grade, as to natural capacities and powers is mere slang, the flimsy pretext of slaveholders, to conceal their pride and avarice. Christianity and providential circumstances make the difference; but the former has already been given to Africa and the latter will, e'er long be turned in their favor.

All the prominent nations in the world have traits of character and occupations in life which are peculiar to themselves; and the African character is as strongly marked in these respects as that of any other people. They may not be a warlike people but they will exhibit the milder virtues in greater perfection than any other portion of mankind. They have mingled very little with other races; and they will have more homogeneousness of feeling and more concordant views than any other nation. Their national, political, and Christian character will be formed, not like that of most other nations by a very gradual process and amidst the incessant conflicts of interest and passion, but in a short space of time and under the influence of the highest civilization yet attained by mankind. Then the extent of the continent and its geographical position; it accessibility to Europe, Asia, Australia, and America; and it soil productions, all indicate a future destiny for it of no ordinary greatness. If the slaves of this country were returned to their fatherland and the slave trade were abolished and no calamity should befall the noble enterprise now begun we have no doubt that in half a century from this time the hundred millions of Africans there ready for organization and improvement will form one of the most commercial and important nations in the world. The descendants of Abraham were six generations in Egypt, about the length of time that the Africans have been in bondage here and during the latter part of that time, probably about the half of it, they were sent to the lowest depths of degradation and wretchedness; but in a short time they were raised up to be the most prosperous, powerful, and honored nation on earth; and the degradation of the African race for the last two or three centuries we regard as a certain indication of a corresponding elevation to national prosperity and greatness.

Bibliography

Barker, William S. "The Social Views of Charles Hodge: A Study in Nineteenth Century Calvinism and Conservatism." *Presbyterion* 1 (1975) 1–22.

Bassett, John Spencer. *Antislavery Leaders of North Carolina*. Baltimore: Johns Hopkins, 1898.

Calhoun, David. *Princeton Seminary: Faith and Learning 1812–1868*. Carlisle: Banner of Truth Trust, 1994.

Caruthers, Eli W. *A Sketch of the Life and Character of the Reverend David Caldwell, D.D.* Greensboro, NC: Swaim and Sherwood, 1842.

———. *American Slavery and the Immediate Duty of Southern Slaveholders*. Durham, North Carolina: Special Collections Library of Duke University, 1862. Microfilm.

Guelzo, Allen C. "Charles Hodge's Antislavery Movement." In *Charles Hodge Revisited: A Critical Appraisal of His Life and Work*, edited by John W. Steward and James H. Moorhead, 299–325. Grand Rapids: Eerdmans, 2002

Murray, Ephraim C. *A History of Alamance Church 1762–1918*. Greensboro, NC: Alamance Presbyterian Church, 1918.

Noll, Mark. *America's God: From Jonathan Edwards to Abraham Lincoln*. Oxford: Oxford University Press, 2002.

Scott, Annie V. "A History of Alamance Church." *State Normal* 18, no. 2 (1913) 82–98.

Wilson, Joseph M. *The Presbyterian Historical Almanac*. 10 vols. Philadelphia: Wilson, 1866.

www.ingramcontent.com/pod-product-compliance
Lightning Source LLC
Chambersburg PA
CBHW051743230426
43670CB00012B/2144